Rewards That Drive High Performance

REWARDS THAT DRIVE HIGH PERFORMANCE

Success Stories From Leading Organizations

Thomas B. Wilson

AMACOM

American Management Association

New York • Atlanta • Boston • Chicago • Kansas City • San Francisco • Washington, D.C.
Brussels • Mexico City • Tokyo • Toronto

PUBLISHED IN COOPERATION WITH AMERICAN COMPENSATION ASSOCIATION

Library of Congress Cataloging-in-Publication Data

Wilson, Thomas B.
    Rewards that drive high performance : success stories from leading
organizations / Thomas B. Wilson.
        p.   cm.
    Includes bibliographical references and index.
    ISBN 0-8144-0428-6
    1. Industrial management—Case studies.   2. Business enterprises—
Case studies.   3. Success in business—Case studies.   I. Title.
HD31.W5576   1999
658—dc21   98–47845
                                           CIP

Printing number

10 9 8 7 6 5 4 3 2

For my wife, **Fran**, and children, **Robert** and **John**:
You give me adventures to fill a lifetime.

In memory of my brothers, **Jim** and **Larry**:
You taught me all I know.

Contents

List of Contributors

AlliedSignal
Scott Pitasky
former Human Resources Manager
101 Columbia Road
Morristown, NJ 07962

Amazon.com

Joy Covey
Chief Financial Officer
1516 Second Avenue
Seattle, WA 98101

Scott Pitasky
Director, Human Resources
1516 Second Avenue
Seattle, WA 98101

Avid Technology, Inc.
Judith Oppenheim
Senior Vice President of Human
    Resources and Corporate Services
Avid Technology, Inc.
One Park West
Tewksbury, MA 01876

Baptist Health System, Inc.

Douglas Dean, CCP
Corporate Director,
    Compensation & Benefits
Baptist Health System, Inc.
P. O. Box 830605
Birmingham, AL 35283

Suzanne Thorn, CCP, PHR
Compensation Manager
Baptist Health System, Inc.
P.O. Box 830605
Birmingham, AL 35283

**Blanchard Training &
  Development, Inc.**
Bob Nelson
President
Nelson Motivation, Inc.
11848 Bernardo Plaza Ct., Suite 210B
San Diego, CA 92128

Boone County National Bank
Bo Fraser
President and Chief Executive Officer
Boone County National Bank
P. O. Box 678
Columbia, MO 65205

Burke, Inc.
Rod Cober
Senior Vice President
Burke Customer Satisfaction
  Associates
805 Central Avenue
Cincinnati, OH 45202

Joe Ottaviani
Senior Vice President
Burke Marketing Research
805 Central Avenue
Cincinnati, OH 45202

CIGNA HealthCare
Michael Jaques
Vice President of
  Compensation & Benefits
CIGNA HealthCare
900 Cottage Grove Road, A 145
Hartford, CT 06152-1145

Cisco Systems, Inc.
John Radford
Director, Organizational Effectiveness
Cisco Systems, Inc.
255 West Tasman, Building J
San Jose, CA 95314

The Coca-Cola Company
David Cheatham
Manager, Strategic Compensation
The Coca-Cola Company
P. O. Drawer 1734
Atlanta, GA 30301

Colony Communications, Inc.

Daniel V. Donahue
HR Consultant
124 Daniel Drive
North Kingstown, RI 02852

Bruce Clark
former CEO
154 Edmund Drive
North Kingstown, RI 02852

Community Health Plan

Dr. Paul Jarris, M. D.
Medical Director, Vermont Region
Community Health Plan
7 Park Avenue
Williston, VT 05495

Dr. David Jillson, Ph.D.
Director of Health Services
Community Health Plan
7 Park Avenue
Williston, VT 05495

Copley Pharmaceutical, Inc.

Barbara Morse
Vice President, Administration
Copley Pharmaceutical, Inc.
25 John Road
Canton, MA 02021

Corning Incorporated

Harold Altmansberger, CCP
Goal-Sharing Consultant
HNA Consulting
2736 County Line Drive
Big Flats, NY 14814

Cummins Engine

Theo Smith
Director, Human Resources
Cummins Engine
901 South US Route 23
Fostoria, OH 44830

Dirk Taylor
Plant Manager
Cummins Engine
901 South US Route 23
Fostoria, OH 44830

DuPont Corporation

Robert McNutt
DuPont Human Resources
DuPont Corporation
Nemours 10460-8
Wilmington, DE 19898

Fleet Financial Group, Inc.
Michael Irons
Senior Vice President,
Director, Corporate Compensation
Fleet Financial Group, Inc.
111 Westminster St., RI MO M14H
Providence, RI 02903-2393

Jane M. Buonocore
Assistant Vice President,
   Corporate Compensation
   Manager
Fleet Financial Group, Inc.
111 Westminster St., RI MO M14H
Providence, RI 02903-2393

Genzyme Corporation
Jo-Dee Gentile
Compensation, Benefits & HRIS
   Manager
Genzyme Corporation
1 Kendall Square/Building 1400
Cambridge, MA 02139-1562

Harvard Pilgrim Health Care
Larry J. Gibson
Senior Vice President, Human
   Resources, Information
   Technology, and Quality
   Management
Harvard Pilgrim Health Care
10 Brookline Place West
Brookline, MA 02146-7229

Harvard University Health Services
Mary Hennings
Director for Administration
Harvard University Health Services
75 Mt Auburn Street
Cambridge, MA 02138

Dr. Maureen Lynch, MD,
   Chief Associate of Pediatrics
Dr. Christopher Coley, MD,
   Chief of Medicine
Carie Michael, Assistant Director for
   Clinic Operations
Gioia Barry, Assistant Director for
   Human Resources

**Health Services Medical
   Corporation**
Ellen G. Wilson
Vice President Human Resources
   and Communications
Health Services Medical Corporation
8278 Willett Parkway
Baldwinsville, NY 13207-1399

Jennifer Fulton-Vacco
Director, Human Resources
Health Services Medical Corporation
8278 Willett Parkway
Baldwinsville, NY 13207-1399

IdeaScope Associates, Inc.
Kimberly Kelley
Vice President
IdeaScope Associates, Inc.
Union Wharf, Suite 214
Boston, MA 02109

Keane, Inc.
Renee Southard
Vice President, Human Resources
Keane, Inc.
10 City Square
Boston, MA 02129-3714

Key Private Bank
W. Lawrence Gilmer
Senior Vice President and Director
   of Compensation & Benefits
KeyCorp
127 Public Square
Cleveland, OH 44114-1306

Michael Garelik
National Chairman-Financial
   Industry Group
William M. Mercer
1717 Arch St
Philadelphia, PA 19103

K/P Corporation
Chuck Parsons
522 West Mercer Place, Suite 403
Seattle, WA 98119

Patricia Ellsworth
365 Reflections Circle, Suite 23
San Ramon, CA 94583

Levi Strauss & Co.
Steve Epstein
Vice President, Global Remuneration
Levi Strauss & Co.
1155 Battery Street IH2/3
San Francisco, CA 94111

The MathWorks, Inc.
Jeanne O'Keefe
Chief Financial Officer
The MathWorks, Inc.
24 Prime Park Way
Natick, MA 01760-1500

Naomi Couino
Director of Human Resources
The MathWorks, Inc.
24 Prime Park Way
Natick, MA 01760-1500

OSRAM SYLVANIA, Inc.
James R. Stokely
Director of Compensation and
    Organization Development
OSRAM SYLVANIA, Inc.
100 Endicott Street
Danvers, MA 01923

Royal Bank Financial Group
Peter H. Tucker
Senior Vice President
Royal Bank Financial Group
Royal Bank Plaza,
11th Floor North Tower
Toronto, Ontario, Canada, M5J 2J5

Saturn Corporation
Dennis G. Finn
Director of Human Resources
Saturn Corporation
100 Saturn Parkway, P. P. Box 1500
Spring Hill, TN 37174

Sears, Roebuck and Company
Steve Kirn
Vice President, Organization
    Learning and Development
Sears, Roebuck and Company
3333 Beverly Road
Hoffman Estates, IL 60179

Southwest Airlines
Elizabeth Sartain, SPHR, CCP
Vice President of People
Southwest Airlines
P. O. Box 36611
Dallas, TX 75235-1611

Starbucks Coffee Company
Leslie Thornton
Director, Total Pay
Starbucks Coffee Company
2401 Utah Avenue South/
    MS S-HR3
Seattle, WA 98124-1067

SunLife of Canada
Ray Waldron
Compensation Officer
SunLife of Canada
1 SunLife Executive Park
Wellesley Hills, MA 02181

Techneglas, Inc.

Robert Reynolds
General Manager
Techneglas, Inc.
RR #4, Box 60
Pittston, PA 18640

Ronald L. Drennan
Administrative Manager
Techneglas, Inc.
RR #4, Box 60
Pittston, PA 18640

Ticona, LLC

Ann Lane
Executive Director, Sales America
Ticona, LLC
P. O. Box 819005
1601 West LBJ Freeway
Dallas, TX 75381-9005

Margaret Batcheler
Human Resources Manager
Ticona, LLC
1195 Centre Road
Auburn Hills, MI 48326

Wilson Group, Inc.
Thomas B. Wilson
President
Wilson Group, Inc.
100 Main Street
Suite 240
Concord, MA 01742
E-mail: info@wilsongroup.com

W. W. Grainger, Inc.

Gary Goberville
Vice President, Human Resources
W. W. Grainger, Inc.
455 Knightsbridge Parkway
Lincolnshire, IL 60069

Jackie Barry
Director, Compensation
W.W. Grainger, Inc.
455 Knightsbridge Parkway
Lincolnshire, IL 60069

Acknowledgments

This book was truly a team effort. The case studies were developed in close collaboration with representatives from the companies included. A list of these contributors is included on pages xi through xvii.

In addition, there are a number of individuals whose continual efforts have made this material possible. They are individuals who are members of the Wilson Group, Inc., and they added greatly to the preparation of these case studies. In particular I would like to acknowledge Lauren Sagner, Jackie Shaw, and Lynne Kondracki for their tremendous efforts in preparing this book. In addition, I wish to thank Jack Dolmat-Connell, Julie Kniznik, and Carole Greer, who added much guidance, assistance, and support to me in preparing this book. Finally, I thank Dave Kowal of Kowal Communications, Northboro, Massachusetts, for his assistance in working with my materials for this book.

Together they have produced a book that I believe will be of great value to the readers of today, and those in the future who are interested in what high-performance organizations were like in this era.

T.B.W.

Rewards That Drive High Performance

1

The Quiet Revolution

We are witnessing a revolution in the workplace. It is taking place in the United States—and likely occurring throughout the world. It is a quiet revolution, one that is barely being discussed in the media. It is so profound that it is reshaping those who are part of it and those who are affected by it. And its impact is gradual, so few people even notice it.

The globalization, reengineering, restructuring, and downsizing that took place in the 1990s left organizations in more demanding circumstances. Competition intensified from a wide variety of sources. In response, organizations engaged in massive cost reductions, reconfigured their structures, made major investments in technology, and sold operations while acquiring others. They formed alliances, partnerships, and joint ventures, even with their competitors. They sought to find their competitive advantage or core values as an enterprise. People were often demoralized, alienated, and frustrated. Loyalty and commitment dropped to their lowest point, and the people who remained employed held little commitment to the organization. Many organizations did not survive, but some prospered; many people lost their jobs, but some found unique opportunities. Every organization has somehow been changed by these forces.

From this chaos a new organization model is emerging. Organizations are fundamentally changing how they manage their activities and relate to their people. Organizations are becoming more responsive to their customers, reducing costs, and improving quality. As a result, they are becoming more competitive. They are generating higher returns for shareholders and more opportunities for employees. The most fundamental realization is that people are making the difference in organizational performance. This is what the quiet revolution is all about.

The new organization that is evolving places a greater value on employees than organizations have in the past. It achieves more by creating a process for employees to share in the results that they help achieve.

This book provides a series of stories that offer a window into today's organizations. While the focus is on the reward systems that these organizations devised and implemented, the true picture goes much deeper. Each story reflects an organization that was facing a need to change the way it conducted its business and developed a process to support and reinforce change. So, the reward systems are manifestations of a new set of values and practices within organizations. In their own way, reward systems have modified the fundamental spirit of these organizations, the relationship between the employer and the organization's members, as well as their competitiveness and vitality.

These organizations have demonstrated that the actions of people, the things they do or fail to do, often define the difference in the organization's performance. They have also demonstrated how reward systems play a significant role in changing or guiding organizations.

Many people make assumptions about what motivates people; they also have assumptions about what drives successful organizational change. The message from these leading organizations is that there is no simple formula for high performance—but involvement, commitment, and a stake in the outcomes are essential ingredients.

Each of the organizations profiled in this book had to adapt to changing market conditions. Some had a well-articulated strategy. Others were more general in their approach. Some companies used a set of specific performance measures. Others translated their strategy and the values of the organization into programs. Some had leaders who actively supported or promoted change. Others did not. Common to each organization, however, was a holistic approach to rewards that was highly integrated with how the business and people were managed.

Defining Rewards in a Strategic Manner

Reward systems are not merely compensation or recognition programs. They are processes that translate strategic goals and values into actions and define how people will be reinforced for these actions. They can create alignment. Rewards may focus on actions or results. They include salary programs, incentive or bonus programs, a performance management process, and many forms of personal recognition. They exist as management systems and practices within organizations. They define for the individual, "What's in it for me?"

Reward systems create a connection between the employer and the employee. They define the employment contract and the nature of the employer-employee relationship. If they are effective, they do not just distribute cash to employees but reflect the contributions made by the employees and build a renewed sense of commitment. They create a mechanism for sharing the benefits of success and form a link between what is expected from people and the results that are achieved.

Reward systems do not exist in a vacuum. They are part of the strategy and cultural fabric of the organization. They work when they are well designed and well managed. They enable an organization to attract and retain the talent needed to succeed, and they can make the difference in the degree of commitment and discretionary effort employees contribute to their organization.

Why Organizations Should Be Concerned With Rewards

Some people believe money will not drive desired performance. They cite research and examples where financial rewards pressured employees into actions that hurt the organization, its people, and its customers. They use these as evidence to reflect their own values and opinions. The problem is that without some form of meaningful exchange, desired performance does not endure. The reward does not necessarily need to be in cash or even externally provided; some of the most meaningful times occur when someone gains internal satisfaction from an external action. Unfortunately, the work environment does not inherently contain this alignment between personal needs and job accountabilities.

It is true that when a reward system is used to control or manipulate, it can work against an organization and the person. Some programs are more influential than any manager would be in daily practice. However, the answer is not to eliminate rewards but to apply the reward system that's right for the organization. Reward systems that are exploitative, focus on punishment, or fail to require accountability never build successful, enduring organizations.

This book demonstrates that there is a better alternative—one in which rewards give employees a stake in the success of the enterprise. If an employee's performance supports the organization's mission, values, and strategy, and these actions improve financial or market performance, then it is only "right" that the individual be "enriched" fairly for the contribution. The rewards-enriched workplace is characterized by achievement, excitement, and fulfillment. But this does not just happen. A strategy and set of targeted programs need to be created and integrated into the everyday life of the organization. The best reward systems are those that do not appear as formal systems but rather as "the way we do things around here." But there was careful, strategic support behind these practices.

Stories Make a Lasting Impact

Research on the development of human intelligence concludes that greater learning takes place when concepts are presented as case studies rather than as lists and narrative descriptions. Every civilization uses poems, songs, and stories to pass on traditions and values. Stories create mental images. Images burn deeper and last longer than lists that are memorized. They form a connection between an emotional memory and reality.

In one study, when history was taught using a collection of stories, high school students were able to recall up to three times more information than they did after reading traditional text. Stories spark the imagination and may evoke an emotional response. They create a personal relationship to a sequence of events. They live longer in the mind of the reader.

So this book presents success stories, or case studies, from some of North America's leading organizations. In my previous book, *Innovative Reward Systems for the Changing Workplace* (New York: McGraw-Hill, 1995), I explain how to develop a wide variety of reward systems. This book, then, presents a demonstration of how organizations have approached, developed, and implemented reward systems to improve performance and shape their culture.

Situations with very different applications are illustrated. Some of the case studies are sophisticated; others are simple. Some are directly compensation related; others provide a wide range of cash and noncash, formal and informal processes in which people are rewarded. But each company has invested considerable time and effort to address how people can share in the achievements of their own and their organization's performance.

By reviewing many of these case studies, the principles of successful reward systems and high-performance organizations can be learned and hopefully remembered.

Real-Life Situations

The case studies in this book were developed with representatives of these organizations. They are true, real-life descriptions of what goes on inside these companies. A List of Contributors is included in this book.

Those who chose to participate did so for several reasons. First, they want to share their success with others who may have similar issues. They want to show what can be done. Second, they want to contribute to the marketplace of ideas by demonstrating that reward systems can play a crucial role in an organization's business strategy. Finally, they realize that people within their organization, as well as those who do business with them or wish to do business with them, may read this book and connect with the philosophy, values, and unique style of the organization.

Many organizations declined to participate because they were concerned that their competitors would learn their secrets to success, which in itself demonstrates the role reward systems can play in an organization's competitiveness. Some details in the cases presented were eliminated for similar reasons, without compromising the reader's understanding of the concepts involved.

A Collection of Best Practices

Many books have been written about companies that are leaders in their industries. It seems that it is usually not long after being profiled in such a book that the company is overtaken by the competition, sold, or somehow overwhelmed by changing market conditions.

The organizations represented here are not all leaders in their industries, although some certainly are at this point in time. The organizations profiled are from across the landscape of North America. Some have reward systems that have existed for many years. Others have just implemented them. In some cases, rewards have had an incredible impact on performance. In others, the impact has been modest yet important. Some cases describe the company's philosophy of compensation and how it has evolved. Others describe a specific program that was used successfully.

Organizations and case studies were excluded if they did not engage people in positive ways, were too discretionary and arbitrary, or were based on after-the-fact judgments of performance. Generic profit-sharing programs were also excluded, unless they reflected an active management process.

These are success stories. They were selected because they had the desired impact on the culture and performance of the organization. They each provide a special message about what made them successful and about the organization they represent.

Making the Most of This Book

While this book can be read from front to back, it was not written to be read in a traditional manner. It may be useful to take a non-linear approach, jumping from one section to another. Recognizing that reward systems are created not because companies need to develop programs, but because they need to address issues, the book is organized around themes. The chapters with the theme that best matches your current situation may prove most useful as a starting point. Then consider the following:

1. *Set realistic expectations.* This book is not intended to represent the best practices of the best companies, although it often

does. It is a book about reality. It may not include the design for the perfect reward system, but it should give you ideas and approaches that will change the way you think about, develop, and manage rewards.

2. *Look beyond your current situation.* It may prove fruitful to read about companies outside of your industry and to read cases that address themes other than those that relate closely to your situation. Much can be learned from what others do when they face situations different from yours.

3. *Realize that there is no perfect system.* Think about what people did, why they did it, and what they learned. You'll find that each company made trade-offs and found the best approach given conflicting circumstances. There are no blueprints here for designing perfect reward systems for your company. Every situation is different. While you need to find your own answers, this book should provide you with important clues for finding them. The cases are meant to spark ideas; they should stimulate inspiration, not create imitation.

All of the companies represented have taken bold action to change the course of management, creating programs that have had a profound impact on their organizations. But keep in mind that these companies represent only a sampling of what is taking place in business. Capture the spirit represented in these stories and accept the challenge of creating your own approach to rewards. Doing so will give your company a competitive advantage, but only if your approach is better than that of your competitors.

Before You Begin

Millions of people have been affected by the programs presented in this book. Millions more, including customers and suppliers of these companies, have benefited from the actions people have taken because of these programs. Many other organizations have yet to be touched by the quiet revolution that is taking place in the global marketplace.

This book gives these companies an opportunity to share their experiences. If you have a "story to tell" or would like to discuss any of these situations in more detail, please contact me (info@wilsongroup.com). I, as well as those who contributed to this book, are listed at the beginning. You may contact any of us directly, but the pressures and priorities of a high-performance organization may limit their availability.

This book was written with a purpose. It brings together ideas and approaches that a wide array of organizations have used to be competitive and successful—to create their own quiet revolution. My hope is that the stories presented here can influence what you do, why you do it, and how you do it, so that you can make a difference in your workplace in a manner that benefits your customers, fellow employees, other stakeholders, and of course yourself. I hope this book helps you become part of this community of global change.

2

Building an Entrepreneurial Spirit

How does an organization instill or retain the entrepreneurial spirit that it had when it was small? One of the characteristics of an entrepreneurial culture is the strong relationship between the customer and employees, employees and the managers, and shareholders with everyone. People are in a common boat dealing with the turbulence of a dynamic marketplace. They feel the pressure of survival every day. They are innovative because innovation is required to be competitive. People take initiative to address issues because the company cannot afford to wait. There is a spirit of action and collaboration.

If the organization is successful, it grows. As it becomes larger, formal organizational structures and systems emerge to manage the complexity. However, these changes can limit the spirit of the organization. People can no longer easily converse with executives, and decisions need approval. People start performing tasks that are specialized and have limited direct benefit to the customer. They see their boss as their customer rather than the person they serve. The spirit that made them strong as a young organization—responsiveness, flexibility, and commitment to common goals—becomes faded in the memory of the organization's members.

You will see in this chapter how Amazon.com has experienced meteoric growth and yet has retained a small organization culture. The reward systems have been key to retaining the feel of this organization. MathWorks has created a stakeholders program to create a share in the company's success and personal accountability for contribution. Ticona developed a sales incentive program to encourage customer focus and align a common sales force with multiple lines of business. This practice has been key to Ticona's growth as a company. Southwest Airlines places emphasis on its selection process and culture. It uses a broad spectrum of rewards in subtle and powerful ways to reinforce its culture. Finally, the Wilson Group is an emerging company that is building reward systems to retain its values and spirit in the future.

Although these companies are at different stages of their development, they all have a common concern about retaining their entrepreneurial culture. They are using reward programs to build this spirit in unique ways. For some, this has meant change; others seek to get their systems right from the beginning. They all value their culture, and this enables them to define their uniqueness in the marketplace. In this way, they are leaders.

SHAPING A HIGH-PERFORMANCE CULTURE THROUGH HR AND REWARD SYSTEM DESIGN

AT

Amazon.com

Company Background

An explosively growing company headquartered in Seattle, Washington, Amazon.com is the world's largest Internet bookstore and one of the most visited sites on the World Wide Web. Founded in 1994, it also sells CDs, having recently launched its online Music Store, as well as videos and audio tapes. Customers can search by author, title, subject, or keyword. Sold at discounts of up to 40%, books and CDs are ordered directly from distributors or publishers after the customer makes the selection. However, the company is increasingly carrying inventory based on forecasted demand. Books and CDs are generally delivered within two to three days from one of the company's two massive warehouses.

Sales, which were $511,000 in 1995, climbed to almost $16 million in 1996 and $147.8 million in 1997. Revenues in the first quarter of 1998 were $87.4 million, an increase of 446% over the first quarter of 1997. The company has yet, however, to turn a profit, focusing instead on expansion and the capturing of market share. The customer base has also experienced dramatic increases, from

340,000 in March 1997 to more than 2.2 million in March 1998. Amazon.com went public in May 1997 at an initial offering price (IPO) of $18 per share. Its shares were trading in the mid- to upper-$90s (after a recent two-for-one stock split) in June 1998.

The Founder

Jeff Bezos is the founder and chief executive officer of Amazon.com. At age 33, he is one of the true success stories of today's information age and IPO craze, with a net worth of more than $1 billion. Bezos, who graduated from Princeton University with a B.S. in electrical engineering and computer science, always wanted to be an entrepreneur. He realized the Internet was his path in 1994, while he was working at D. E. Shaw on Wall Street and learned that usage of the World Wide Web was growing at 230% a year. He realized that this was faster than anything he had ever seen, so he decided to try to find a business plan that would make sense for the Web. Seeing that you can build a unique bookstore online, as there is no way to have 2.5 million titles in a physical world bookstore, Amazon.com was born.

The Culture

Bezos has worked hard from day one of the company to build a strong and powerful culture at Amazon.com. It is a frugal culture, given the intensely competitive nature of the business and the resultant low margins. To this day, all desks within the company are made of recycled wooden doors, phone books serve as computer monitor stands, and plastic milk crates serve as filing cabinets. This allows the company to invest more in its growth and continue to be able to scale the industry rapidly, as opposed to investing in its physical assets.

It is a culture characterized by intense and hard work. Rapid growth, stiff competition from Barnes & Noble and Borders, international expansion, and entrées into new markets create a supercharged environment where employees want to win and are willing to go to great lengths to ensure that happens.

The culture is also characterized by a balanced short- and

longer-term orientation, in which Bezos sets the trend. Wall Street, typically focused on short-term profitability, is enamored with this company that is looking to revolutionize Internet commerce as a much longer-term perspective. However, Bezos also knows that long-run success is only possible by executing flawlessly in the short-term. Thus, he demands both in the organization—delivering short-term results that will help guarantee long-range success.

It is a culture that is passionate about what it does—transforming the way in which people buy products over the Internet. Bezos does not want a culture at Amazon.com that will appeal to everyone—rather, he wants it to be a culture that will appeal to those who truly want to make a difference and who are willing to do what it takes to make that kind of difference.

The Employees

Along with spectacular revenue growth has come a rapid expansion of the employee population, rising from approximately 150 at the end of 1996 to more than 600 at the end of 1997 and almost 900 in mid-1998. What has remained constant, however, is the quality of people that the company hires.

Amazon.com has one of the brightest workforces. While the company does not screen people out due to their Scholastic Aptitude Test (SAT) scores, it does ask for them in interviews and ends up hiring people who were top graduates at Princeton, Dartmouth, Harvard, Stanford, Berkeley, and other top institutions. It is also hiring top up-and-coming talent from such companies as Microsoft and Wal-Mart—all organizations that know something about high growth.

The average age of the workforce is 28, not unlike many other highly successful Silicon Valley, high tech start-ups. It is a passionate, energetic, highly motivated collection of individuals who are out to change Internet commerce. While the average age of the workforce is relatively young, Bezos knew that to scale a company as rapidly as Amazon.com, he needed a senior management team that had experience building a rapidly growing organization. Executives and senior managers come from organizations such as Wal-Mart, Microsoft, Avid Technology, Apple Computer, Cisco Systems, and Sun Microsystems.

The Reward System

The reward system at Amazon.com is definitely aligned with its business strategy, employee base, culture, and position in its growth cycle. Amazon.com pays base salaries that are slightly less than competitive on average—competitive at the lowest levels of the organization and then increasingly behind the market as employees move up the organization. The company also has no short-term incentive system, so total cash compensation is also slightly lower than the competitive marketplace. This cash compensation strategy fits well with the competitive business environment in which it operates (relatively low margins and high levels of competition driving the need to capture market share in order to best compete). The strategy also fits well with the growth cycle position of a company (high growth needing cash to finance its expansion) and with its culture of wanting to be long-run focused.

When Bezos founded the company in 1994, he believed that to be successful in the longer term, all employees had to retain "ownership" in the organization. As a result, every employee in the company, from executives down to the hundreds of employees working in the warehouse operations, receives new-hire stock options at highly competitive levels. In slightly more than a year after going public, with the stock having climbed to nearly $200 a share (adjusting for the stock split), many employees have accumulated substantial option gains. Even some $18,000-per-year warehouse operations workers have paper gains of more than $50,000. This option strategy has allowed Amazon.com to attract and retain the kind of workforce that it wants and needs to grow, to conserve cash for expansion, and to allow all employees to have a key stake in the long-term success of the company.

There are no perquisites within the company, reflecting its egalitarian culture. Executives' offices are furnished the same way all others within the company are (e.g., desks made of recycled doors). Before acquiring additional space recently, many offices were doubled- or tripled-up, and Bezos told the executive officers that they would not be exempt from this change as well. The benefit plans are typical of most start-up and high-growth organizations—covering the major areas of need but not fully comprehensive. There is also significant cost sharing in the medical arena, again to conserve cash for expansion.

The Reward System/Employee Linkage

The reward system is unmistakably linked to the company strategy, business environment, culture, and position within its growth cycle. How does it link to employee needs and expectations? The company is out to hire a certain profile of individual—aggressive, bright, forward thinking, someone out to make a real difference and invested in the long-term success of Amazon.com. It is able to get and keep this kind of individual through the design of its reward system. Relatively low base salaries, no short-term incentives, and generous levels of stock options attract people who are hungry, willing to trade short-term economics for the potential of far greater long-term gains, and unafraid to work incredibly hard to make success a reality.

Conversely, the compensation system also acts as a highly effective screening tool for people who don't have the profile that the company is looking for. Those unwilling or unable to take a risk, to trade off short-term for long-term potential, and to live in an egalitarian, no-perquisites organization are going to select out due to the structure of the reward system.

What the Future Holds

Amazon.com has already begun looking at what the future holds for its reward systems. What is clear, and what will not change, is the type of people that the company wants to attract and retain. What will need to change, however, is the specific reward system mix, and undoubtedly the amount and types of components in the reward system. Given the explosive employee growth, stock option dilution must be considered. Given the necessity of attracting a diverse workforce, benefit strategies will have to be looked at. Given the competitive pressures inherent in the labor market, greater pressure to be competitive on cash components will arise. What is gratifying to see, however, is that the company is proactively considering these areas and not waiting until an issue or crisis arises. Will things need to change? Certainly. However, one can be assured that the reward system at Amazon.com will continue to be linked to critical strategies, the culture, and the desire to attract and retain exceptional talent.

RETAINING THE SPIRIT OF AN EMERGING COMPANY AT

The MathWorks, Inc.

The software industry is dynamic and continually undergoing change. If an organization is successful in this industry, it grows and matures and may lose its edge. The factors that lead to success at one stage of growth often form the seeds of the organization's demise in later stages. The challenge of growth in this dynamic marketplace is being addressed by The MathWorks, Inc., in unique and important ways.

Company Background

The MathWorks was founded in 1984 to address a need among engineers and scientists for a more powerful computing environment than was available with FORTRAN, the then-popular programming language. Founders Jack Little, the current president of The MathWorks, and Cleve Moler, the current chief scientist, were experts in mathematics, engineering, and computer science; they were also driven to start a new business. They created MATLAB, a high-performance technical software environment with a comprehensive set of functions for computations and graphics. The products have been used by companies for the design of cars and air traffic systems, for medical research, and as education tools for scientists. The MathWorks has become the world's leading provider of tools for engineering and scientific professionals.

The company has grown to more than 450 people and has been profitable every year since its inception. It is privately held and does not depend on venture-capital funding. Growth has been financed through strong cash flow management. This has given the company a unique ability to focus on customers, employees, and the products that will retain its market leadership. It does not need to produce a return on investment (ROI) for external constituencies; it does need to remain profitable in order to support growth plans and investments. Consequently, the firm has been able to establish a culture that is driven to serve the needs of a complex marketplace and, in turn, make an impact on its customers' ability to use technology in ways that have never been applied before.

One of the important hallmarks of The MathWorks has been its commitment to keeping people involved and dedicated to the success of the company. This philosophy is embedded in many aspects of the organization, from recruitment and selection, to work assignments and structures, to communication about the company and its actions in the marketplace. Employees are kept highly informed and involved in every aspect of the company's operations. This has led to a responsiveness and continual process of change and development seldom experienced by established companies.

One of Jack Little's common refrains is, "If we're happy and motivated and doing our jobs, the customer's going to be happy." This commitment to an informal, customer-oriented, fun place to work has shaped the firm's culture. The structure is dynamic, and the company favors cross-functional teams. All levels of management are actively engaged in promoting new ideas and methods both to improve products and services delivered to customers and to reduce costs. These actions are reinforced by the company's compensation systems as well.

Building Shared Rewards

One of the most powerful reward systems in the company is the Stakeholder Program. This is an incentive program where all employees share in the company's financial performance. It has changed and evolved over time and continues to develop as the organization changes.

The precursor of the Stakeholder Program was started as a year-end bonus, profit-sharing type program. The payouts, while based on performance, were made on a discretionary basis by the senior management team. As the firm grew, the correlation between the performance of an individual and the amount of the bonus payout was not well understood. The program began to be seen as a holiday bonus or entitlement program that was nice to have but did not reflect individual or company performance.

The executive team, lead by Jeanne O'Keefe, the chief financial officer, researched alternatives to change the program. The executives realized that it was important for people to share in the performance of the company and to see how their own contributions made an impact. They considered performance-based stock options, stock appreciation rights, and employee stock ownership programs. Each one of these initiatives seemed to increase dysfunctional pressures on the organization or management's decisions.

The executive team decided not to use stock-related programs because it wanted The MathWorks to remain a privately held company. While one could establish an "internal market" for the private stock in these programs, the greatest gain to individuals would come when the company did an initial public offering and went public. The stock-related programs would place pressure on management to take the company public and to generate capital in the external markets to support the compensation payouts. The executives were also concerned that it would take considerable time to generate sufficient payout under an equity-based plan, and they wanted the incentive plan to have a more immediate impact on behaviors.

Developing a New Approach

To that end, they developed a new approach called the Stakeholder Program. The program is structured to pay out each quarter with no holdback for annual performance. There are three factors that determine payout:

1. The profitability of the company (net operating income before taxes)
2. The individual's current salary
3. The performance rating of the individual

The payout is determined by the following steps:

1. Of the company's profits, 10% is set aside and paid out each quarter for the Stakeholder Program pool. While the quarters vary

in profitability, the pool varies as well. This communicates to all staff members that there are cycles to the business and their payouts will vary accordingly. Furthermore, if there is a large investment or expenditure during a particular quarter, there will be effects on the payouts, but these actions should lead to increased payouts in subsequent quarters, thereby promoting a longer time horizon.

2. A share of the pool is determined for each individual based on the percentage of one's salary to the total payroll of all participants (i.e., eligible employees). As the number of people in the firm grows, the percentage share of any one will be reduced. Thus, individuals that are added to staff need to make a contribution to the company in growing its profitability. An individual must be with the company for one and a half years to receive a full vested interest in the program.

3. The share that individuals receive is "modified" by their performance rating. The following are the ratings used by the company:

- ▸ Outstanding
- ▸ Excellent
- ▸ Very good
- ▸ Meets requirements
- ▸ Needs improvement

Each rating is assigned a weighting factor from 0.5 to 2.5.

4. The payout is then determined by combining the modified amounts of all stakeholders and calculating each individual's percentage share. This percentage is applied to the pool dollars and the amount of the payout is determined.

5. Each manager gives out the payout checks personally. Some groups meet as a team to discuss overall results and then discuss the achievements of each individual during one-on-one sessions; other managers meet one-on-one with each staff member. As a company, there is always excitement the day the stakeholder payouts are made.

Integrating Pay and Performance Reviews

The performance review process is done by managers and continues to develop and change as the organization becomes more complex. The evaluations are based on a set of performance indicators that reflect the functional area and/or project team in which the individuals work. The performance indicators tend to be based on specific objectives or technical contributions. In some cases, units have developed team-based performance plans, and all members on the team have input to an individual's performance rating. Furthermore, managers review the evaluations of their people annually with a peer group of managers. This is done in a discussion session with the objective to increase the quality and reliability of the assessment. Frequently, peer managers push back on a manager who either is overly harsh or generous in the performance ratings. Managers need to correlate their unit's performance with ratings of the individuals within the unit. This process enables the distribution of ratings to be achieved without reverting to forced ranking controls.

Recently, The MathWorks has begun a pilot project to institute a multirater assessment process to expand the information on which the stakeholder performance is judged. This was done because of a successful experience with using this feedback process to assess the performance of the executive team. The feedback made a powerful influence on how executives provide leadership, and the factors were adopted for a broader application in The MathWorks. The results will be integrated into the performance ratings of individuals and should be reflected in their stakeholder payouts.

This program has become an integral part of the way people are managed and rewarded at The MathWorks. Although the structure is relatively simple, the supporting actions require concentrated effort. The company has gained an important tool that has contributed greatly to growth and profitability. As stated earlier, the firm has achieved a steady, above-market-average growth for most years since its inception. It has continued to achieve impressive net income results, which has enabled The MathWorks to finance growth and provide attractive payouts to the stakeholders.

The Impact of the Stakeholder Program

From an organizational perspective, this program has achieved the following important outcomes:

1. *People think and act like stakeholders in the company.* People receive monthly updates on the financial progress of the company. Because this information affects their payouts, employees have become keenly interested in the results. This timely information has led many to examine decisions and to exert peer pressure to control costs or increase revenues. Often people are heard asking whether a given action is the "stakeholder-friendly thing to do."

2. *The program shares the profits of the company with those who helped create them.* From the beginning, the executives wanted to create an environment where people shared in the fortunes of the organization. They act to support this principle. However, they did not want to create pressures to take the company public or create ownership rivalries. Thus, the program enables people to be part of the organization, add to its competitiveness, and share in the results.

3. *Performance is rewarded in meaningful ways.* The MathWorks executives realized that a merit pay program alone simply does not always have sufficient impact on people to make a difference. The Stakeholder Program provides a direct link between the performance of individuals, the financial performance of the company, and one's payouts. It has established a strong link between performance and rewards.

4. *The program requires significant management attention, which is one of the most important activities in which managers are engaged.* Setting performance targets, tracking performance, making product and process improvements, and communicating progress have become important to building a competitive organization. By requiring monthly reports on the progress of the business, and reviewing individual performance on a frequent basis, the culture of the organization has become highly performance oriented. The factors encourage people to focus on customers, market leadership, new product development, and cost management. Everyone is engaged. A major management challenge is to help people see how their actions contribute to or detract from the company's ability to be competitive in the market and effective with customers. They have created an alignment that many organizations would envy.

The Stakeholder Program is not perfect and will most likely undergo changes as the organization becomes larger and more complex. It needs to retain the ability to encourage cross-functional collaboration while providing people with the line-of-sight between their actions and desired results. As the organization grows, the number of participants will grow. The pressure on profits will increase to sustain the desired payout levels. For now, however, the style and nature of The MathWorks management is reflected by the success of this program and the company. An emerging business needs to keep its spirit alive and keep people engaged in the process of growth. This is a continual struggle at The Mathworks, and they have many of the tools to make it worthwhile.

THE CHALLENGE OF INTEGRATION: ALIGNING SALES STRATEGY WITH MULTIPLE BUSINESSES AT

Ticona, LLC

One of the most critical issues of any organization is to align the sales process with the strategic objectives of its business. This becomes even more complex when the company operates several product lines but the customer wants a single point of contact. Such was the challenge facing Ticona.

Company Background

Ticona LLC is a wholly owned subsidiary of the Hoechst Group, a German-based multinational industrial company. Ticona markets, manufactures, and distributes engineering resins to a wide variety of industries, including automotive, high technology, healthcare, electrical/electronics, consumer, and appliances on a worldwide basis. The marketplace for its products is highly competitive and many product lines face increased pricing pressure. It sells directly to industrial customers and also uses an active distribution channel for marketing and servicing customers with needs for smaller quantities. Ticona maintains market leadership through its ability to collaborate with customers on the development of applications (using materials to enhance the customer's competitive advantage) and to provide solutions to the customer's design problems and account servicing.

After the company completed a major strategic assessment, it discovered several critical issues necessary to retain its market leadership:

- ▸ Customers want the sales professionals to have a better understanding of their business and to work more closely with the company to enhance their competitiveness.
- ▸ Customers want a single interface with Ticona to simplify the account relationship responsibilities and increase responsiveness to customer needs.
- ▸ Customers want more focused applications development projects that will build competitive advantage for the future.

To this end, Ticona reorganized its sales force into a set of industry-focused teams. Ticona identified two critical roles in these groups and organized accountabilities to better serve the customer. Account managers have accountability for the sales and overall relationship with the customers, and they use their industry knowledge to identify trends and opportunities that enhance Ticona's competitive position in the market. Applications development engineers have responsibility to develop longer-term applications with clients. This involves working closely with members of the customer engineering function to examine new ways that Ticona's materials can improve their products or reduce their costs.

Ticona has five product-based business units with full profit and loss accountability for their sector of the company. These units include business lines such as Nylon, Celcon polyacetal, Celanex, and Impet polyester. These business units develop strategic plans to grow their market share and generate desired operating income to the corporation. The business lines share the same common sales force. The Americas sales organization serves customers in North, Central, and South America and the business lines work on a global business basis.

This organizational structure utilizes the sales force as the primary linkage between the customer and Ticona, and the business lines have accountability for product development, pricing, manufacturing, and delivery. This dynamic tension positions Ticona to be highly responsive to the needs of the market while achieving economies of scale and integration where needed. The sales organization seeks to identify opportunities where the products portfolio can help solve the customers' application needs and deliver growth and profitability to each of the businesses.

Creating Business Alignment

To make this strategy and organization work effectively, it is essential that the sales organization and the various lines of business work together to achieve market leadership. If the sales organization did not collaborate with the business lines, or the business lines did not tie closely with the customer needs, then Ticona would lose its competitive advantage. Ticona has sought to achieve an optimal balance between product line focus and an integrated face to the customer. This will in turn stimulate growth and keep Ticona in a leadership role for innovations and services with its customers.

While this strategy and organizing concept is relatively clear, the critical task is implementation. If people do not take the desired actions, then the strategic plan will be at risk. For this reason, the sales organization decided to "reinvent" its sales compensation program, with the simple concept that it needed to encourage and reward strategic behaviors.

Developing a New Sales Compensation Program

To accomplish this task, Ticona identified a sales compensation design team to work with an outside consultant to assess and develop a new model of compensation for the account managers and applications development engineers. The program had three principal objectives:

1. Encourage and reward sales and profitable growth in Ticona's businesses.
2. Attract and retain highly skilled and successful sales and applications development engineer talent.
3. Align the objectives of respective business lines with sales objectives through integrated measures of performance.

The design team worked for several months on the plan. Many alternative approaches were examined, and the group developed an approach that balanced sales with business lines, individual with team performance, and account managers with applications development engineers. Although on the surface the program appears complex, it is actually quite simple in concept.

The sales compensation plan is composed of two or three elements, depending on one's role. The combined level of compensation (salary plus target payout for incentives) should be highly competitive in the market and reflect desired market pay levels for desired performance philosophy.

The first component is the base salary. All members of the sales organization retain their base salary, although future increases depend on the implementation of the plan. Furthermore, the company is investigating linking the base pay levels to the definition of critical competencies necessary for successful account manager's or applications development engineer's performance.

The second component is the team incentive. A "team scorecard" is developed for each industry team within the sales organization. The measures are tied to both sales and business line objectives. Figure 2-1 is a sample of the team incentive scorecard. The focus of the team incentive is to encourage both revenue and profit growth in the businesses. The score from the performance of the industry team would apply equally to the account managers and the applications development engineers. The measures include:

- The combined operating income from the business lines that the sales team serves
- The revenue growth generated by the industry team
- The revenue generated from commercializing new programs

This ties them together to ensure they support each business line and work closely with customers to identify sales opportunities and new applications for Ticona's products. For the account managers, this represents approximately half of their variable compensation.

The third component applies to the account managers only and is based on individual sales results. Since each account man-

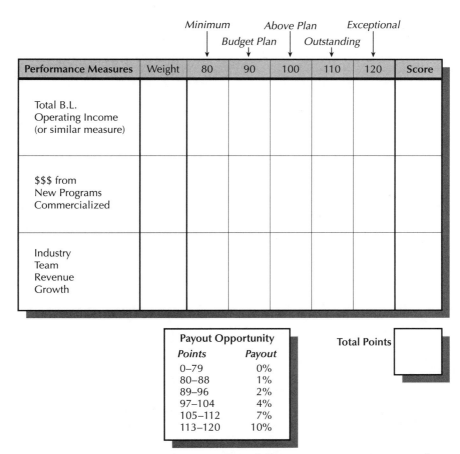

| | | Minimum | | Above Plan | | Exceptional | |
| | | | Budget Plan | | Outstanding | | |
Performance Measures	Weight	80	90	100	110	120	Score
Total B.L. Operating Income (or similar measure)							
$$$ from New Programs Commercialized							
Industry Team Revenue Growth							

Payout Opportunity

Points	Payout
0–79	0%
80–88	1%
89–96	2%
97–104	4%
105–112	7%
113–120	10%

Total Points

Figure 2-1. Team incentive scorecard for account managers and applications development engineers.

ager may serve some or all of the business lines and the mix of business needed by each individual may vary, Ticona needed a process to tailor the program to different roles. To that end, an "individual scorecard" was developed (see Figure 2-2). This scorecard allows each business line to select one measure for their business that serves their sales development and growth objectives. Most business lines utilize net revenues, but they may also utilize contribution margin, number of new accounts, or operating income from new programs, for example. Sales management and the business line leaders would work together on selecting the measures and developing the range of performance needed by each

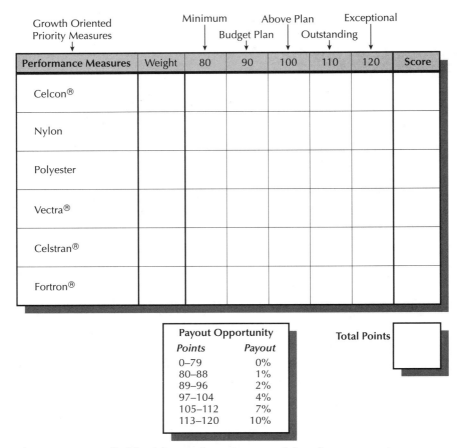

Figure 2-2. Individual incentive scorecard for the account managers and sales team leaders.

account manager. Because this process is done in an open fashion, in close collaboration between sales managers and others, each individual scorecard reflects an optimal balance between the performance requirements of the business lines and the overall people resource allocation priorities of the sales organization. This component of the sales compensation plan is based on individual performance and available only to the account managers.

The Scorecard

The scorecard is an integrating tool used in both the team and individual incentive components; the process of performance planning is key to achieving the right balance of alignment between priorities and needs. The scorecard serves as the catalyst for important decision making and resource allocation. Each scorecard is structured in a similar manner. There are between three and six measures for each card, a weighting of each measure, and five levels of performance. The performance levels range from minimum threshold, to budget plan, and to exceptional. The score (80 to 120) is computed by identifying the level achieved during the performance period, multiplying this amount by the measure weight to determine performance score, and then adding the score for each measure to determine the total score. This is a relatively simple mathematical process. The total score is then compared to the "payout opportunity table" and payout is determined. The payout percentage is applied to the individual's total earnings for the performance period.

The payouts are determined every six months. The first six months' payout is based on the performance for the first half of the year and the second six months' payout is based on the total year, less any payout in the first half. This allows the plan to operate on an annual basis yet provide for half-year performance payouts.

Implementing the Plan

The sales compensation plan has been approved, communicated, and implemented throughout the organization. After the first performance period, the company exceeded its growth objectives for both revenues and profits. The number of development programs that can be commercialized has increased and changes needed in the sales process are taking hold. The trend of results is clearly in a positive direction, but the timeline of the plan's impact on behaviors of all parties concerned, both inside and outside the sales organization, is just beginning. It was expected that the plan would cause an immediate change in behaviors and results. Reality has shown that it takes time to redirect performance and change entrenched behaviors. The commitment to the program remains high, and although the payouts were on target, people expected them to be significantly higher than target. Furthermore, they discovered that it takes more time to develop effective measures, create the systems needed to support the process, and establish fair performance targets. However, the time spent appears to have had multiple benefits, in building strong industry teams, improving trust and communication with the business lines, and establishing strong sales leadership. These are the foundation elements of a successful organization.

Numerous organizational changes were happening at the same time the compensation plan was being implemented. Would it have been better to wait until the changes were completed before implementing the new compensation program? Many challenged the wisdom of moving ahead with changes in compensation before all the other organizational alignment issues had been resolved. But Executive Director of Sales Ann Lane pushed back, indicating that there was never a good time and that the changes would take longer if people could put off the hard decisions that impact compensation. She was proven correct.

The Impact and the Future

Perhaps one of the greatest benefits of the plan has been in how the performance-planning process was created. The scorecards have caused discussions and decisions that were only "talked around" in the past. The business lines needed to finalize their strategic plans and identify the priority performance measures and then integrate these with the sales organization's plans. The sales organization examined its allocation of resources and determined "who best fits with whom"— on an industry and account basis. It defined its mission, vision, and values as an organization, and developed a sales strategy to support the business lines as well as the overall corporation. There were changes in the people serving as sales leaders, development of new sales support information technology, and a redefinition of the relationships with the distributor channels. The sales leadership team identified priority accounts and focused people on strengthening the collaboration between sales and customers, and sales with business lines and account managers and applications development engineers.

Like many organizations, Ticona is undergoing a fundamental transformation to make itself more competitive in a changing market, create closer ties to its customers, and be more efficient in how it uses resources. The sales compensation plan has served to stimulate important actions, but the real driver for change has come from the sales leaders. They have realized the importance of providing focus to and collaboration within the organization. They know the importance of setting fair, well-understood, and challenging performance goals. They are working closely with their staff members to think beyond a narrow definition of the performance measures and see how today's actions will build a more competitive (and rewarding) organization of tomorrow. They are well into their journey of change, and everyone knows that the success of this effort will yield greater success for the company and they will share directly in the benefit.

FINDING THE FORMULA FOR SUCCESS AT

Southwest Airlines

Few companies have achieved the performance and consistent awards that Southwest Airlines has. It has been able to develop an organization that is highly desirable to both employees and shareholders. While many companies attempt to study and emulate this organization, few have been able to achieve it.

Let's review a few of the results this 25-year-old airline has achieved.

1. Southwest was named by *Fortune* magazine in 1998 as the number-one Best Place to Work, and it is consistently selected for other attributes such as best airline, most admired airline, and safest airline by other publications.
2. It has been the most profitable airline in the industry in the 1990s and has been profitable every year since 1973.
3. Southwest has been the fastest-growing company in revenues of all major airline carriers.

4. Southwest earned the Department of Transportation (DOT) "Triple Crown," which is the highest DOT ranking of all major airlines for on-time performance and fewest mishandled baggage, five times in a row. Best customer satisfaction was earned for seven straight years.
5. Southwest has one of the lowest operating costs of all major airlines, achieving around seven cents per available seat mile. This has enabled the airline to offer low-cost fares that routinely beat the competition.

While the list can go on, the important point is that Southwest Airlines has achieved remarkable performance by almost any standard. This is within an industry environment that is undergoing major change. The airline industry is both consolidating, as the major carriers form alliances and mergers, and experiencing many new entrants in local markets. While the current cost of fuel is low for recent historical standards, the competition is becoming more intense. This has kept prices relatively low and offered passengers more choices. The pressure on margins is quite intense. The cost of equipment is growing and labor costs continue to be an important component of the total operating costs. Deregulation of the markets, with intense regulations of operations, equipment, and procedures, requires multiple responses to regulatory pressures. Many experts indicate that this is the most difficult industry in which to compete.

So what has been the secret to Southwest's success? The answer is not due to any particular technology, equipment, market niche, or program. The success of Southwest Airlines is due to its culture. But a culture does not just happen; it is created. This case study will examine how reward systems have played a supporting role to building and sustaining this culture of high performance.

Overview of Southwest Airlines

Southwest Airlines was started in 1971 by the current chairman, chief executive officer, and president, Herb Kelleher, and board member Rollin King. The concept was to build an airline that provides lower-cost point-to-point services delivered with more efficiency and service than any of the major airlines. The company has grown from a regional airline to a major national force. The company has been able to survive recessions, oil embargoes, and de-regulation. It achieved a profitable operation after three years from start-up. The company has had no furloughs or layoffs in its history and seeks to continue this track record. More than 85% of its 26,000 employees are unionized. The relationship with the unions is clearly one of mutual commitment, trust, and support.

The culture of the company can be characterized in many ways. First, there is a great deal of freedom and responsibility. People are encouraged to contribute ideas and take actions that will serve the customer and improve the organization. People know the regulations of the industry and maintain an intense commitment to meeting these core requirements. By maintaining a high commitment to the industry regulations, people are able to focus on serving the customers.

Second, there is a high level of involvement throughout the company in making decisions and recommendations for change. People see their ideas seriously considered and many implemented. The company prides itself in constantly renewing and seeking better ways to do things. For example, there are more than 120 people on the Corporate Culture Committee, and even more in culture committees established in each department and location. People at all levels are involved making improvements to promote and enhance the culture—operations and services are addressed in their functional areas. These committees have formed the backbone of the culture-building process for the organization.

Third, most of the culture is sustained by hiring people who match the profile of the desired employee of the company. There is perhaps no more important decision than who is hired for the organization. Even with the tremendous growth in the company and decreased availability of qualified workers, Southwest has not lowered its standards to fill jobs. Herb Kelleher believes the culture starts with the hiring process. The recruitment and selection process involves a great number of people and reflects the commitment by sustaining the desired culture and retaining the individual. Much of the interview process is based on examining how people have handled various situations in their experience and how they would address current situations. From these in-depth interviews, the true character of the person emerges, and the selection team can determine the degree of fit with the organization. They want people to be successful and to be themselves during the interview process. This applies to how they select pilots, operations staff, and administrative support staff. Every hiring decision is a commitment to the person and a statement about the company's culture.

Fourth, training is strongly supported and emphasized at all levels in the organization. But training goes beyond skill development. The purpose is not to train people to just do their jobs, but to "color outside the lines" and to use their initiative to fill the gaps in functions, departments, and operations to better serve the customer. So, even in the training process, the culture of involvement, action, and customer service is reinforced.

Finally, Southwest seeks to remain flexible in how it utilizes employees and to respond to career aspirations of their people. New hires usually join the company at an entry level in the organization, including the pilots, who join as first officers. They are then expected to progress within the organization as they acquire better skills and become proponents of the culture. People are selected for internal promotions and transfers based on a combination of technical skills and personal style. Managers who are not strong reinforcers of the firm's culture seldom advance and usually leave the company. Managers are leaders within the organization and need to operate consistently with the values and principles of Southwest Airlines.

Consequently, the hiring, training, placement, and development of people have become the key levers by which the organization sustains its culture of high performance. Libby Sartain, vice president of people, has said, "The Southwest Airlines culture is designed to promote high spirit, avoid complacency, and prevent a hierarchy or bureaucracy from slowing down creativity and innovation. Breaking the rules is often rewarded, and employees are expected to do the right thing when tough situations arise—they do. It's the airline's philosophy that employees with a sense of ownership in the company usually will make the right decisions for the company."

Integrating Rewards Into the Fabric of the Organization

Southwest Airlines has characterized its reward systems as basic. However, they are viewed as a process for supporting and reinforcing the airline's philosophy. In a 1992 letter to shareholders, CEO Kelleher stated, "Material rewards are important—to a point—but they also prove hollow unless accompanied by the satisfaction of pride, excitement, fun, and collective fulfillment. Our people provide these essential intangibles to each other and to our customers." Hence, Southwest views salaries, variable compensation, and recognition programs as part of the process of management and highly integrated with the things leaders and people do on a day-to-day basis.

Since unions represent most of Southwest's employees, the wages and salaries are covered by union contracts. For most people this means that pay is related to seniority. This is important because Southwest values retention and long-term commitment to the organization. Furthermore, pay levels are either consistent with or slightly below the wages for various markets. In fact, starting rates are low relative to the market, but they progress more rapidly than others to desired market levels. This keeps the salary costs in line with the low-cost provider philosophy of the company.

The CEO is compensated at below the median of the market for executives in companies of similar size. Other senior managers are paid slightly higher relative to the market, but they retain a smaller portion of the company's stock. The philosophy is to underpay the executives for cash compensation but let them share in creating greater value for the shareholders by building a stronger, more competitive airline. The stock options are not discounted, and executives have the same opportunities for stock purchases as other employees. The emphasis is on long-term growth and development of the corporation. Furthermore, there is a strong commitment to make the compensation levels and pay opportunities internally fair.

There are limited variable pay programs. Perhaps the most inclusive is a corporatewide profit-sharing program. This program was started in 1973 and encourages everyone to keep costs as low as possible. Everyone shares equally based on their earnings and the company's profits. Those who work longer hours or fly extra trips receive a larger piece of the profit-sharing payouts. Historically, the program has paid a mix of cash payments and deferrals to retirement accounts. Employees requested several changes in the program and, in 1990, the total contribution was made on a deferral basis. This enables employees to build a larger nest egg for their retirement.

The retirement plans offer a variety of investment options, including Southwest stock. The employees currently hold between 9% and 10% of the company. When the stock performs well, everyone gains. Many long-service employees have retired quite wealthy from this investment. But once again, individuals need to take responsibility for their own retirement; the corporation makes the process easier (a further reflection of Southwest's culture).

Company stock is an important device for sharing the risks and rewards of the company's performance. In addition to profit-sharing investment options, employees can purchase stock with payroll deductions at a discount through the employee stock purchase plan. Furthermore, the recent pilot union contract enables pilots to gain even greater investments in the company through stock options and deferral of wage increases. The profit-sharing and stock options programs have encouraged everyone to share in the task of holding costs down and working together to benefit the airline and the customer. Finally, it is important to note that the stock price is displayed in each facility, and people watch it every day.

Southwest makes limited use of team or unit-based incentive programs. Instead, it relies on an extensive series of special recognition programs to encourage and reinforce desired behaviors. These programs have limited the need to provide special incentive compensation programs, and they have supported the cultural values of Southwest.

There are a wide variety of both corporate and local-unit-based recognition programs. They change every year and remain exciting, involving, and fun. For example, "Heroes of the Heart" is a way to recognize teams of individuals whose behind-the-scenes work make a major impact on customer service. They may be groups from maintenance, service, or support roles. They are selected through an extensive nomination and review process. They are honored by having the group's name painted on an airplane for one year. The award ceremony is one of the major events of the company, and many people share in the excitement of the presentation.

The senior executives acknowledge every commendation made to both the person who received it and the person who gave it. This enhances the importance of the awards given to individuals and reinforces those who provide them. Furthermore, there are numerous programs to recognize and reward individuals, teams, and entire departments for their contributions. These programs are encouraged and supported with advice, financial resources, time, and experiences from other locations. Space does not allow for a full description of these programs, but note some of the titles:

Together We Make It Great
Ticket to the Future
Walk a Mile
Helping Hands
Stuck on Service
Go See Do
Winning Spirit

Furthermore, some of the awards are as creative as the programs. These include:

Joe Cool Award
President's Award
Top Wrench Award
Superstars
A Shining Star
Voice Award

Many of these programs were developed and managed by local committees of employees. The "people department" provides advice and assistance as needed and may refer developers to other locations for ideas and solutions to problems. The key concept is to reward everything that people like; they celebrate everything—birthdays, anniversaries, promotions, and especially special efforts. For example, when Southwest Airlines took over several Midway Airlines operations in Chicago, the transition team discovered that another airline had taken over some of Southwest's gates. The Southwest Airlines employees took the facilities and properties back and created the logistics for the airline to operate at the airport. When they returned to their home base, they were welcomed with banners that read: WELCOME HOME, CHICAGO BANDITOS! People in the crowded lobby cheered when the team entered, and everyone took great pride in their achievements.

Recognition is part of everyday life. Celebrations occur daily and weekly somewhere on Southwest property. They have taken the spirit of recognition to new levels of excitement and involvement. It is an important responsibility of managers to support these activities, and many, many people are involved. Furthermore, the awards are presented in a meaningful and fun manner. Some of the awards include small cash awards, gift certificates, savings bonds, books, tickets to events, champagne, watches, extra time off, extra breaks, T-shirts, flowers, and whatever is creative and meaningful to employees. The awards are always changing. The important message is to not rely on a single program or a single award; they must be continually refreshed with spirit and innovation.

Have You Discovered the Secret Yet?

Southwest Airlines indeed has a secret. It can share this information because the answer does not lie in the programs. Instead, the culture fosters a process and the process fosters a culture. It is an environment where people can experiment, make mistakes, learn, and try again. Initiative is expected, encouraged, and rewarded.

They have transformed compensation into rewards, pay programs into appreciation. They gain a high positive impact from the various reward programs because of the way they are delivered. There are many avenues by which people are told they are valued by the company. In turn, people value the customers and the company. Consequently, commitment is high and employee turnover remains one of the lowest in the industry. This has resulted in an organization that is highly competitive, resourceful, and achieves remarkable results.

Herb Kelleher has stated, "The difference is in the dedication and spirit of our people. And, that is very hard for our competitors to emulate."

SHAPING CORE VALUES WITH REWARDS
AT
Wilson Group, Inc.

When a company is formed, it has no culture—it is a clean slate. It lacks traditions, practices, or a reputation. There are only the founder's vision, commitment, capabilities, and values. The company's success depends on how successfully the founder can create the desired capabilities and culture that create a competitive advantage and customer commitment in the marketplace.

The advantage of being a new company is that it is far easier to shape a new type of organization than it is to transform an existing culture into something new. The founder of the Wilson Group, Inc. (WGI) recognized this opportunity when he formed the company as a consulting firm specializing in developing performance-based rewards and other people management systems. He also wanted to create an organization that lived by what it advised its clients to do, and to build a desirable place to work for everyone–including him.

To accomplish this, reward systems were structured to align with the organization's strategy and values. As demonstrated in the book *Built to Last* (New York: HarperBusiness, 1994), vision and values drive the success of high-performance companies. The common characteristic of high-performance companies is their ability to integrate their core ideology and drive for success into the fabric of the organization. They build a total environment around their values and achieve alignment in everything they do. When there is integration between the corporate culture and the factors necessary for its success, the organization is always at a competitive advantage. The Wilson Group found that it could utilize the lessons of high performance for its clients as well as itself.

A Simple Mission

The mission of the Wilson Group is simple and focused: to help clients align all their performance-based reward systems with their strategies and core values. These systems then encourage and reinforce the behaviors the companies need to achieve a competitive advantage in a complex marketplace.

The Wilson Group's services include reward strategy development and assessment, base and variable compensation programs, strategic measurement systems, and recognition and performance management programs. These services may be applied to an entire organization or to select groups, such as key executives, the sales force, operations, managers, or specialized talent (e.g., information technology, engineers, physicians, and customer service staff). The Wilson Group consultants work in a wide variety of industries, and most engagements are highly customized to meet special client needs.

The organization has grown dramatically since its inception and has experienced both the pains and the joys of growth. Initially, the principle concerns were those typical of any new business—developing the desired client base, creating high-impact methodologies and tools, and managing cash flow. As the organization's client base and demand for services grew, attracting and retaining staff that shared the organization's values became a priority.

The firm has been tested by tough competition and situations that challenged its core values. But these situations have provided opportunities to bring the character of the company into clear focus. While the Wilson Group is still an early-stage company, what it does today will determine the culture and image the organization will have in the future. Therefore, the leaders are careful to create the organization they want so that future change can be minimized.

The Marketplace Context

The Wilson Group's market is complex but attractive. Opportunities are growing because few organizations are satisfied with their compensation systems. As organizations increasingly recognize that their reward systems do not fit with their business strategies and success factors, they want change. When they realize the impact reward systems have on their culture and their ability to compete, they search for advisors that can provide new ways of thinking about their people management systems.

The compensation consulting industry has several tiers of competition. One tier is composed of several large companies that have a broad network of offices and extensive capabilities and talents. The second tier includes smaller, specialized firms built around specific services or a geographic or industry market niche. The third tier is made up of individual practitioners, including academic professors, with a special interest and expertise in compensation.

Many companies have become disillusioned with large consulting firms, having experienced a lack of responsiveness, creativity, and commitment to their needs. This has created opportunities for smaller firms that are more focused and more responsive. While the smaller firms may lack the depth of resources of larger firms, they often provide better value for the client.

Another factor benefiting second-tier firms is the changing requirements for consulting. Clients want solutions that are custom-tailored to their needs. They don't want boilerplate. Clients want to work with the seasoned professionals who gain their trust and confidence during the selection process, not the junior associates that the larger firms often send in after the contract is signed. Clients want to work with consultants who have in-depth experience and specialized know-how, and whom they will enjoy working with. Ego-centered consulting is no longer acceptable. They also want the security and confidence of knowing that the solutions presented will address their needs and work effectively. If a small firm can demonstrate these desired capabilities, it can often effectively compete for the same assignments as the larger firms.

Because there are few barriers to entry, the Wilson Group recognized that it could compete successfully by focusing on an attractive niche and establishing a reputation for exceptional value and responsiveness. To grow, the Wilson Group needed to build an organization that distinguished itself in the marketplace and win clients in head-on competition with regional and national firms.

To accomplish this, the Wilson Group needed to establish a competitive advantage that could not be easily replicated by other firms, small or large. While competing on price can help a firm gain market share, it is not a viable long-term strategy in the consulting industry. A better approach is to create greater value for the client than the competition. This requires innovative, high-quality services, a proven set of tools and methodologies, and resources to invest in growth. It also requires the ability to attract and retain better people than the competition.

Reward Systems for an Emerging Company

Early in the life of the Wilson Group, the founder realized that a certain kind of person was essential to the company's success. The staff members needed to have the requisite technical expertise, and they needed an interpersonal style that is consistent with the firm's core values. They also needed people who want to work for a small consulting firm, rather than starting their own business or working for an established company.

To be effective in attracting this kind of individual, the Wilson Group needed to create an environment where talented people feel truly valued for their contributions. A variety of reward systems, formal and informal, had to be created to shape the desired culture. Compensation is important, but so are flexibility, opportunity, challenge, and the knowledge that you are valued for your contributions. Since the Wilson Group is in the business of developing reward systems that align with strategy, it needed to follow the same framework it prescribes to others. It developed a reward strategy.

Realizing that desired performance needs to be rewarded quickly, the core (or base) compensation program should reinforce the individual's efforts to generate revenues. The amount paid should reflect the individual's competencies and performance. In addition to rewarding individual performance, there needs to be team-based incentives to reinforce working together to build a strong organization. This program should encourage the firm's growth and implementation of its annual business plans. There should be both cash and stock options opportunities to create a meaningful stake in the future of the business. The value of the rewards should reflect the firm's growth and competitiveness over time.

Finally, both formal and informal recognition should assist in reinforcing special actions of individuals or teams that support the company's core values. The cash compensation plans reinforce the firm's strategy and business drivers, and the recognition practices reinforce the firm's values and desired culture. Each element thereby operates as part of a total system, which translates the firm's key success factors into action.

Description of Reward Programs

In professional service firms, compensation is the organization's largest expense and cash flow is always a major concern. At the Wilson Group, consultants are paid an established commission percentage of the revenues they bill to clients each month. Their billing rate is established by the degree of competency they have in practice areas, project management, and consulting. The commission rate reflects the competencies and degree of risk in the compensation package. The revenue consultants generate is a reflection on their performance in providing highly valued services to clients. Thus, the monthly pay reflects both competencies and performance.

By paying the consultants as projects are billed, they receive a nearly immediate reward for their performance. The company then serves a banking function and is responsible for collecting amounts billed. In months when consultants perform well, they receive a large check. When client activity is limited, and the company has limited revenues, the check is smaller. The challenge of the company is to retain sufficient projects so that each consultant's monthly income does not fluctuate too widely and they achieve a target compensation level.

This unique variable base pay system is altered for new consultants, who typically need a transitional period. New consultants usually receive a guaranteed draw and can earn additional income when they exceed specific revenue levels. This encourages increasing applied time, but does not penalize new consultants as they learn and develop their portfolio of client projects. The threshold level and duration of this guaranteed pay system depends on the background of the consultant and project opportunities. Consultants who are on total commission receive a larger percentage commission than those who are on a guaranteed or draw pay.

In addition to their monthly income, all staff members participate in the companywide incentive plan. The plan is designed to encourage individuals to work collaboratively and reward contributions to grow and develop the organization. This program uses four to five performance measures tailored to the individual's role and personal interests. Two measures are common to all members. The first measure is growth in company revenues. If business opportunities can be shared with others, and revenues grow as a result, everyone receives benefits. The second measure is based on the total score from the company's customer satisfaction survey. A questionnaire survey is distributed to clients after the completion of each project; it provides feedback on a variety of performance indicators that reflect the firm's values and strategy and key success factors. The responses are tabulated and analyzed and the results added into the group's performance results.

For some consultants, a third measure is personal sales volume, which credits them for generating sales of client projects. The company pays a sales commission only to a few key business development consultants, but others are compensated based on a sales credit system. If two or more consultants work together to develop a new client, they can split the sales credit based on the role each performed. The sales credit can range up to 200% of the project's total revenues; no one can receive greater than 100% credit. Each consultant has sales goals that are greater than what the individual can bill personally. This encourages collaboration on all sales efforts.

Some consultants use revenue credit from projects they managed as a measure. This performance reflects revenue generated from client projects or from specific tasks within a major project, where the consultant plays a leadership role. As with sales credits, the goals are greater than what one can produce alone. This encourages individuals to assume responsibility for clients and projects and involve others in one's projects.

Individuals may also have personal measures related to important assignments that will benefit the company without directly producing revenues. These efforts include:

- Conducting conference presentations
- Writing for publication
- Implementing new technology or systems within the company
- Implementing practice areas or industry-based business plans
- Learning or developing something for the company

Finally, when individuals designate a specific major goal, such as earning a special certification or having an article accepted by a major publication, they can earn special achievement points as well as recognition. These special goals are developed collaboratively with each consultant and reflect business objectives for the specific year. In some cases, individuals share the same measures, such as implementing business plans or installing new systems in the company. The combined set of measures balances individual and team performance, revenue generation with building infrastructure, and strategic with tactical goals.

To organize all these factors, the program uses a scorecard for displaying measures and setting specific goals (see Figure 2-3). All consultants have their own scorecard, and the resulting total score is applied as a percent to the individual's target incentive payout. For example, a 100% score means the individual receives 100% of his target incentive. Payouts range from a minimum of 60% to a maximum of 150% of target. Payouts are made twice a year; the first six months' payout is based on that period's performance, and the second six months' payout is based on total annual performance.

Individuals receive feedback on all revenue-based measures monthly. They discuss other measures during staff meetings as appropriate. The scorecard provides active performance measures, and individuals can easily determine how well they are performing.

Although the company is privately held, all staff members are eligible to receive stock options in addition to their cash compensation. Stock gives staff members a tangible stake in the success of the company that grows in value as the company grows in value. The company's value is determined annually by the board of directors using a formula based on total annual revenues and profitability. The number of shares and when they are presented (every one to three years) are based on the staff member's contribution to the growth of the company. Stock options are likely to be granted if the individual generates significant revenues in excess of personal billings, develops new tools and methodologies in key practice areas, or enhances the capabilities of the company's infrastructure. The board of directors determines stock option awards after discussions with key individuals within the firm.

Stock options represent an important, symbolic stake in the company, but they are beginning to take on greater meaning as the company grows in value. For some, stock options may provide a substantial future income opportunity if the company is sold or recapitalized. The firm may create an employee stock ownership plan (ESOP) or provide other opportunities for cashing in stock in the future where payouts would come from retained earnings.

The limitation with each of these reward systems is timing.

Measures	X Weight	60%	70%	80%	90%	100%	110%	120%	130%	140%	150%	Points
Total WGI Revenues	40	$AAA	$BBB	$CCC	$DDD	$EEE	$FFF	$GGG	$HHH	$III	$JJJ	
Companywide Customer Satisfaction Survey Results	10	75	80	82	84	86	88	90	92	94	96	
Revenue from Projects Managed	20	$AA	$BB	$CC	$DD	$EE	$FF	$GG	$HH	$II	$JJ	
Strategic Projects Completed (see checklist)	30	1	2	3	4	5	6	7	8	9	10	

Total Score

Special Achievement Opportunities:

_____ _____

_____ _____

_____ _____

Payout Opportunity Table

Target Incentive: $ _____

Total Score: × _____ %

Payout = $ _____

Figure 2-3. The consultant's performance scorecard.

While monthly commission income reflects personal effort, other performance rewards are significantly delayed. To address this, the Wilson Group also provides informal, spontaneous rewards to people when appropriate. One consultant, for example, was given a personal fax machine for her new home office after selling a major new project to a difficult client. Another consultant, who is a wine connoisseur, was given an especially good bottle of wine after signing the company's largest contract to date. Project demands kept a third consultant from spending time with a visiting parent on several occasions, so she was given round-trip airfare to visit her parent. This gift reflects one of the Wilson Group's core values, that people lead a balanced life.

Recognition rewards are provided for important contributions to the organization. While they are often made after the fact, they are based on clear, consistent actions by individuals who help achieve company goals, such as reinforcing client relationships, bringing in new business, and fulfilling client commitments. Rewards must be based on several important principles. They must be:

- Tied to actions that support company values
- Made immediately after, or as soon as possible after, the action was taken
- Highly personalized and meaningful to the individuals who were rewarded

Informal rewards are becoming increasingly important to the company. In combination with cash-based compensation, they help create a portfolio of rewards that shape the company's desired culture today and in the future.

Aligning Rewards With Values

Over a series of strategic planning meetings, members of the Wilson Group developed mission, vision, and value statements that serve as a cornerstone for decisions and actions. As a relatively new company, it is critical to articulate these concepts and integrate them into all activities. The alignment between these principles and the rewards, informal and formal, is of paramount importance.

The Wilson Group's five core values are:

1. Deliver exceptional value to clients.
2. Collaborate with clients and each other.
3. Be innovative and creative in providing solutions.
4. Be honest and demonstrate integrity in all actions.
5. Have fun and lead a balanced life.

These values are reinforced by a combination of several reward practices within the company. The cash incentive compensation plans focus on revenue growth, which is achieved by providing exceptional value to clients. Selling new projects to existing clients, as well as achieving high customer satisfaction survey results, are additional demonstrations of this core value.

Collaboration is reinforced in many ways. Conducting regular staff meetings, involving others in projects, collaborating on sales efforts, and sharing company information on project staffing and financial performance contribute to a collaborative culture. Many client projects are conducted with design teams and special task forces within the client organization, reinforcing collaboration not just internally but externally.

Innovation and creativity are also encouraged in many subtle but important ways. During staff meetings, consultants share innovations or new approaches that have benefited their clients. They also periodically prepare guidebooks on different practice areas, and others use these materials in other projects. Distributing and utilizing innovative ideas is more important than "owning" them. Support staff members look for ways to improve operational efficiency, increase positive customer relationships, and experiment with new systems or processes. In addition to traditional support functions, they research processes that can help consultants work to their maximum potential. Ideas are frequently discussed in open forums and short-term task forces are established to handle specific issues. Innovations that increase the growth of the organization can also be rewarded with stock options. The company also invests heavily in internal and external training, and all staff members attend major conferences.

Integrity and honesty are recognized as important principles of conduct. Integrity begins at the top of the organization and is important in everything people at the Wilson Group do. Some company members have assumed the role of the company's conscience and they highlight situations when others act as role models or fail to act in a manner consistent with the core values. This form of dialogue creates healthy exchanges and is encouraged. While mistakes occur, they are treated as opportunities to learn, clarify values, and reinforce commitments.

Having fun is one of the most important values of the organization. This is reflected in promotional materials used for marketing and recruitment, and it is demonstrated in everyday actions. Laughter is encouraged through spontaneous and genuine fun activities. A sense of humor is an important criterion for hiring and is important in how members act with each other and with clients.

To achieve a balance between home and work, the company is highly flexible about work hours, time commitments, and dress. The focus is on the client commitments, not on some arbitrary time or dress requirement of the company. Technology, such as e-mail, voice mail, and office networking, enables consultants to work from home or other locations without sacrificing client service. Staff members are not judged based on the "face time" they put in at the office. Some work part-time or have flexible hours to address personal or family needs. While policies are in place, individual situations dictate the proper response. Staff members are not expected to work excessive hours, but they are required to meet client commitments.

The company respects the individual's personal time. Staff meetings take place during normal business hours, and evening phone calls, while sometimes necessary, are infrequent. Weekend hours are expected only when necessary to meet tight client deadlines. Creating a workplace that is fun, balanced, and personally fulfilling is a deliberate part of the firm's everyday culture.

The Results and the Future

In a recent study comparing the Wilson Group with other consulting firms, it was found that the Wilson Group has grown faster than its competitors, pays higher compensation, has a higher profit margin, and has competed more successfully for new business.

The firm has created a distinctive workplace and a national stature in a short period.

The future of a new company is always uncertain. Marketplace and internal challenges test every company. The Wilson Group will face situations where short-term pressures outweigh long-term investments. The economy will not always grow at the rate it is growing today. As new people join the firm, they will change the culture. The evolution of the organization as it grows will require more structure and control, more systems and procedures. Growth may challenge the highly personal feel of the organization. However, if companies such as Southwest Airlines, Starbucks, Amazon.com, and Keane (whose case studies are discussed in this or other chapters throughout this book) can sustain a culture of high performance, so can this company. The challenge for the Wilson Group's leaders will be to continue to reinforce the company's core values as the company grows.

The Wilson Group has emerged as an attractive firm in the consulting industry and a strong competitor. It has articulated its values and remains committed to fulfilling them. It has established programs and practices that are building the desired culture. Working and behaving according to the core values has become a priority for all staff members. The Wilson Group will need to continue attracting people whose work style is consistent with the company's principles of success. The market for creating high-performance organizations is immense and growing daily. The Wilson Group's continued success depends on its ability to be an innovative thought leader, to deliver exceptional value to clients, and to be a highly attractive place to work and work with. This means people, tools, and culture are key to its future. People in this company are making a difference to their clients, their company, and themselves.

3

Creating a Stake
in the Enterprise

One of the common themes of the companies presented in this chapter is how they seek to create a bridge between the requirements for success and each individual. The factors of corporate success are very different. The approach each company uses is different. Yet they have a common desire to share the risks of performance with the individuals who will create success.

Each company understands how important are the actions of individuals. You will see a combination of stock-related programs as well as the use of multiple reward systems. This stake in the enterprise goes beyond a symbolic representation and defines a process for linking people to the organization.

You will see how DuPont has developed an all-employee stock option program. Coca-Cola uses a critical set of metrics to drive performance that has produced a significant increase in the value of the company. Saturn has developed an incentive-pay program that supports a culture of quality, collaboration, and service. Saturn has created a different kind of car company. Boone County National Bank has implemented a similar all-employee incentive program and created a different kind of bank. IdeaScope Associates has developed an innovative array of financial and recognition-based rewards. Finally, Cisco Systems has established multiple strategies to connect people to the business of the organization, and all have benefited from this alignment.

Each story is different, but each organization has found a way to create for their members a common stake in the organization. This process has enabled each organization in its own way to create a connection and achieve success.

CREATING A SHARE IN THE SUCCESS OF THE CORPORATION AT

DuPont Corporation

Have you ever wondered how to create a stake in the success of a large enterprise? How does a large company provide a mechanism for all 136,000 employees to share in the ups and downs of the organization? DuPont has developed such a program and integrated it into the culture of a performance-oriented culture.

In the late 1980s, DuPont looked for a way to share both the benefits of a successful company and the responsibilities for achieving growth objectives with the employees. A design team of representatives from across the company developed the program. They explored several options, including what companies such as Pepsi-Cola were doing. They concluded that the best system was to provide stock options to all employees. The program was entitled the DuPont Shares Program.

Chairman of the Board E. S. Woolard, Jr., said, "If we are to be a great global company, we cannot separate the ideas of valuing people and achieving financial success—they are two sides of the same coin." His support of the program and demonstration of commitment to all employees worldwide made this program possible.

The DuPont Shares Program

The program was inaugurated in 1991. That year every full-time employee across the world received an award of 100 stock options in DuPont. The value of the options would be based on the growth, profitability, and performance of the company in the marketplace. Each employee has a role in achieving these results. Along with the option grant, employees received considerable education about what a stock option is and how an individual employee's performance can impact the value. Company management discussed the reason for the plan and how it was part of an overall series of reward systems targeted to creating a meaningful stake in the company for each employee. Employees in countries where there are legal requirements against owning U.S. securities had an account established in their name that would mirror the stock performance and provisions of the program, only the payout would be made in cash (local currencies covered from U.S. dollars).

The program has several important provisions. First, an employee needs to retain the options for one year before he or she can exercise them. Second, the employee then has up to 10 years to transfer the options into actual stock in the company. At that time the option would expire. Third, an individual can exercise the stock option by paying cash for the stock at the exercise price or utilize some of his or her options to purchase the stock in a cashless transaction. All transactions are made in U.S. currency and are available to all employees worldwide.

A fourth provision is that a distribution of stock options is not provided annually. Unlike other programs, the design team did not want to create an entitlement of annual grants. The Office of the Chairman must determine whether there should be a distribution based on the performance of the corporation. This makes it a discretionary program and creates a degree of uncertainty about the program.

Finally, all employees participate in the program, including DuPont's executives. Even though they receive additional options based on performance, their participation in this program is included in determining the target number of options they receive. This reflects an important value of equity in the participation of this program.

Transferring Value to the Employees

The value of the options is based on the growth of the stock price. The price of the option is based on the current market rate of the year in which the options are granted. If DuPont continues to perform well in the market and the stock market favors this growth, then the value of the stock increases. During the period from 1981 to 1990, the value of DuPont stock increased an average of 10% per year. In fact, it increased an average of 21% a year from 1985 to 1989. In other words, if an individual had invested $1,000 in Du-

Pont in 1981, the money would have been worth $2,625 by 1990. With the initial grant price in 1991 at $37, the stock has increased in value by 1997 to more than $120 (on a 1997 pre-split basis), which is almost a three times growth in shareholder value. This opportunity for growth in shareholder value is exactly what the design team intended for each employee.

The value of the DuPont Shares Program has been in how it has changed the mind-set of employees and how they perceive their relationship with the corporation. The program was intended to create a sense of shared destiny, of a common fate between the employee and the corporation. As the fortunes of the company rise and fall, so too does the impact on employees. The impact goes beyond their employment status or their direct compensation, but depends on the value of their "stake" in the company.

Some argue that this program is ineffective in influencing individual behaviors. The designers did not intend for the program to impact individual performance. DuPont maintains and continues to develop a wide range of specific incentive and recognition programs that influence the actions of people. The executives wanted this DuPont Shares program to be an additional element in a broad portfolio of rewards available to employees. It is difficult to ascertain the link, if any, between an individual who views the stock price in the morning paper over breakfast and the actions she takes that day to make DuPont a more successful company. DuPont has created, in some measure, a process that links employees with the concerns of management and all shareholders.

There are those that criticize the program for not placing more risk in the program. The critics point out that DuPont has provided employees with an opportunity without withholding some other tangible reward. The design team considered a wide range of issues in developing this program. A central objective was to create a positive impact on employees and encourage them to consider DuPont as their own company. The risk is that without growing the value of DuPont's shares there will be no gain. Hence, the program is more focused on opportunity than risk.

Overcoming the Concerns

The wide use of stock option programs has also been criticized by some for diluting the impact on share price (i.e., if more shares are on the market and the value of the company does not grow accordingly, the value of each share will be reduced) and creating unrealistic expectations of gains. The market value of a company is not always dependent on the firm's performance; hence, there is a risk of stock devaluation because of broad external market forces over which people have little control. If people have an expectation that the stock price always rises and the firm expects people to share in this growth, both may be severely disappointed.

The dilution impact of the program has been minimal. At the launch of the program, only 100 shares were provided to each of the 130,000-plus employees; this represented less than 5% of the outstanding stock. Furthermore, if the company grows, the impact is minimal. If the company does not grow, no stock options are awarded. So there is a self-regulating feature to the program.

In terms of the fluctuations of the marketplace, DuPont has clearly communicated this risk to its employees. The company frequently communicates share price to all employees, as well as explains events in the company and the market that may influence the price. The company also provides a 10-year time frame in which individuals may exercise their options, and then they may retain the shares or sell them. Furthermore, if the company does not perform well, there is no guarantee of a stock option distribution. An interesting challenge to the company arises when the stock price falls below the exercise price of the option. People will realize that this program is for the long-term. Since this program is only one element in an array of reward programs, the stock price may have only limited impact.

Stock options were distributed to employees in 1991, the initial year. They were again awarded in 1995 and 1997. There is anticipation on whether they will be provided in 1998 and beyond. The overall objective is to achieve growth in stock value of the company so that each employee will realize significant gains.

The Future of DuPont Shares

The program continues to be modified as market and business conditions change. For example, there was a special provision for stock options awarded in 1997. The stock must achieve $75 per share for five days before individuals will be able to exercise the options. The value at the grant of the options was $52.50 per share.

This needs to be achieved by 2002 or they will be forfeited. Consequently there is significant pressure to grow the value of the company. To this point, DuPont is well on its way to achieving this goal.

The principal challenges to developing this program were in three areas. First, the company applied this program to all employees worldwide. The design team needed to research and comply with the investment laws of each country in which DuPont operates. Furthermore, they established a global partnership with Merrill Lynch to administer the program.

Second, many employees did not understand what a stock option was or what it meant to own one. There was a significant investment in training and education about stock, stock options, and the drivers of DuPont's performance. This had many important benefits to building the culture and "common fate" philosophy the executives sought from this program.

Finally, DuPont wants the program to be dynamic and alive with employees. Therefore, there is ongoing communication about the company and the stock's performance. Often discussion points are made in relation to the share price, and this provides common ground for all members of the corporation. There is risk associated with this program, not in terms of loss but in terms of not realizing a desired gain.

There is also a great deal of excitement about the DuPont Shares Program. It has aligned the interest of executives with all employees; it has created a connection between employees and shareholders. Both have a common goal of building DuPont into one of the world's leading companies and sharing the gains that are realized by this achievement. This gain is not guaranteed, but it can be achieved if people take the actions that lead to the corporation's success. At least for now, it has created a common bond.

LINKING INCENTIVE COMPENSATION AND EVA TO DRIVE SHAREOWNER VALUE
AT

The Coca-Cola Company

The Coca-Cola Company leads the worldwide beverage industry in terms of volume, profitability, growth, and innovation. Its primary objective as a company is to grow shareowner value over time, and it has been extremely successful in recent years in achieving that objective. The total market value of its stock grew from $15 billion at the end of 1986 to $165 billion at the end of 1997.

However, from the company's perspective, much remains to be done. Around the world, the company still supplies less than 2 of the 64 ounces of liquid intake the average person needs each day. And the company's focus remains resolutely on going after the other 62!

To do so, it operates in accordance with three guiding objectives. First, it works to fuel growth within the industry, increasing overall demand for beverage products. Second, it focuses on innovation in every area of the business, including marketing, packaging, and people management. Third, it manages for the long-term, making investments today that will pay off in the future.

Setting the Strategic Measures

To ensure that every decision it makes is sound from a financial and shareowner value perspective, the company is managed from an economic value added (EVA) and economic profit viewpoint. EVA and economic profit are closely linked and serve as decision-making tools that allow all associates to ensure they are creating shareowner value with every decision they make and every action they take. EVA is defined as the change in economic profit from one year to the next. Economic profit is defined as net operating profit after taxes (NOPAT) minus a charge for operating capital.

In the mid-1980s, the company's financial systems began tracking, measuring, and reporting aggregate economic profit. Through refinements and enhancements, by the early 1990s economic profit data became available on a regular basis at the operating division level (approximately 25 worldwide, geographic units that report in to corporate).

With the availability of the financial data now ensured, and with the increasingly focused effort on creating shareowner value at all levels of the organization, the compensation group of the company led an effort to realign variable pay programs to focus on economic profit. The process was a straightforward one consisting of essentially four steps:

1. Review overall business strategy and key business drivers.
2. Assess alignment of current incentive and stock option programs with those drivers.
3. Redesign incentive and stock option programs to more closely match business needs.
4. Implement and communicate the changes.

The outcome of that process included several key conclusions:

1. Financial measures are the most critical measures of the company's success.
2. Volume and profit results are equally important.
3. Each division should stand alone in its performance and not be rewarded or penalized based on total company performance.
4. Each division should have flexibility to determine the exact distribution of incentive and stock option awards.
5. One universal program design should apply consistently to headquarters and all operating divisions and to all levels of associates.

The resulting program design is best described as a funding pool with flexible distribution to individuals based on value-added contributions to the results. The programs are consistent on a worldwide basis and all associates from mid-level professional and above are eligible to participate. A specific description of the annual incentive and stock option programs follows.

The Annual Incentive Program

Each division, working with senior management, determines an objective for unit case sales of company products (volume) and economic profit (profit). These two objectives become the target for the division for annual incentive purposes. For corporate associates, the target for incentive purposes is the objective for the total company.

At the end of the year, the performance of each division is assessed versus its objectives for the year relative to a funding matrix. The matrix weights volume and profit equally. If divisions meet their objectives exactly, then incentives are funded at 100%

of target. If they exceed objectives, they are funded at greater than 100%, and if they fall short, they are funded at less than 100%. The targeted pool itself is simply the total amount required to award each participant in the plan their exact target, which is expressed as a percent of base salary (e.g., 10%, 15%) based on job grade level.

Once the pool for the division is funded, then division management decides how the exact pool will be distributed. Each division has the responsibility to set specific team and individual objectives that link into the total division objectives. Based on individual and team performance against those objectives, each participant then receives a specific annual incentive award, which falls within a broad range from no award to the maximum award. It is the responsibility of each division to make sure that total incentive awards do not exceed the amount allocated and that the total awards balance against the pool.

The Stock Options Program

The process for stock option awards is similar to that of annual incentives: Option pools are funded based on performance against unit case sales and economic profit objectives, and individual option grants are determined based on specific contribution to those objectives. Stock option awards are considered annually and fall within a minimum to maximum of a specified range, which varies by grade level and is driven by targeted total compensation levels versus the marketplace. Division management considers each eligible associate each year for an appropriate grant and then recommends that amount for approval by the compensation committee of the board.

For both annual incentives and stock options, awards for corporate associates come from and must balance against the corporate pool, which is based on total company performance.

Impact of the Programs

The effect on the business of the clear linkage of incentive and stock option awards to economic profit has been very positive. Some of the benefits include the following:

- ▸ More attention is given in the planning process to the amount and cost of capital required to deliver volume and profit results.
- ▸ Managers and associates now focus more daily attention than ever not only on generating volume and profit, but doing so in a way that covers capital costs and enhances shareowner value.
- ▸ The communication efforts surrounding the importance of value-based management are reinforced financially twice a year through incentive and stock option awards.
- ▸ The economic profit levels of the company and the resulting increase in shareowner value continue to grow at healthy rates. Figure 3-1 shows that as economic profit grew an average of 20.2% per year for 10 years ending with 1997, stock price grew an average of 30.2% per year for the same period.

Even though the plan is working well and the company's financial results are strong, there are still aspects of this approach that Coca-Cola continues to work to improve.

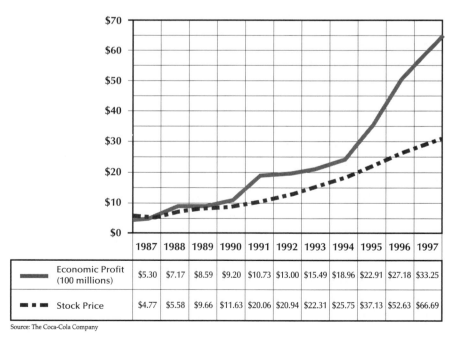

	1987	1988	1989	1990	1991	1992	1993	1994	1995	1996	1997
Economic Profit (100 millions)	$5.30	$7.17	$8.59	$9.20	$10.73	$13.00	$15.49	$18.96	$22.91	$27.18	$33.25
Stock Price	$4.77	$5.58	$9.66	$11.63	$20.06	$20.94	$22.31	$25.75	$37.13	$52.63	$66.69

Source: The Coca-Cola Company

Figure 3-1. Relationship between economic profit and stock price growth.

One of these is the budget process. Since so many financial rewards are directly tied to performance versus budget (at both the division and corporate level), the company works constantly to ensure that business plans are set with the same degree of difficulty across all divisions. In other words, senior management has regular dialogue with the operating units to make sure they are planning on capturing all available growth in volume and profit in both the short-term and the long-term. Such judgments are rarely simple ones, but they are necessary to ensure both business growth and equitable opportunities for financial rewards for those divisions that perform well.

A second constant challenge relates to communication to the individual participant. Since both the pool funding and individual or team performance can vary, it is difficult to explain to an individual precisely what his exact reward would be under different performance scenarios. For instance, a participant could perform exceptionally well, but if the division does poorly, then his payout could be reduced significantly because the overall pool is lower. Explaining this team-based, zero-sum approach in a simple and easily understood manner is a constant challenge.

A final challenge relates to making sure that every participant has some line-of-sight between his or her actions and the financial rewards received from these plans. Part of this endeavor involves general education about value-based management (a major priority of the company) and how decisions should be made. Part of it involves clear objectives that relate to and drive portions of the volume or economic profit equation. The final piece involves demonstrating how the individual's reward links back to the overall value added to the business.

A fundamental communication to all associates at the company is: "Everything you do today will either create or destroy value for The Coca-Cola Company." With that level of focus on value creation, the close linkage of incentive and stock option programs to EVA currently in existence is exactly right for the company. The programs are working well, are fully aligned with business needs, and no major changes are planned.

However, since another shared value is continuous discontent with the immediate present, the company will continue to be vigilant in monitoring all aspects of its rewards programs to ensure they improve, evolve, and change as necessary to support the company on its infinite journey to create shareowner value.

BEING A DIFFERENT KIND OF COMPANY
AT

Saturn Corporation

How does a different kind of car company remain a different kind of car company? This is the challenge facing Saturn, a wholly owned subsidiary of General Motors. Saturn had the luxury of creating a company with strong financial investments by the parent organization. Since its inception in 1985, it has created many new models for management and labor relations. It has been able to create a culture that truly lives by values of customer focus, collaboration, and market responsiveness. But as it faces increasing competition and a changing marketplace, there are pressures to return to "traditional" ways of operating. The important conclusion is that Saturn cannot go back to old practices because the changes have been fundamentally integrated into the very fabric of the organization.

One of the major contributors to the process of change and the organization's culture has been its reward systems. However, as Dennis Finn, Saturn's human resources advisor points out, the reward systems support the new process of management but do not determine it. One needs to fully understand the cultural dimensions that characterize Saturn before one can appreciate the value of this statement.

The Formation of Saturn

The genesis of Saturn's formation was based on a simple reality—the American automobile industry had lost significant market share over the 1970s and 1980s to foreign car companies, principally Japan. General Motors, which was perhaps the most resistant to change, decided to create a skunks-works organization to develop a new car model and a new manufacturing process. Roger Smith, chairman of General Motors, sponsored this effort at the highest level of the corporation. He was joined in the sponsorship by Don Ephlin, the then vice president of the International United Auto Workers (UAW) and the representative to the General Motors Corporation. A group of 99 individuals from across the corporation and the union were brought together to research high-performance work sites, analyze customer needs and preferences, and develop a new car model. They were chartered under an entity known as the Saturn Study Center with a simple but powerful mission to recommend the best approaches to manufacture a small car for the United States based on the integration of people and technology.

This massive study effort resulted in the preparation of a paper, which some have referred to as the equivalent of a constitution or Declaration of Independence, entitled "Memorandum of Agreement." This 1,600-word document laid out the principles and practices necessary to develop a new car for the American marketplace. The key points included:

- ▸ People want to and should be involved in decisions that affect them.
- ▸ People care about their jobs and those they work with.
- ▸ People take pride in their work and their contributions to the company.
- ▸ People should share in the success they help create.

These simple statements of philosophy became the basis for the organization in practice today and the reward systems that support the process of the organization. Furthermore, the Memorandum defined goals for quality, cost, and customer satisfaction. It was a business document as well as a statement of organizational success factors.

The UAW representatives were highly involved in the Saturn Study Center, drafting the Memorandum and defining the staffing process for the new company. When the UAW ratified the Memorandum, it achieved a commitment that the organization would be highly committed to the labor organization. This meant that more than 6,000 people would be drawn from other parts of General Motors and moved to Spring Hill, Tennessee. They had no facility, car designs, or dealer networks. Each of these would need to be built, but these tasks would conform to the principles and spirit of the Memorandum.

A Different Kind of Reward System

From the start, Saturn wanted to build on the concepts of collaboration and sharing in the success of the enterprise. This also meant that people would have clear goals, accountabilities, and contributions to make the company highly competitive in the marketplace. New people would be hired based on consistent hiring criteria and they would work within the guidelines of the Memorandum. One key objective outlined in the Memorandum was that pay would ultimately be at-risk and that 20% of the target total compensation would be variable. This meant that base pay would be set at below market levels and the difference would be made up through variable compensation. After the initial start-up phase of the company, it was determined that the at-risk portion of pay would be phased in, but that the company would have an active variable compensation program.

The variable pay program was implemented in 1992. In this initial year, the incentive target was set at 5% of pay. Individuals could earn this amount if they successfully completed specific critical training activities to enable the teams to handle nontraditional responsibilities such as budgeting, workplace organization, materials management, scheduling, safety, and housekeeping. This was important as a precedent-setting measure for several reasons. First, the company was in a start-up mode and new work practices needed to be established. The focus of work would be through teams, and employees needed to understand the production process, have strong communication skills, and be highly effective in working with others as a team. Second, Saturn established a goal to be a learning organization. By emphasizing training as the initial focus, this reinforced the point of learning within the culture of the new organization. Finally, there was little baseline from comparable manufacturing plants on which to establish reliable goals. By using a fairly conservative approach initially, the program was able to get up and running and establish standards of performance that would be set once the process was understood.

By 1998 the pay at-risk portion has grown to 12%. The variable compensation program was structured in two parts. The first component, the pay at-risk portion, focuses on three key goals:

1. *Quality performance (4% of pay).* The goal is to build Saturn cars that meet or exceed competitive quality levels. This was measured by an audit team using International Uniform Vehicle Audit (IUVA) standards. Saturn needed to at-

tain 9.0 discrepancies per vehicle (DPV) or lower to achieve maximum payout of 4%.

2. *Achievement of training goals (4% of pay)*. The goals included performing an approved individual training plan (50%) and receiving a minimum of 92 hours of training credit during the year (50%).

3. *Team effectiveness goals (4% of pay)*. The focus is on strengthening the effectiveness of teams and their contributions to the performance of the company. Teams are defined by functional groups and need to complete a minimum of one communication meeting per quarter and to identify and solve at least three high-priority safety problems. The guidelines and review process for these goals have been thoroughly defined.

The second component is the reward pay. This component is based on exceeding budgeted earnings before interest and taxes (EBIT), matrix production schedule, and quality goals. The EBIT threshold is adjusted based on production schedules to account for changes in market conditions. The financial payout is based on a sharing of actual cost reductions versus current year budgeted cost; individuals share 50% of any cost reductions above the budget. There is no cap on this sharing. However, the payout may be modified by the quality performance (based on the IUVA ratings) and on-time delivery schedule performance.

The program makes payouts quarterly. Data is charted and displayed daily and weekly so that individuals are continually aware of the performance standing and the opportunity for their additional pay. Based on the overall results, all members of the organization receive a common payout as a percent of their total earnings.

Remarkable Results

The marketplace has clearly appreciated the quality of this automobile. For several years Saturn was the only small car within the GM line that was profitable. It achieved a profitable status three years after the plant start-up; this is unprecedented in the automobile industry. The company has established a leading reputation for its cars as well as the sales and service process that supports the products. This "experiment" has changed GM as well and has served as a model of what the American autoworker can accomplish.

Members of the organization have benefited as well. The variable compensation program was established in 1992. Payouts have been achieved each year, as follows:

Year	At Risk	Payout
1992	5%	$ 1,800
1993	7%	5,000
1994	10%	3,200
1995	10%	10,000
1996	10%	10,000
1997	12%	2,100

Base salaries have increased with the market and have retained 88% of the average GM compensation. There was a $10,000 cap on the program; this was increased to $12,500 in 1997.

To illustrate the impact of the performance capabilities of the organization, one needs to review productivity results in 1996. At one point during the year, Saturn was 40,000 cars behind production schedule. This was due to strikes at part suppliers that brought work nearly to a halt. By year-end, the Saturn team had produced 314,000 cars, which was 4,000 above target. This required careful coordination among all elements of the organization and was a testimony to the leadership and involvement by many in the organization.

A Challenge to the "Memorandum of Agreement"

In March 1998, the UAW members at Saturn voted again on whether to retain this "very different" agreement between labor and management. At issue was the decline in the payouts for 1997 in relation to previous years. Since sales for small cars have declined, some hourly workers pressed for the UAW to void the agreement and replace it with a conventional wage contract. This vote was watched carefully for its test of commitment by the UAW to the partnership and whether this philosophy of compensation would endure hard times. The program is perhaps the most innovative labor contract in the U.S. auto industry. Furthermore, the market segment for small cars has cooled greatly as American consumers have become attracted to larger luxury and sport utility vehicles. Thus, would a pay program that targets base wages 12% below market and provides opportunity for incentives remain a viable pay philosophy in light of declining market growth?

The agreement implied that when business was strong, members of the Saturn organization would share in the benefit. When times were weak, would they also suffer on the downside? The union vote would test not only this philosophy of compensation but in some measure the core values of the organization.

The vote on March 11, 1998, was strongly in favor of the "Memorandum of Agreement." The margin was nearly 2–1, with 4,052 voting in favor of the agreement and 2,120 voting to change it. Both union and management leaders felt that this demonstrated that the "partnership is alive and well in Tennessee."

Although this represented a decline in the margin of victory, given the prospects of the immediate future, it remains a strong statement of support. In 1992, the union voted for the compensation contract by a margin of 87%. At that time the Saturn car was strong in the market and the prospects of payouts were high. Today, the market has changed and market success will be more difficult. It is no wonder that the average employee is concerned about the pay, but the commitment to the principles of the partnership remains intact.

The Future Will Be Different

Saturn has clearly demonstrated that a partnership in working together and sharing in the results can be highly effective. The reward system is an important element of the culture, but it is not the driving force. Instead, the focus is on a commitment to the customer, the quality of the cars, and effectively utilizing resources. Actions taken on a daily basis demonstrate how the organization is different. For example, the hiring process involves people from all levels, training is extensive and applied to the work setting, and marketing involves people in organization. This is an organization that leads by its values.

While the market for small cars may not hold the same opportunity in the future, GM is committed to keeping the success record of the company. There are efforts under way to modify the existing product line, introduce new products into this company, and expand Saturn's market reach on a global basis (e.g., manufacturing right-handed cars to fit the Japanese market). Other strategies are being developed to retain Saturn's long-term leadership in the marketplace.

The success that Saturn has achieved has given it confidence that it is indeed a high-performance organization. Among the major positive attributes are the trust and partnership established at all levels of the organization. This is perhaps the most important outcome of the management and reward process. With this characteristic as a cultural foundation, Saturn does not need to worry whether the organization can produce on commitments. It will seek new opportunities and address challenges in a manner that will retain its uniqueness. In the future, Saturn may not be a different kind of a company, only because other organizations will follow its lead.

SHARING THE BENEFITS OF PERFORMANCE
AT

Boone County National Bank

"The key issue for us," stated Bo Fraser, chief executive officer, "was to encourage the behaviors we needed to be successful in this competitive market. We are in the people business. If we are to be successful we need to be perceived by our employees as fair and willing to share the risks and rewards." Like many other community-oriented financial service companies, Boone County National Bank (BCNB) did not have the resources or network of a super-regional or nationwide bank. Yet it faced increasing competition from local, regional, and national financial institutions. The competitiveness of the marketplace was increasing and BCNB wanted to maintain and strengthen its leadership position.

However, one of the problems with creating a sense of urgency was that its employees and parent company regarded the bank as highly successful. It achieved a 55th percentile ranking on performance of peer banks and had been quite profitable for many years. Few beyond the senior executives realized that the bank needed to improve its effectiveness in the marketplace or face a more difficult struggle in the future. They needed people to take actions that would retain the bank's leadership in the marketplace. To place arbitrary goals such as a 10% cost reduction was unwise because some areas should reduce costs by 15% while others should not reduce costs at all. There were few levers by which to motivate people to take purposeful and meaningful actions.

Finally, if the bank was able to improve its performance and achieve a stronger market position, how could the bank make people feel good about it? Bo Fraser used the concept of "fairness" to describe the dilemma. If the executives and shareholders benefited from the improved performance, why shouldn't the people who made it happen share in the gains as well? It simply became a concern about fairness.

Background of the Bank

Boone County National Bank is a strong, community-oriented bank located in Columbia, Missouri. It has a long history of service and investment in the community. It has assets of $617 million and employs 344 people. It is owned by a regional bank holding company but operates in a highly autonomous manner. The organization has retained a relatively low level of turnover by offering attractive salaries, progressive management systems, and a highly supportive and personalized workplace. For example, the service award ceremony involves all employees of the bank and is highlighted by personal presentations by the CEO to each award recipient. The bank has been open in communicating its performance and maintains a strong culture of communication, collaboration, and service.

The Development of GainSharing and TEAM

The challenge was to create a process that would encourage and reward performance improvements. This led the CEO and the senior management team to decide to develop an incentive compensation plan. The overall purpose was to create a vehicle that could

create a meaningful stake in the needed improvements and develop a strong sales-oriented culture within the bank.

The design process used a team of representatives from
throughout the bank to develop the program, with guidance from
an external consultant. The membership included individuals
from senior management, commercial lending, retail banking, operations, finance, systems, and human resources. They worked
together over four months to develop the measures, payout
mechanisms, incentive opportunities, eligibility criteria, and the
costs/benefits of the program. They recommended the program to
the chief executive and senior management team and received
strong endorsement. The program was communicated through a
series of meetings and a brochure that captured the purpose and
spirit of the program. The program was titled GainSharing because it provided a way to share the gains achieved by the performance improvements. The design team has continued as
the steering committee; the overall effort, which included the
GainSharing program and other performance improvement efforts, became known as TEAM—Together Everyone Achieves
More.

Overview of GainSharing

One of the first tasks of the design team was to examine why the
bank needed the program and to develop a purpose statement that
reflected the core theme of the program. The team developed the
following statement:

> The purpose of the Boone County National Bank Incen-
> tive Program will be to recognize, reinforce, and reward
> employees for serving the needs of the Bank's customers
> which result in increased profitability and growth.

They also developed a set of guidelines for the program. The
guidelines included the following:

- ▸ Measures must align with the key success factors of the
  bank.
- ▸ The program should be easy to understand and administer.

> ▸ Measures must be objective, meaningful, and achievable.
> ▸ The program should encourage teamwork and cooperation across all areas of the bank.
> ▸ The program should communicate the business goals, the progress being made, and the results achieved in the most reinforcing manner possible.
> ▸ Feedback should be communicated in as timely a manner as possible.

The design team considered many alternative approaches during the development of the program. They concluded that the best way to reflect the complex nature of the business was to use a balanced scorecard approach to the measures. This would entail a multiple set of measures. These measures were:

> ▸ *Return on beginning equity* (the key financial measure of the bank)
> ▸ *Deposit growth* (reflects growth and market position)
> ▸ *Efficiency ratio* (an operational, well-established set of indicators)
> ▸ *Customer satisfaction* (based on a survey of customers)
> ▸ *Number of services per household* (reflects "share of wallet" or market position of the bank as well as customer retention and satisfaction)

To communicate, display, and determine payouts, the design team decided to use a performance scorecard. An illustration is shown in Figure 3-2. Each of these measures represented a major functional area of the bank. Although a significant amount of education was needed to help people understand the measures, they took great interest in the information. The scorecard therefore became a useful tool to communicate the program to employees and clarify the performance goals.

The GainSharing program is an annual plan. The payouts are made annually as well. One of the questions that arose during the design team sessions was how to ensure employees felt the payouts were fair and equitable. After much discussion, the team made the payouts as a common percentage to all eligible employees. Although people would receive different amounts of incentive

Measures	X Weight	Threshold 50	60	Budget/Plan 70	80	90	Target 100	110	120	130	Exceptional 140	Points
Customer Satisfaction (survey score)	10%											
Number of Services per Household	15%											
Deposit Growth	15%											
Efficiency Ratio	30%											
Return on Beginning Equity	30%											

Total Score

Payout Opportunity Table	
0–69	0
70–79	2%
80–89	3%
90–99	4%
100–109	5%
110–119	6%
120–129	7%
130–139	9%
140+	12%

Figure 3-2. The performance scorecard.

payout, they would all receive the same percent of the salary. All employees of the bank were eligible to participate in the plan unless they had unacceptable performance.

Keeping the Attention Focused

One of the concerns about having annual payouts was retaining the attention of employees throughout the year when the payouts may seem very distant. Then, once the program had been thoroughly communicated and employees knew how the program worked, the steering committee identified that employees had a difficult time understanding what they could do to impact the results. While they understood the measures, many employees did not know what actions they should take.

To address these two issues, the steering committee developed several effective solutions. First, the steering committee conducts a monthly meeting for all employees to review the performance of the bank and the progress on the GainSharing program. Different members of the committee present the data; this demonstrates that the program is a concern for the whole organization, not just for senior managers. Usually about one-third of the employees attend these meetings.

These meetings review the progress of the bank in each of the measurement areas. They discuss the factors that contribute to the measures and use these sessions to further educate people on the performance drivers. People frequently ask questions. These sessions have become an important element of managing the GainSharing program.

In addition to the monthly meetings, the steering committee contributes to the monthly newsletter within the bank. This newsletter reviews the results as well as describes activities that were taken in different areas of the bank to improve performance.

A second important performance improvement process implemented within the bank is brainstorming. These are quarterly sessions conducted by each department manager to develop ideas to improve the performance of the unit. The CEO reviews the minutes and action items recommended by each department and the actions are often discussed in the senior staff meetings. The steer-

TEAM	Dept:		Date:	

| | **IMPACT** | | | |
IDEAS PLANNED	Reduce Costs	Increase Income	Improve Customer Satisfaction	Improve Service Quality

| | **IMPACT** | | | |
ACCOMPLISHMENTS	Reduce Costs	Increase Income	Improve Customer Satisfaction	Improve Service Quality

Figure 3-3. Idea record sheet for brainstorming.

ing committee developed the idea of the brainstorming sessions, and the impact has been significant. Figure 3-3 is an idea record sheet.

An important learning from the brainstorming sessions is that no idea is too small or insignificant. In fact, the bank has found that many small ideas added together often lead to large savings or improvements in performance. The process first focuses the group on a single measure, and then the participants generate a list of actions that would improve performance in this area. The participants then review the ideas and determine the ones that would have the most effective impact. Some of the ideas implemented include:

- Putting all forms on a PC and sharing with other facilities
- Initiating a monthly contest based on a product or TEAM goal
- Writing a program for balancing traveler's checks to save two people two days' worth of work
- Working with customers on deposit preparation to save time
- Asking processors to work four 10-hour days for efficiency and less overtime
- Making changes on the Web site to include loan and job applications

The Impact of GainSharing on the Bank

GainSharing has had a significant impact on the bank and all employees. However, the process has not been easy. In the early stages of the program, people were excited by the opportunity of sharing in the performance improvements of the bank, but many did not know what to do differently. Even the monthly feedback session provided little clarity about the applicable actions. The bank did improve performance, and while everyone may not have changed, there was sufficient attention to the critical measures of deposit growth, customer satisfaction, and expense control that people began changing some of their actions. The brainstorming sessions showed many people the things they do that affect the bank's performance. People now question many actions and decisions, asking, "Would this be good for GainSharing?"

Measures are continually revised to improve their accuracy and validity. For example, the bank conducts regular customer satisfaction surveys and uses this tool to provide rich information to those departments with direct customer contact. The number of services per household has encouraged people to refer business leads to other areas of the bank. The senior managers update the goals each year, but the program has essentially remained unchanged over the last three years.

Perhaps one of the most memorable elements of the program is the payout celebration. After the closing of the fiscal year, the performance results are finalized and the bankwide award ceremony is scheduled. This event usually occurs around Valentine's Day. They often have fun with the images of this holiday. The steering committee organizes the sessions, identifies the theme, and outlines the roles for the senior managers. These events have become a major "happening" in the bank, one that most people look forward to for months and talk about months afterward.

For example, in one of the first sessions the meeting began with a review of the performance data by the Senior Vice President of Operations Vicki Dunscombe. Then the CEO discussed many of the exciting challenges of the year and how people were able to be successful. He discussed the importance of these results in terms of the bank's customers, the history of the bank, and his personal objectives. Then he called for the exchange of checks that had already been distributed—people did not receive their own checks but someone else's. They were instructed to find the person belonging to the check, tell them about something they had done for the bank, or just give them a simple thank-you. "For without the combined performance of everyone," as the CEO stated, "these checks would not be." The process was met with great humor, excitement, and laughter. After the cake and refreshments, employees left the meeting feeling that they had made an important contribution to the bank and shared in some important way with this success. Events like these have strengthened the culture of the bank in remarkable ways.

Today the bank is performing at record levels. It has improved its peer group position to over the 70th percentile. The bank is able to attract and retain most of the talent it needs to be successful. While challenges remain and the competition continues to improve, Boone County National Bank is ready. The key will be to sustain the level of energy and commitment into the future.

The bank has created a spirit that is unusual and reflects the sincere, active engagement of its senior executives. The GainSharing program has contributed to this success, but the real contributors have been the steering committee and each employee. For without their efforts, the performance excellence would not have been achieved.

Building Rewards for Those Who Facilitate Change at

IdeaScope Associates, Inc.

In some organizations "innovation," like other management fads, has lost its meaning and ability to inspire action. Yet most companies are challenged to develop new products, enter new markets, or address threats to their market position in new and creative ways. This often requires an organizational culture that is focused on being competitive, taking risks, and supporting new ideas.

Company Background

Strategic innovation, a process developed by the consulting firm IdeaScope Associates, Inc., of Boston and San Francisco, enables companies to see new markets, invent new product categories, and develop the discipline to implement bold ideas. The question is, does the "doctor" practice its own medicine? IdeaScope has used a variety of reward systems to create its own culture in which all staff members share in creating for their clients what they have achieved for themselves—an exciting, innovative, and highly successful company.

IdeaScope has developed a variety of reward systems that are built around a common set of principles. The five core principles are:

1. Reaching bottom line profitability goals
2. Reaching revenue growth goals
3. Delivering excellent consulting that leads to additional consulting work and advances their methodologies
4. Growing the intellectual property of the firm through both professional development and recruitment
5. Making a contribution to the field of strategy and innovation

A Total Approach to Rewards

Within this context, IdeaScope has developed and applied a total rewards concept to the organization. It is composed of three elements:

1. *Base pay.* Each "IdeaScoper" has a salary that is sufficiently competitive with the market to attract and retain desired talent. The pay levels reflect the general role within the firm, but should not foster complacency. Base pay provides stable, economic secu-

rity to individuals. Employees at higher levels, however, should not be comfortable earning only their base pay.

2. *Variable pay.* Everyone in the firm is eligible for incentive compensation. The payouts reflect both individual and firm-wide performance. The variable pay program was founded on a simple principle: Everyone should benefit from the financial success of the firm in proportion to their contributions. Although it is described in more detail below, the essential design provides a pool based on companywide profitability, with a requirement that revenue growth goals need to be achieved, and then the payout is based on each individual's contributions. Variable pay components increase at higher levels in the firm (i.e., lower levels, less variability; higher levels, more variability).

3. *Special contributions.* There are two additional noncompensation rewards programs. The first is a special spot dollar award for writing articles, getting an article published, delivering a conference speech, or bringing in a new employee. The second is a program called IdeaScope Dollars, whereby individuals can nominate other employees for going beyond the normal call of duty and/or contributing directly to one of the five core principles. Individuals are selected monthly and given IdeaScope Dollars. These dollars are exchangeable for items that improve one's quality of life. These items include weekend trips with one's family, dinner nights out, gift certificates for shopping sprees, massages, scuba gear, camera equipment, VCRs, and other items that are of special value to the individual.

The significance of these programs is how they work in combination. Each one has an impact on individuals, but working as a total system they reinforce a set of cultural values that make IdeaScope a unique environment.

How the Programs Work in Combination

The variable compensation program has a significant impact on individuals. On a monthly basis, a certain percentage (ranging from -25% to $+30\%$) of the firm's total salaries is contributed to a pool based on a sliding scale of the profit margin of the company (ranging from −40% to +40%). Then, if the company achieves its revenue growth goals for the quarter, a payout is made. If a payout is not made for a given quarter, then the pool gets carried forward. If a negative balance exists, it is carried forward until a positive balance eliminates it. If the revenue goals are exceeded, the pool may be increased. Individuals have a certain percentage of their base pay as a target incentive in the pool; whether they receive this amount depends on their individual contribution.

Individual performance is judged by two measures: the delivery of services and providing consulting excellence. For delivery, $x\%$ in personal consulting revenues (i.e., days billed at one's personal rate) is added together for each consultant to determine a "consulting day delivery" score. The percent that individuals contribute to this pool determines their share of the bonus pool. Adjustments are made for those whose work requires extensive, nonbillable travel time and for those in support roles to the consulting project.

For the excellence in consulting measure, IdeaScope uses a team incentive program. This is determined by several factors: the quality of the project (based on the average client survey feedback score), the profitability of the project, and the complexity of the team assignment (as compared to standard consulting engagements). First, a consulting project is given a client feedback score. This score is then modified by the profitability of the project (0.60 to 1.15) and by the complexity of the assignment (0.85 to 1.25). The resulting team score is then given to each member of the team. An individual will likely serve on many cases during the year and will then earn points for each engagement. The average total will determine one's overall performance rating for allocating an annual bonus.

The case team director (or project manager) will earn a score in a similar fashion except the factors include client feedback, case profitability, and the case team evaluation of the director (to include such performance criteria as availability, ability to foster applied creativity, information sharing, goal achievement, mentoring, and encouragement of teamwork).

The executives of IdeaScope share in this performance-oriented set of reward systems as well. Every individual at the director level and above has personal goals that link directly back to the five critical success factors of the organization. They have a direct impact on the decisions, resource allocations, and coaching of staff members, which can be attributed to these factors. In this way, the reward system is directly aligned with the elements needed for IdeaScope's continued growth and development.

The company is currently developing an employee stock ownership program for all staff and an incentive stock option for key leaders. This will continue to support the principles of commitment to the organization and create an environment that excels for its clients and its own future.

In professional service firms such as IdeaScope, the customer has a significant impact on everyone. If clients are not highly satisfied, the firm's reputation will not grow. If the reputation does not exceed that of competitors, the firm will not be able to obtain new business. The satisfaction of the clients is often dependent on the impact of the intervention on the organization and the ability of the client to strengthen the organization's market position. If the client organization can improve its competitiveness because of the consulting firm's assistance, both organizations benefit. Consequently, there can be an intertwined relationship between the client and the consulting firm, where their futures are inexorably linked.

Using the Guiding Framework

The reward programs that IdeaScope has developed and implemented seek to foster, in as direct a manner as possible, the five core philosophies. The programs have become a solid framework for guiding the actions of all staff members and providing them with recognition and rewards in relation to their direct actions.

Innovation is key to IdeaScope's future. The company continues to develop opportunities and services that enable its clients to command a competitive advantage. The programs outlined above are built to provide staff members with rewards that reflect growth of the business, a culture of innovative thinking and development, and the satisfaction of clients. By so doing, everyone achieves desired results.

CREATING A SHARE IN THE SUCCESS
AT

Cisco Systems, Inc.

Growth, the common characteristic of successful high technology companies, is not achieved by merely having a "hot" product. The commercial landscape is strewn with companies that had an attractive idea, developed the market, and fell prey to competitors or their own resistance to change. Sustained growth is a continuous effort of strategic actions. One company, Cisco Systems, Inc., has been able to achieve remarkable growth and maintain its leadership in the emerging market of Internet networking.

Cisco was founded in 1984 when Leonard Bosack developed a technology to link his computer lab system with his wife's system at the graduate business school. They believed there could be a market for networking systems. With money from their mortgage and a few friends, they developed a networking router product in their garage.

In the early years they depended on word of mouth for marketing and personal relationships for generating customers. In subsequent years, they used venture capital support and acquired professional management talent. Their sales exploded from $1.5 million in 1987, to $28 million in 1989, to $69 million in 1990 and $6.4 billion in 1997. Cisco is now the leading company in the computer networking market, the third-largest company on the NASDAQ and among the top 40 companies in the world. Its growth is continuing to rise as the market for Internet and networking products expands.

Success like this creates enormous challenges. Maintaining a clear focus, sustaining a strong stream of new products, and managing the financial cash flow needed for operations and investments are but a few of the challenges Cisco has faced. Attracting and retaining people is also a critical issue; Cisco's employee population has grown from 254 in 1990 to more than 13,000 in 1998. Product offerings have broadened from networking routers to an extensive line of integrated solutions—oriented equipment and services. These challenges are compounded by the fact that Cisco has achieved much of its growth by being one of the most aggressive and successful acquirers of small companies. Prospecting and integrating these companies have become elements of everyone's job. Cisco's ability to sustain this growth is part of its overall business strategy.

This is the case study about how Cisco has been able to keep the organization intact and focus on core strategic drivers of success. Other firms in this industry have attempted similar feats, but few have accomplished what Cisco has done. This company has created a common spirit and commitment to an organization with a clear purpose, and provided a process whereby people share in their success. It has become a great company.

A Business Founded on Growth

Cisco Systems is the worldwide leader in networking for the Internet and for organizations. It provides solutions that connect computing devices and people, allowing information to be transferred without regard to time, place, or operating environment. Its mission is simple: to change the way people work, play, live, and learn. With the prevalence of computer-connected networks emerging in almost every organization—private or public, government, or educational—and the transformation of communication technology into the home, this mission is not so far-fetched. In fact, all these networks of computers require technology to manage the signals and transfer of data—the products of Cisco Systems.

At this point 80% of Internet transactions flow through Cisco's products. Cisco focuses on offering solution services to companies seeking networking capabilities. It prides itself on being the leading example of the global network business. By using networked applications, the Internet, and its own applications, Cisco has saved hundreds of millions of dollars on operating costs while improving customer interface and satisfaction.

Successful Acquisitions as a Key to Growth

There is perhaps no other company that has so successfully capitalized on the consolidation of the networking industry. In the late 1980s and 1990s, the network industry grew rapidly through start-up and new ventures. Then, like other hyper-growth industries, consolidations started occurring as alliances and mergers enhanced an organization's ability to compete. Cisco's aggressive acquisition program began in 1993 with the exchange of about $95 million in stock for Crescendo Communications, another California-based networking services company. In 1994 it bought Kalpana, the leading maker of Ethernet switches. Cisco strengthened its position in the ATM (asynchronous transfer mode) switching market when it bought LightStream and StrataCom. The company also formed alliances with Hewlett-Packard, Dell, and US West to offer an integrated set of products to the growing networking market. Over the next few years, Cisco acquired Ardent Communications, Global Internet Software Group, and Precept Software to strengthen its suite of software products to support the components and systems solutions.

Cisco has used these acquisitions to position itself for the future directions of this market. Rather than relying primarily on internal research and development, Cisco has used the acquisitions to integrate promising new technologies into its market offerings. This has enabled it to penetrate new market segments and provide a highly attractive set of services to the market.

Although most organizational research studies indicate that mergers seldom produce desired results, Cisco has been able to capitalize on the integration of the new companies. Its key to success is to minimize the controls or processes it imposes on these new companies and to invest in their development and expansion. The Cisco culture has been highly adaptive and attractive to these new organizations and their people.

Because acquisitions have been so remarkably successful to Cisco, the organization has created a culture where people are continually "on the lookout" for attractive partners. Frequently people in a variety of roles, from marketing, manufacturing, advanced development, and human resources, will investigate new companies as potential partners and recommend some of them to Cisco executives. In some cases these "prospects" form alliances with Cisco, which leads to a trial arrangement. If this early-stage relationship is successful for both parties, then they pursue formalizing the ownership change. This often has a positive effect on the new acquisition candidate and makes Cisco an attractive acquisition partner for many firms in this industry. Participation in the significant growth of Cisco stock value has provided an additional reward for members of the acquired organization as well.

Utilizing Rewards to Support Cisco Values

Cisco approaches the challenge of managing growth and integration of new companies in a deliberate manner. It has established a culture that serves as an organizing framework for adaptive, flexible management systems and processes. Then it uses cash incentives to reward company performance and individual contributions. It uses stock options to give people a direct, meaningful stake in the long-term success of the company. The culture of the firm promotes three key themes in all its activities:

1. *Focus on the customer.* Listen, respond, and solve the problems or meet the needs of the customers.
2. *Teamwork.* Support and collaborate with others in the company and with strategic partners to provide the best products and services possible.
3. *Achieve stretch goals.* Set high standards for performance, never be satisfied with second best, and get results that make a real difference.

These three attributes have served as an important organizing frame of reference for the company's business integration, performance management, and reward systems. They have become components in the assessment for new acquisitions. Executives, managers, and employees take these three cultural values very seriously and make things happen that support them.

Cisco uses two principal reward systems as drivers of performance. Each program works to provide a meaningful stake in the success of the organization. One is a cash incentive program and the other is the stock options program.

Every Cisco employee participates in a cash incentive program. There are a few different programs depending on one's role in the company. Essentially, each program is an annual incentive, but there are midyear or quarterly payouts. The performance measures are tied to two key variables—company revenue and profitability and individual performance contributions. At the end of the performance period, managers assess the performance of individuals and make payout decisions. Senior managers review these decisions to ensure the assessments are fair and the top performers are effectively rewarded. The award is made in relation to a target payout level of individuals based on their role within the company. The payout opportunities are heavily leveraged and have been the source for significant payouts.

One issue that often emerges with the incentive plan is the desire to have it focused more at the operating-unit level rather than the total company. John Chambers, chief executive officer, strongly feels that a total company focus is critical to reinforcing Cisco's common culture. He believes—and the results have demonstrated strong support for this position—that the people need to see that Cisco is their primary unit for contribution rather than business units or functional areas. This enables executives to move talent around the organization without restraints on the incentive pay opportunity. It also enables people to share directly in the success of the company.

The second reward system Cisco uses is the stock options program. Each year the company provides 4.75% of outstanding shares in stock options to employees. Individuals receive these options based on several key performance factors. First, an individual is eligible to receive stock options that correspond to the overall level within the corporation. Managers are given a pool of stock options commensurate with the total number of people and eligible number of options. Then the number of options an individual may receive ranges around a target level for the position and may go up to 200% of target. Managers are able to allocate the shares as appropriate for their area, as long as the total number does not exceed allocated number of options. Approximately 10% of the people are designated not to receive any options for a given year. This encourages managers to make important assessments of each of their people. The task is taken very seriously.

The number of options an individual receives is based on several factors. First, the target number of options reflects the relative value and role of the job in the organization. The range from 0% to 200% is the same for all levels. Next, the number of options is based on the contributions of the individual to the success of the organization and on the growth potential of the individual. Specific annual performance is handled through the cash incentive program; so stock options reflect the contribution and growth potential.

Third, managers consolidate the recommended shares and review them with their vice president. The vice president reviews the recommendations, makes adjustments as needed, and finalizes the award allocations. Senior vice presidents review the allocations and can make additional allocations to top performers. The human resource managers work with each level of the organization in this decision process and ensure that the decisions are based on fair, objective, and performance-oriented criteria. Cisco has automated this process so that all 13,000 people can be reviewed and awarded stock options within nine days.

These reward systems give each organization within Cisco significant flexibility to encourage and reward high performance. As John Radford, director of organizational effectiveness, indicates, "This works to send the right messages to people and provide them with a meaningful stake in the success of the company. People feel and act like owners, because they are."

The Impact of Rewards

Cisco's growth and success in the marketplace is unparalleled. The reward systems have been key to Cisco's ability to acquire and integrate new businesses, retain critical talent, and reinforce actions that are consistent with the corporation's strategy and values. This alignment has been critical to its success.

The impact of the stock option program has been quite significant from several points of view. While most of Cisco's stock is currently owned by institutions (66%), the number of shares going to employees of the company has been significant. This has helped to create the "one company" John Chambers seeks to promote. Furthermore, the growth in the value of the shares to the individual has been incredible. The table on the next page shows several key growth indicators of Cisco from 1993 to 1997.

When a company uses stock options, it is important for people to retain the options or the stock so there is a direct relation to

Fiscal Year	Revenues (in millions)	Net Income (in millions)	Number of Employees	Share Price (at FY close)
1993	$ 649	$ 172	1,451	$ 8.65
1994	1,243	315	2,443	7.00
1995	1,979	421	4,086	18.59
1996	4,096	913	8,782	34.52
1997	6,440	1,049	11,000	53.07

company success. Whereas in other high-growth companies individuals sell their stock once a vesting period lapses, people at Cisco are retaining their stock. The previous table clearly indicates why—return on investment. Institutional investors appreciate the high degree of stock retention because it creates a connection between employees, managers, and shareholders. It also demonstrates the confidence people have in the company and its leadership.

Finally, the effective use of cash and equity-based reward systems throughout the company has enabled Cisco to retain its most critical employees. These systems support the other opportunities and challenges available to employees. Where other companies often need to implement special recognition or "golden handcuff" programs, Cisco has not. The strength of the culture, the challenging opportunities, and the impact of the reward systems have been credited with Cisco's ability to retain key talent. Cisco puts its money and stock into what it values, and the results speak for themselves.

As in other industries, there will come a time when the growth is not sustained. The impact of stock-based rewards may lessen, and the aggressive use of cash incentives may be more difficult. Executives and human resources managers understand this eventual condition. However, until that comes, Cisco will continue to focus on what it does best—changing the way we work, play, live, and learn. The flexibility of the organization and its ability to respond to changing conditions will likely be a core competence to continue this growth and success well into the future. One point is clear: Cisco has the commitment of the people in its organization because they share in the success they help create.

4

Keeping a Focus on the Customer

Customers define the importance of work and the nature of the tasks in organizations. While other companies have lost sight of their customers and the markets they serve, the companies in this chapter keep the customers' needs clearly in focus. Whether their customers are internal or external, the customer orientation has renewed and transformed these organizations.

Each of these organizations integrates the philosophy of meeting customer needs with their reward systems. This encourages collaboration within the organization and keeps the focus on serving others. As a result, these organizations become highly competitive and attractive places to conduct business.

In this chapter you will see how the Royal Bank Financial Group (part of the Royal Bank of Canada) has modified a broad-based profit-sharing program into a process for integrating people with the corporation's strategy. The strategy emphasizes customers and performance. Colony Communication transformed its culture from a fragmented "utility minded" company to a highly competitive set of teams. It built a variety of customer-impact measures into its team incentive program and achieved remarkable change. Copley Pharmaceutical built a customer-focus mentality into its base pay program. To progress to higher grades, individuals need to demonstrate stronger collaboration and impact on the customer. Starbucks has created an unusual culture that closely links the organization to the customers it serves. These case studies ought to provide useful tools and strategies on how to retain a customer focus so that people collaborate and strive to perform better. In this way, the customer benefits and so do the members of the organization.

QPI AND PERFORMANCE: BETTER WAYS TO MEASURE SUCCESS AT
Royal Bank Financial Group

Preparing for the twenty-first century, the financial services industry finds itself in a period of sweeping change. Banks and other financial services providers must adapt to changing demographics, growing customer needs and expectations, rapidly evolving technology, the globalization and re-regulation of financial markets, and increased competition alongside industry consolidation. As Canada's leading provider of financial services, Royal Bank Financial Group (RBFG) has earned customers' business by anticipating and meeting their needs, providing them with what they want at a competitive price, as well as being committed to delivering to shareholders superior, consistent returns on their investment. Moving forward, RBFG has clearly defined goals and strategic priorities to ensure the continued growth, future success, and enhancement of shareholder value (source: RBFG 1996 Annual Report.)

An Overview of Royal Bank Financial Group

RBFG is Canada's leading provider in most financial service markets, with growing and profitable global operations in 36 countries. RBFG is composed of three major business segments: Personal and Business Banking, Wealth Management, and Corporate and Investment Banking. It provides products and services to nearly 10 million consumer and business customers and has a leading market share in residential mortgages, consumer and business loans, and personal deposits. RBFG is the largest money manager, third largest in mutual funds, and Royal Bank of Canada (RBC) Dominion Securities is the largest and most profitable full-service investment dealer in Canada. Action Direct, RBFG's discount brokerage arm, is the second largest in Canada, and RBC Insurance is a significant provider of creditor life and disability, individual life, and travel insurance. RBFG operates 1,400 branches, more than 4,200 automated banking machines, more than 570 self-service account updaters, and some 84,000 point-of-sale merchant terminals. Over 1.3 million customers use Royal Direct telephone banking, and the company recently launched PC home computer and Internet banking.

RBFG's vision is to be Canada's premier financial services provider, with close to 58,000 committed employees working as a team to exceed customer and shareholder expectations. The focus is on continually improving performance in each business to achieve consistent and superior returns for shareholders. To achieve this, RBFG's strategic priorities are to grow and diversify revenues, improve efficiency, and maintain a quality risk profile.

Background of the Bank

In 1989, Royal Bank introduced the Quality Performance Incentive (QPI) Program, a broad-based incentive program designed to reward employees for their contributions to Royal Bank success. QPI led the financial services industry and was one of the first programs of its type in North America. The main objectives of QPI was to focus the efforts of all employees on the bank's strategic business plans and to tangibly reward all employees for their individual and team contributions toward helping to meet those plans. Each year, if the bank met a planned level of financial performance, a pool of funds was created to reward employees. The size of the incentive pool was determined by the degree by which the bank achieved its business objectives.

The value of individual awards was based on several factors:

- ▸ The performance of the bank as a whole
- ▸ The performance of the business or geographic area
- ▸ The employees' pay level, which determined a QPI opportunity range (i.e., the minimum and maximum amounts that could be earned under the program)
- ▸ The employees' contributions in achieving their key priorities

The program has evolved over the years with a major redesign in 1996 to meet the challenges of the changing work and business environments and maintain leadership in performance-based compensation.

Nature of the QPI Redesign

In the spring of 1996, employee focus groups were conducted with close to 400 employees across Royal Bank Financial Group to share ideas, concerns, and suggestions about QPI. In these groups, most employees said they liked QPI. They felt it was an effective way of paying for performance. But employees also asked:

- ► Were results relative to the annual business plan the best way to determine the amount of QPI available for payment?
- ► Could there be more consistency in the way individual QPI awards were determined?
- ► Could there be a clearer link between personal performance and QPI?
- ► Could QPI earnings become pensionable?

The redesign of QPI took these questions into account. RBFG reviewed its own business needs to create a set of principles for the new program. These principles were:

- ► QPI should reward what is good for shareholders, customers, and employees.
- ► QPI should be clearly linked to results and reflect individual contribution to those results.
- ► QPI should be based on the employee's ability to influence results.

With these principles in mind, QPI was redesigned to achieve one clear objective: to focus all efforts on meeting business priorities and beating the competition.

New Measures of Success

The original QPI used only one measure—return on equity (ROE)—to determine the pool of QPI funds available for payout. The new QPI adds a second financial measure—revenue growth—in line with RBFG's strategic priorities. However, another set of measures was added—RBFG performance against the competition. Because the financial services industry in Canada operates in a highly competitive environment, it is no longer practical to measure success by internal standards only. It became apparent during the redesign process that performance against the competition in terms of financials, customer satisfaction, and employee commitment would give a balanced scorecard adding up to increased value for shareholders, customers, and employees.

Why Measure Employee Commitment, Customer Satisfaction, and Financial Performance?

1. Studies reveal high levels of employee commitment translate directly into improved customer service and satisfaction.
2. Customers who are very satisfied do more business and also help attract other customers.
3. By doing more business with existing customers and attracting new customers, financial performance can improve.
4. Better financial performance enables companies to reinvest in new technologies, new services, new jobs, more learning opportunities, and a better work environment.
5. Studies also show that employees who have the tools to provide customers with the best possible services and who feel good about where they work have high levels of employee commitment.

Every step in the cycle reinforces the next. If managed well, the combined power of high employee commitment translates directly into improved customer satisfaction leading to better financial results and improved shareholder value.

How the QPI Program Works

The redesigned QPI program has two major components:

- ▸ Total QPI for all of RBFG is determined by performance relative to annual business plans and against the competition.
- ▸ The size of individual QPI awards is determined by personal performance relative to the key goals of the business unit.

Performance Against the Annual Business Plan

This is the foundation of the QPI model. At the beginning of each fiscal year, RBFG sets goals for both return on equity and revenue growth. Every quarter, a QPI scorecard is distributed to each employee as a pay statement insert updating them on how RBFG is doing against these measures. ROE and revenue growth performances are added together to determine how well RBFG performed relative to plan. Here's how the scorecard is calculated.

50%	+	50%	=	100%
ROE Performance		Revenue Growth Performance		Financial Performance Relative to Plan

Performance Against the Competition

If Royal Bank Financial Group is to succeed, it must keep a close eye on the competition. When consumers deal with RBFG, they have expectations of quality based on the experience they've had elsewhere. They don't just make comparisons with the other bank down the street. They make comparisons with the high standards they find elsewhere in the marketplace. Customers measure RBFG against the competition, so RBFG must make the same comparison. Those measurements are in three areas: financials, customer satisfaction, and employee commitment.

Financials: RBFG's relative performance in terms of return on equity and revenue growth

	compared to the five other major Canadian banks
Customer satisfaction:	RBFG's relative level of customer satisfaction measured by independent surveys with other major Canadian financial institutions, including credit unions
Employee commitment:	RBFG's relative level of employee commitment as measured by an independent survey with other high-performing companies across North America

With the introduction of the new competitive measures, QPI can be increased by as much as 25% through any combination of superior or improved performance on the three competitive measures. Superior performance is defined as placing in the top third of the companies RBFG measures itself against. Improved performance is defined as a move from below average to average or from average to superior against these companies.

Defining Employee Commitment

Employee commitment is more than employee satisfaction. Employee commitment measures how capable employees feel they are able to do their job, how well managed they feel they are, and how satisfied they are in their work. If an employee has the tools and training to serve customers well, customer satisfaction will increase and customer value is built. It all fits together: Employee commitment leads to customer satisfaction, which leads to financial results . . . a balanced scorecard.

The Full Picture

Taken together, performance relative to business plan targets and performance against the competition will determine RBFG performance for calculating QPI. The following is an illustration of how QPI would increase if RBFG meets its business plans and leads the competition in all three competitive measures: RBFG performance would be 125%.

50% ROE Performance	+	50% Revenue Growth Performance	+	25% Competitive Performance	=	125% Total RBFG Performance

Individual QPI Awards

Individual QPI awards depend on RBFG performance, the employee's compensation band, and personal performance. It is calculated using the formula detailed in Figure 4-1.

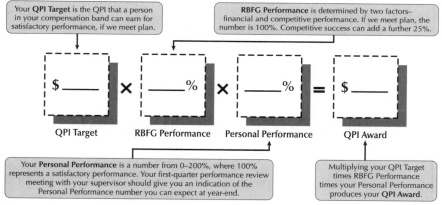

Figure 4-1. Individual QPI calculation.

The amount of the QPI award is directly linked to personal performance in meeting individual goals established at the beginning of the fiscal year. Employees will know exactly how much QPI can be earned for satisfactory performance in their compensation band, if RBFG meets plan. RBFG's financial performance is updated and communicated to employees quarterly. Likewise, employees and their managers are to review personal performance quarterly. By inserting the appropriate numbers in this formula, employees can calculate their QPI award at any time during the year. This was a major improvement over the previous program since employees now have a direct line-of-sight between their personal performance and the amount they can earn under QPI.

For example, a person employed as a customer service representative achieves a Personal Performance of 130%. Here's what the QPI formula would look like:

$750	× 100%	× 130%	= $975
QPI Target	RBFG Performance	Personal Performance	QPI Award

Making QPI Pensionable

With variable pay becoming a growing element of total compensation, RBFG recognized the need to include QPI as a part of the calculation for the noncontributory portion of employees' pension. Previously, only base salary was recognized for pension purposes. Now QPI is added to base salary to determine noncontributory pensionable earnings. All pension plan members automatically receive noncontributory pension with no contributions required, so all members participating in QPI benefit. RBFG was the first Canadian bank to provide such innovative compensation policies for employees.

Communicate, Communicate, Communicate

Don't say it once, say it again! The importance of communication cannot be overlooked, especially in this age of information. RBFG made sure all employees knew and understood QPI by communicating information about it in various ways. At the launch of the revised QPI, all managers were provided with briefing kits announcing QPI. Various materials were included with the kits: full program explanations, staff meeting agendas, overheads, delivery notes, questions and answers. Likewise, a communication package for each employee was distributed that consisted of a QPI program overview, examples of the new program in action, questions and answers, and a quick reference card showing the QPI formula. Each quarter, employees were provided with a QPI scorecard that reported RBFG performance against plan and against the competition. Just prior to the year-end announcement of financial results, a special video was distributed to all units that again provided a complete overview of QPI. A special site on RBFG's intranet was opened dedicated to QPI, and it includes a special feature of a QPI calculator. Also, there is a telephone line set up so employees can call and hear about the program. The communication paid off: More employees were completely aware of and comfortable with the program.

RBFG Performance Delivers Extraordinary QPI

Hard work, supported by favorable economic conditions, produced significant financial performance in 1997, resulting in a record-breaking payout under the QPI program. RBFG placed in the top third of the companies in return on equity and employee commitment. Revenue growth was the highest ever, and customer satisfaction scores remained constant compared to benchmarks established in previous years. In 1997, RBFG performance for calculating QPI was 152%. These powerful results show commitment to creating value for shareholders and customers and provide significant rewards to RBFG employees who are key to success.

Lessons Learned

With an increased awareness of the QPI program, employees were keen on learning exactly what RBFG's financial performance was each quarter, as well as measuring their personal performance. As soon as quarterly results were known and the RBFG performance factor communicated, employees busily calculated QPI. But, more important, employees were beginning to take a shareholder perspective and focusing on opportunities to grow quality business, attracting new customers and adding new profitable business. Improving the line-of-sight for employees was one of the major reasons for the program redesign, and the activity throughout 1997 showed QPI achieved its goal.

QPI is evolving, and further experience will improve the program. Individual goal setting is one area that is undergoing review. Although QPI removed most of the subjectivity, employees still feel some remains when performance is assessed in qualitative terms. Better tools are being developed to assist managers in setting goals and measuring performance against them.

Moving Forward

New, exciting challenges and opportunities are in store for RBFG. The business environment in Canada remains very competitive. The vision is to be Canada's premier financial services provider, with committed people working as a team to create customer and shareholder value. The focus is on improving performance to achieve consistent and superior returns for shareholders. The priorities are to grow and diversify revenues, improve efficiency, maintain a high-quality risk profile, effectively manage the balance sheet and capital, and provide opportunities for capable, committed employees. The Quality Performance Incentive program is one of the tools used to maintain a balanced scorecard for shareholders, customers, and employees that is imperative to RBFG success.

TEAM INCENTIVES TO INCREASE CUSTOMER LOYALTY AT

Colony Communications, Inc.

The changes in the telecommunications and information industry are reshaping the marketplace for cable television operating companies. While these organizations were once protected from competition by maintaining franchises in local communities, developments in information technology fundamentally changed how these companies view their businesses and retain their leadership. A key factor to their success will be the loyalty they maintain with their customers.

Company Background

Colony Communications, Inc., was a large cable television company that was owned by a major publishing company. It operated 27 local cable systems throughout the United States and had approximately 1,500 employees. As competition increased from satellite broadcasting companies and other new entrants to the market, Colony's growth prospects were being challenged. Furthermore, Internet-based communication provided both a significant threat and opportunity to Colony and others in this industry. Although the threats to survival were not imminent, the company needed to change its culture to be more competitive and retain customers. The centerpiece of this change strategy was to increase customer loyalty so that when a customer was offered other choices for television services, they would remain with Colony Communication.

The president of the company, Bruce Clark, and members of his senior management team decided that their current compensation systems were inadequate to support the change needed by the company. They needed a reward system that encouraged individuals to improve the services that were meaningful to the customer, take actions that would grow revenues, and reduce costs. They had implemented a variety of restructuring and reengineering efforts, but to achieve enduring improvements they needed more employee involvement. They believed that their success depended on changing the culture of the organization to make it more responsive to customer needs and competitive in the marketplace. The senior executive group decided to use an incentive compensation to drive the needed change.

Developing the Incentive Program

The incentive compensation program was designed by a group of executives and middle managers. They met for a series of day-long sessions over four months. An external consultant guided the meetings. When completed, the program was entitled SPIRIT, which stood for Superior Performance Increases Rewards and Improves Teamwork.

To set the framework for the incentive plan, the design team asked several critical questions:

- ► Who were Colony's customers and what did they want?
- ► What factors were critical for the organization's success?
- ► What were the best measures of success?
- ► What actions were needed by staff members for the system to excel in these areas?

The design team developed all aspects of the program. Their first task was to determine the purpose and approach of the program. They decided that the primary unit of focus would be the local operating company (or system). These units were relatively self-contained and the line-of-sight between actions and results was relatively clear. Second, they agreed that the primary principle behind this effort was that if the system improved its performance in critical areas, the company would share the resulting benefits with the employees. As the company became more competitive and profitable, individuals would benefit financially and personally. Consequently, they decided to develop a goal-oriented, team incentive plan.

The team next identified a series of performance measures. These measures directly reflected the customer-focused success factors and the company's strategic plan. The measures were:

- *Net revenues* (retention and growth in revenues from basic services)
- *Controllable expenses compared to budget* (excludes purchased programming, taxes, and related special costs)
- *System reliability* (the amount of time the system was fully operational)
- *Customer service* (the degree to which the system exceeded Federal Communication Commission requirements)
- *Customer satisfaction* (the degree to which customers were pleased with Colony Communications' services)

Most of the measures already existed. For example, the system reliability report had been developed several years before, and it was provided to each system on a monthly basis. However, few people used it to take action and employees were generally unaware of its existence. The customer satisfaction measurement process needed to be developed, which had been a priority for the marketing department. The development of the incentive plan served as a catalyst to use measures or implement systems that had been considered important for several years.

How SPIRIT Works

To link the measures into an incentive system, the team decided to use a performance matrix. Each measure would receive a weight, and a range of performance goals from "threshold" to "target" to "exceptional" would be developed for each measure. A total of 10 progressive levels of performance were identified. The matrix, or scorecard, integrated the measures into a single incentive program that could be applied to each cable operating system.

The performance would then be based on how the system did against its own scorecard (see Figure 4-2).

The payout was determined based on the score achieved by the system using the scorecard. All members of the system received the same percentage of their salary as a payout, but actual payments would differ because of the different salary levels. The payout opportunity ranged from 2% of pay to 10% of total earnings for the performance period. Payouts were made quarterly. Each quarter was a separate performance period; there were no reserves or holdbacks. This facilitated the focus on immediate results and encouraged individuals to take action. While this did present a risk that payouts early in the year would not be supported by overall annual results, the considered opinion was that the immediacy of the payout was more important than the risk of overpayment. The program included everyone in each system except for the general manager and ad sales representatives on commissions. The general manager participated in the corporate executive incentive program and the measures for this program were adjusted to create alignment between the corporate and the system's measures. Corporate staff members who did not participate in the executive pay plan were provided incentives based on the cumulative results of the incentive plans for all systems for which they had responsibility.

A special consideration in the strategic plan and the design of the plan was to encourage community involvement by each system. While people were told to become involved in their local communities, this was often seen as a marketing or management responsibility. Yet market research clearly demonstrated that if the system had a positive image in the community, it would have greater customer loyalty.

The design team developed an innovative feature to the incentive program. The system could receive "extra bonus" if it was highly active in some important community-based programs. If approved, team members would receive an additional 0.5% on their SPIRIT payout, assuming that achieved at least 80 points performance. These programs needed both to increase the visibility and positive reputation of the company within the community and involve many members of the system. For example, involvement in Rotary or lunch club meetings did not count; community drives for food shelters, involvement with Habitat for Humanity, or active

SYSTEM _____

LOCATION _____

PERFORMANCE PERIOD

Measures	X Weight	Threshold		Budget/Plan		Target				Exceptional		Points
		50	60	70	80	90	100	110	120	130	140	
Customer Satisfaction Survey Score	20%	60	65	70	75	80	85	88	90	92	95	24
Service Reliability Score	20%	5 pts	8 pts	11 pts	14 pts	17 pts	20 pts	24 pts	27 pts	30 pts	35 pts	24
Customer Service Score (FCC compliance)	20%	70	75	80	85	87	90	93	96	98	100	20
Net Revenue ($ thousands)	20%	900	950	1000	1050	1100	1200	1300	1400	1500	1600	18
Controllable Expense to Budget (% to budget)	20%	110%	105%	100%	98%	95%	93%	90%	88%	85%	83%	20

Total Score **106**

Payout Opportunity Table

0–69	0
70–79	2%
80–89	3%
90–99	4%
100–109	5%
110–119	6%
120–129	8%
130–140	10%

Community Service and Contribution
Extra Points:

Sponsoring Community Special Olympics

Payout : 5% + 0.5% = 5.5%

Figure 4-2. The SPIRIT performance scorecard.

support for the Special Olympics would receive credit. The special contribution bonus was determined by the senior management of Colony based on the recommendations of the system's general manager.

The Impact

The program has had an enormous impact on the company, its culture, and its competitiveness. Of the approximately 27 systems, 24 received at least one payout over six performance cycles. The average payout was 3.5% of pay, and the improved financial results have exceeded the cost of the payouts by more than 6.2 to 1. In other words, if the total payouts were $1 million, the organization realized $6.2 million in above-business-plan operating income.

Furthermore, SPIRIT helped the company to achieve:

- ▸ A significant reduction in customer turnovers, especially compared to industry standards
- ▸ Fewer customer complaints than historically received
- ▸ Lower costs of operating the system (e.g., many budgeted positions were not filled, travel costs were reduced, and supply costs were lowered)
- ▸ Lower employee turnover and a shorter time to fill vacancies

When the program completed its sixth cycle, the president and vice president for human resources wanted to understand why certain systems achieved significant gains (and high payouts) while others were weak performers. An interesting finding was discovered about the program.

There were distinct differences in the way high-performing and low-performing systems managed the team incentive program. First, in the high-performing systems, each manager took the overall system's measures and translated them into small team or individual measures of performance. Managers educated people on the actions they needed to take to improve performance and realize a payout.

Second, the system displayed the overall results on a regular basis. There were large graphic and colorful displays throughout the work areas on the key performance measures. The scorecard was displayed in high employee traffic areas, and the information was kept current. Many work teams displayed their own data as well, even though their payout was based on the overall system's performance.

Third, as data came in from marketing (customer satisfaction), finance (revenues and expenses), and engineering (reliability), employees and managers combed through the data together to understand its meaning. They used the data to create opportunities for greater employee involvement and to develop corrective action plans. Individuals and teams then became focused on implementing changes with little resistance. There was also a better understanding of the data and any inaccurate data was corrected.

Fourth, as individuals or groups began improving the process and achieving better results, they received immediate recognition by both managers and peers. People were frequently recognized in meetings in departments and systemwide sessions. Finally, when the checks arrived, the people in the system celebrated their achievements as a total group. They were recognized as winners, they felt like winners, and they were. They made changes in work structures, increased training and communication, and found ways to improve performance well beyond the target level of expectation. None of these actions occurred in the low-performing systems.

In this company, there were winners all around. The customers received better and more responsive services, well above the standards set in the industry. The organization gained financially through reduced costs, increased revenues, and improved customer loyalty. It became a stronger competitor. The employees were winners because they earned more money and received greater recognition for their contributions. Contributions and performance were highly valued by both managers and peers.

There is an epilogue to the Colony story: The company has been sold to a larger cable television company, and several of the SPIRIT team incentive programs remain in effect. Although Colony no longer exists as an independent company, many of the people who were designers or participants have learned how a program of this nature can impact behaviors, and they have applied this experience to their new endeavors. The SPIRIT is alive.

Establishing the Value of a Job
at

Copley Pharmaceutical, Inc.

When an organization transitions into a professionally managed organization, does it need to become a bureaucracy? This was one of the central issues at Copley Pharmaceutical, Inc., when it was considering how to design a compensation system. Furthermore, it was concerned with how to retain its entrepreneurial spirit in the presence of growth and continued regulatory vigor. Finally, it wanted to integrate the concept of customer relationships in every aspect of the organization, even while managerial controls were key to its success.

These were the paradoxes facing senior managers. Since a compensation program clearly sends messages to every employee about what is valued, they wanted to establish a set of specifications that reflected the values of the company. By so doing, the company could grow and develop professionalism, retain its desired culture, and achieve desired market leadership.

Company Background

Copley Pharmaceutical was started in 1972 by Jane Hirsh, a pharmacist in a major Boston healthcare organization. The company develops, manufactures, markets, and distributes a wide range of generic pharmaceutical products. These products are both prescription and over-the-counter drugs and come in a variety of forms, such as tablets, solutions, creams, ointments, and powders. The company is currently owned 51% by the Hoechst Corporation. Copley ended its 1997 fiscal year with net sales of $121 million and approximately 400 employees located primarily in Massachusetts.

Generic pharmaceutical sales have increased dramatically over the last several years. This is due in part to the increasing role of pharmaceuticals in the treatment and management of disease, as well as the use of therapeutic equivalents for brand-name drugs. Generic drug costs tend to be significantly lower, which is consistent with the current pressures to contain healthcare costs. This market continues to change and become reshaped by many

forces—the healthcare provider industry, the chemical and pharmaceutical industry, the biotech industry, and government regulations. Remaining competitive in this industry requires constant
vigilance.

Copley was one of many new entrants to the emerging market
of generic drugs. Since that time there have been significant concerns by many consumers and regulators about the efficacy of
generic drugs. While they were clearly lower in cost, did they
provide the same high-quality impact on the patient as brand-
name drugs? Experience has shown that these products are of
great value and achieve both clinical and cost objectives.

Copley has always been an organization that is highly responsive to the market situations. Furthermore, it has maintained the
highest possible standards of quality despite the market's cost-
competitive nature. Though there have been challenging times for
Copley, it continues to be a major player in the generic pharmaceutical market.

These market conditions, as well as the traditions of the company, were deeply considered by senior management in defining
what was key to continued success. These key success factors included:

- Providing high-quality pharmaceuticals at attractive market prices
- Maintaining high customer service levels
- Introducing a continuous array of new products that sustain
  market confidence and market share
- Maintaining an operation that supports a competitive cost
  base and ensures end-user value

Developing a New Framework to Compensation

These key success factors were then reflected in the compensation
system that Copley developed. Historically, the company provided
pay levels that were "market priced"—that is, it paid whatever
was necessary to attract and retain the desired talent. While this
worked well in the early stages of the company, numerous internal
pay issues were causing attention to be focused internally rather
than externally. There was simply no way in which managers could

reasonably control compensation costs and provide employees with consistent career opportunities. The variable patterns of compensation were no longer appropriate to the company's needs.

As the vice president of administration and an articulate communicator of the company's values, Barbara Morse outlined the key requirements for the new compensation system. It needed to:

1. Reflect the values of the organization for quality, customer focus, and cost management.
2. Be seen as effective by managers and employees and instill confidence in them that decisions were made in an objective manner.
3. Be simple to manage and maintain.
4. Enable the company to attract and retain the desired talent.

Furthermore, it was important to the organization that people be involved in the development process. An outside consulting firm guided the effort, but the process utilized a design team of senior managers and key professionals. Finally, while variable compensation was important to people, it was felt that the current base compensation program was in most need of development. This would provide the foundation on which other reward programs, including incentives and special recognition programs, would be based. If the company did not have confidence in the basic salary structure, it would be difficult to establish credibility in the other programs.

Key Elements of the New Compensation System

At the time when Copley needed to develop a new compensation program, it had a large number of job titles, a limited number of formal position descriptions, few meaningful compensation surveys, and an uneven process for managing salaries. To that end, the project focused on building the five core elements that would enhance the company's ability to manage pay. The project developed these elements of the new compensation system.

Customer-Focused Job Descriptions

Most organizations have some form of job descriptions. Many of these reflect a command-and-control philosophy by defining the job in terms of reporting relationships, budgetary and staffing controls, and specialized responsibilities. There is usually little emphasis on the customer or collaboration.

At Copley, managers developed a new approach to job descriptions based on the following ideas:

- ▶ Rather than asking workers whom they report to, the questionnaire format asked them to define whom they serve (i.e., their customers) and what they want. Rather than defining tasks or responsibilities, the format asked individuals to define what value they add, and with whom they need to collaborate to make it happen (i.e., individuals could share value-added accountabilities).
- ▶ Rather than defining what resources the worker controls, the format asked one to identify the resources used to fulfill the needs of the customers (i.e., less is better).

By asking a different set of questions, the focus of the job description changed. Furthermore, because job descriptions often imply what is valued by the organization, senior management felt that these questions were a strong reflection of what behaviors or actions should be encouraged.

Values-Based Compensable Factors

The company realized that there was a difference between competencies and compensable factors. Competencies often reflect success factors for performance or entry requirements into the company. They may or may not be applicable throughout the organization, both vertically and horizontally. Compensable factors defined the basis on which the corporation allocates its compensation dollars. These factors coupled with the marketplace defined the dimensions for pay in the organization.

To that end, the compensation design team developed a model that defined in Copley language the requirements for each grade level in the organization. This model used the following compensable factors:

1. Knowledge and skills applied
2. Performance effort
3. Scope of responsibility
4. Critical thinking
5. Collaboration
6. Working conditions

These six factors were then defined and applied to 10 grade levels. An example is provided in Figure 4-3. As jobs were applied to each level, they aided in defining how the key factors applied to the level. Both the criteria and job-level assignments were tested for

JOB LEVEL 6	BENCHMARK JOBS	Knowledge/ Skills	Performance Effort	Scope of Responsibility	Critical Thinking	Collaboration	Working Conditions
	Human Resouce Assistant	Performs work routine(s) requiring some practical experience and specialized training	Tasks and expectations are well-defined; often include written instructions	Accountable for routine activities within a project/unit Work reviewed periodically by supervisor	Thinking within well-defined procedures Offers suggestions for continuing process improvements	Works cooperatively with others in own unit May need to coordinate tasks with other units and functions	Must have a clear understanding of the known hazards of the job Needs to know the proper preventative actions
	Marketing Assistant	Performs multiple detail-oriented work routines	Handles well-defined problems	Should report unsafe work conditions	Derives solutions based on experience and know-how	General understanding of one's customers	
	Lab Technician –R&D	Knowledge of computerized applications in one's functional area	Assistance is readily available Works within established deadlines and schedules with frequent review of work	May initiate routine corrective actions Varying degrees of most liability limited by internal control systems	Plans and organizes own work		Follows appropriate safety procedures
	Lab Technician –QC						
	Accts. Payable/ Receivable	General understanding of regulatory and business requirements related to their particular area					
	Quality Assurance Inspector						
	Customer Service Representative	Requires frequent verbal communication and/or written documentation with others Two-year Associate's degree or equivalent preferred					

Figure 4-3. Copley Pharmaceutical's definitions by grade level.

validity through the application of benchmark positions. The compensation design team led this effort with assistance from the consultants. The primary outcome was a set of well-defined grade levels that could be used to assign positions in an objective, rigorous, and open manner.

Market-Based Salary Ranges

Like every organization, Copley needs to compete in various labor markets for talent. The project included an analysis of the current pay relationships and the development of a new grade structure based on sound market data from a number of external compensation surveys. The design team examined compensation surveys for their relevance to Copley and discussed the current competitiveness of salaries. In addition, they articulated with senior managers the desired market position and degree of internal equity necessary to provide a sense of fairness and opportunity within the organization.

The outcome of this process was a set of 10 salary ranges that corresponded to the grade levels developed earlier. These ranges were broad in traditional terms (50% minimum to 80% maximum) and defined the pay opportunity for managers and employees. While the organization could establish special ranges for "hot market jobs," these ranges were sufficiently broad and market-based to provide a high degree of flexibility for attracting and retaining desired talent.

A Simple Salary Management Process

Consistent with the themes of the organization, managers needed guidelines by which they could manage compensation. Managers were accountable for managing the compensation of their people consistent with these guidelines. The human resources function served in a consultative, problem-solving role.

To support the development of these guidelines, Copley needed to establish its compensation philosophy. Although many of the key principles were defined early in the development process, this task focused the design team on articulating the compensation philosophy (see Figure 4-4). Each element of the compensation program was then reexamined to ensure that it was

> ☑ Because employees are critical to Copley's competitiveness, our compensation program should provide an opportunity to share in our success as a corporation.
>
> ☑ The compensation program should encourage employees continually to seek ways to improve their service to their customers, increase their contributions, and enhance their capabilities.
>
> ☑ The program needs to be fairly and effectively managed to the benefit of employees and the company.
>
> ☑ To minimize our fixed costs, we need to trade off high market rates of pay with an aggressive combination of at-market salaries with above-market total pay opportunity.

Figure 4-4. Copley Pharmaceutical's compensation philosophy.

consistent with this philosophy. Senior managers appreciated this quality assurance.

The guidelines related to hiring, transfers, promotions, and salary action policies. Accountabilities of managing the program were well defined. Although these have been adjusted somewhat over time, the essential principle was that managers are to manage their people and their pay, while human resources provides the tools, administration, and guidance to ensure this task is done effectively.

Communication That Is Honest and Open

Managers are expected to understand the principles and guidelines of the new compensation program. Employees need to understand how the process works and to support their managers in ensuring that individuals are compensated fairly. To that end, many of the elements of the new compensation program were communicated openly to all managers, supervisors, and employees. While at first there was great concern about issues of equity, fairness, and opportunity, over time these issues have diminished as people have gained confidence in the system and the system has adjusted to unique circumstances. Managers know the grade-level model and the salary ranges. They are expected to use these tools when creating new positions or when counseling employees on how to progress with their careers in the company. It is simple, they are trusted, and the process works.

The Impact Endures as the Organization Changes

Copley is an organization under constant change. It has grown rapidly and continues to face the pressures of an unforgiving marketplace. The one issue executives and managers do not need to deal with is the base compensation program. By the fact that it is seen as lending support to strategic efforts, the program has added value to the company. Furthermore, many managers can easily use each element of the system and see how it empowers them to continually shape and improve their business units. The job description process has clearly reinforced the customer-focus philosophy of the company and made managers mindful of relative position values.

Individuals and managers that are new to the organization quickly learn how the process works and find new, creative ways to apply the criteria and values in managing performance. In this way, it has become an important tool of management and one that has contributed to Copley's ability to compete in the marketplace—for talent and for market share.

The Future of Compensation at Copley

The company has used the salary management system well. It has established confidence and credibility. There are continual pressures to make exceptions for individuals that are in high demand in the marketplace. Managers find the model has aided in the process, and they've applied the model in a flexible manner. In the marketplace for generic drugs, effective management of compensation requires continual vigilance.

The company continues to change and develop new programs for incentives, special recognition, and attractive employee benefits. Communication has been a key element to the success of this program, as has treating everyone in a responsible and responsive manner. As Copley's executives focus on what it takes to remain competitive in the marketplace, they continue to support a compensation practice that rewards their people for what's important.

BUILDING A UNIQUE TOTAL REWARDS AND HR SYSTEM FOR A UNIQUE COMPANY
AT

Starbucks Coffee Company

Since Starbucks isn't your typical company, this isn't a typical case study. Rather than focusing on a single reward program or even the entire reward system, this case focuses on how the entire total reward and human resources (HR) systems at Starbucks are linked to the business objectives and reinforce the company's strong culture and values. Working in mutual support of the business, the culture, and values, this integrated HR system has helped shape a powerful success story that didn't rely on conventional thinking and trends with respect to the treatment of its workforce.

A Brief History of Starbucks

Starbucks Coffee Company, as we know it today, began in 1987, when Howard Schultz, the current chairman and CEO, acquired the assets from the original founders, whom he had worked with from 1982 to 1985. In 1987, Starbucks had 11 stores. The original business plan, and promise to the investors, was to have 125 stores within five years.

From 1987 to 1992, the company remained private, growing at the astonishing rate of 80% per year to more than 150 stores. In June 1992, the company went public, and it was one of the most successful initial public offerings of the year. Today, Starbucks is the leading retailer, roaster, and brand of specialty coffee in North America. It operates more than 1,800 retail locations in North America, the United Kingdom, and the Pacific Rim and has established joint-venture partnerships with Breyer's (to produce coffee ice cream) and PepsiCo (to produce Frappuccino, a bottled coffee drink). Sales for fiscal year 1997 were $967 million, an increase of nearly 39% over the previous year, and the company employed more than 25,000 partners (the company's term for employees). The company goal is to have more than 2,000 locations in North America by the year 2000. The company mission is to "establish Starbucks as the premier purveyor of the finest coffee in the world while maintaining our uncompromising principles as we grow."

Starbucks' Culture and Values: The Driver of HR and Reward Systems

Starbucks is a values-driven company, with a firmly established set of principles that are widely shared within the organization. It is also a company that puts its employees first and invests a tremendous amount in them. None of this is by accident. It all stems from the values and beliefs of its CEO. Says Schultz, "I wanted to establish the kind of company that gave people a form of equity (ownership) and comprehensive health insurance, and most importantly, give them self-esteem in the workplace. People feel that Starbucks is a place that gives them self-respect and values the contributions they make, regardless of their education or where they are in the company."

The company believes that if it puts partners first, the result will be exceptional customer service, and by extension, if it has highly satisfied customers, the financial returns will follow.

Reinforcing Culture and Values Through HR and Total Rewards

In order to reinforce and help drive the Starbucks culture, leading-edge compensation and benefits programs have been put in place. Full- and part-time partners (who meet eligibility criteria) are offered health, dental, and vision insurance, as well as access to an employee assistance program (EAP), reimbursement accounts, short- and long-term disability, and Working Solutions, Inc. (a resource and referral service) to help manage work and family issues. This is very atypical of the retail industry, which for the most part does not pay the costs associated with providing benefits to part-time employees. Even though the costs of providing these benefits to part-time employees raises the overall cost of benefits at Starbucks, the average cost of providing benefits to an employee, vis-à-vis the competition, is still lower. While this investment is significant, it pays tremendous dividends. The people who receive these benefits greatly appreciate and value them and, as a result, provide customers with better service.

Second, all partners have an opportunity to become owners of the company. The company instituted the Bean Stock (i.e., broad-based) stock option program in 1991 and the Stock Investment Plan (SIP) to purchase stock at a discount in 1995. Part-time employees who maintain a minimum number of hours are again eligible for both programs. The Bean Stock program provides stock options on an annual basis, in an amount up to 14% of base salary, for any partner employed from April 1 to the end of the fiscal year, working at least 500 hours during this period, and employed with the company when the options are distributed in January. As Starbucks stock price has continued to climb, the value of the options provided to employees has been significant; more important, when combined with the education the company offers relative to creating value and profits, it has linked employees to shareholder value.

Reinforcing culture and values is more than just a total rewards issue, however. The total rewards system, while a powerful lever to help drive the business, is but one element that cannot be viewed in isolation from other key human resources levers that have been put in place. These other levers include extensive employee education, an open and highly communicative environment, and a unique program called Mission Review, which is part of a broader program called Partner Snapshot. Partner Snapshot is a comprehensive effort aimed at getting feedback from the company's partners. It parallels the Customer Snapshot program aimed at getting customer feedback. Partner Snapshot includes company-wide surveys, Mission Review, and a relatively new telephone-based survey system on key company and partner-related issues.

Mission Review is a formal program that was set up in 1990 to ensure that the company is living up to its mission statement. Every location has comment cards addressed to the Mission Review team that employees use when they see decisions and outcomes that do not support the mission statement. Relevant managers have two weeks to respond to the employee and the issue. Additionally, a cross-organizational team meets to review employee concerns, seek solutions, and provide a report at the open forums. Not only does this keep the mission statement alive and well; it reinforces the openness of the culture.

All partners hired to work in a retail position receive a minimum of 24 hours of training during their first month with the company. This training includes an orientation to the company, customer service skills, and the technical skills necessary to work in the stores. An extensive management-training program also exists, focusing on leadership skills, customer service, diversity, and career development.

Open communication is also part of the norm at Starbucks. Open forums, held several times a year, update partners on happenings within the company, explain the financials, and allow partners to ask questions of senior management and provide input to them as well. Additionally, a regular employee newsletter is published that also discusses developments within the company, along with a column on benefits and ownership programs.

The Evolution of HR and Total Rewards at Starbucks

One other thing that has been learned and focused on at Starbucks is that as the company has moved through various stages of its life cycle, the HR and total reward systems have had to evolve as well. For example, in the late 1980s, Starbucks was a regional company with a single product focus. Its HR organization was primarily made up of administrators—smart, people-oriented partners with bright ideas, but who at the same time were characterized as being highly reactive and caught up in manual processing, with a significant amount of the work directed by consultants. Compensation and benefits during this period (it had yet to evolve into a total rewards function) were characterized by part-time coverage of the basics and the implementation of the 401(k) plan.

In the early 1990s, Starbucks became a truly national company with multiple product lines. Human resources became a project manager, moving from administration to HR management, delivering products and tools that supported the business. Certain services began to be outsourced that were not core competencies of the organization. Further automation of HR functions continued. Compensation and benefits was characterized by a move to total rewards that included additional health benefits, maturation of healthcare delivery to managed care, coverage for same-sex partners, and an employee assistance program.

As Starbucks moves into the late 1990s, it will become increasingly international in scope and business focus. Simultaneously, HR has positioned itself to be a business leader: a technology-based organization that is integrated with the business units, providing business consulting and strategic management. Numerous vendor partnerships have been established that have increased the strength and quality of total pay offerings and will allow an integrated national and international HR focus that remains connected to the strategy of the business.

The Results to Date

Have the results of this integrated HR and total reward system that strongly reinforces the culture and values of the organization been worth the investment? It certainly appears that it has. The company was named one of the Fortune 100 "Best Companies to Work For." The financial growth of the company has been exceptional, with revenues of nearly $1 billion in fiscal year 1997. The stock price has increased more than 30 times its original price, including two stock splits. Employee turnover, especially within the stores, is dramatically below the retail industry norms, running at an annual rate of one-half to one-third that of the industry norm. Results of the employee satisfaction survey indicate that partners tremendously enjoy working for Starbucks and feel terrific about the leadership of the company. The external firm that conducts the employee survey said that the results at Starbucks were literally "off the charts" when compared with most other firms.

Can they quantitatively correlate these results of the HR and total reward system efforts? Not likely. However, there is a strong feeling by senior executives, managers, HR, and employees that these programs have certainly contributed a great deal to the growth and development of the company and its employees.

What the Future Holds

As the company continues to expand its stores both nationally and internationally and the employee population continues to rapidly grow, several challenges are posed on the HR and reward systems front. How can the company continue to reinforce and live its strong culture and value system as it gets more diverse, spread out, and bigger? As Starbucks grows larger, how can it maintain a small company feel? How do programs such as Bean Stock, which have been extremely successful, maintain their vibrancy and stay aligned with the changes in the business and the needs of employees?

Providing solutions to these questions in ways that continue to reinforce the company's culture and values and demonstrate commitment to putting employees first, is where HR and total rewards at Starbucks will be focusing today and into the near future. If the future is anything like the past, stay tuned for some exciting and unique developments.

5

Working as a Team

Organizations were created because work can be accomplished more effectively in a group than by independent individuals. The concept of organizing work by teams is not new, but recently it has revolutionized the workplace. This change is more reflective of a new management philosophy than the introduction of a new work structure. With this philosophy, people operate on the "whole job," not incremental pieces. People are encouraged to collaborate with others to improve the process and serve customers better than the competition. The results have been remarkable.

The case study companies presented in this chapter share a common value about teams and have come to learn how they can make a major difference in an organization's competitiveness. One of the interesting aspects of their experience is that they have used rewards to support their philosophy of management. Great performance achievements are made because people start working closer together.

Should they have collaborated in the past? Yes. Did they? Usually not. The reward systems made the difference. They encouraged people to collaborate and provided a share of the benefit if improvements could be achieved. You will see how DuPont developed one of the most publicized variable compensation plans with the Achievement Sharing Program. Then, when the program was discontinued, you will understand why. Cummings Engine has used its reward systems to enhance problem solving and process improvements. Blanchard Training & Development has used noncash recognition in simple and powerful ways to enhance collaboration and customer focus. K/P Corporation has used compensation for business initiatives for greater realization on its vision and mission. Finally,

Baptist Health System, Inc., has used team-based pay to strengthen performance and responsiveness in a highly complex marketplace.

These organizations have focused on teamwork, not teams. One is a process, the other is a structure. They have found the value of collaboration. This value has then been translated into superior performance. They then celebrate these achievements as a team.

LESSONS FROM A PLAN THAT DID NOT ENDURE AT

DuPont Corporation

Profit sharing is a simple, powerful concept. It says that if the organization is able to realize profits above a predetermined level, it will share a portion of this money back with those that created it—the employees. What could be simpler? What could be more compelling? These programs link everyone in the organization to the same focus, making the business more profitable.

However, not every attempt to apply such a program endures. Such was the experience of the Fibers Department at DuPont. This case description will review the development process, plan design, and principle learnings of an incentive plan that was discontinued. This experience highlighted the conflicting choices that are inherent in the development of such programs. Finally, the case provides a powerful design process that made a more lasting impact than the plan it was chartered to create.

Background of the Fibers Department

In 1988 the Fibers Department of DuPont decided to introduce a variable pay program. The Fibers Department was one of the largest business segments of DuPont, with sales at that time of $5.8 billion and more than 20,000 employees, including five unions. It had been a highly successful department of DuPont, but was now facing increasing pressures from global competitors. The company had articulated its core values of quality, leadership, and continuous improvement and sought ways to integrate these values in everything it did. It also believed strongly in teamwork, prudent risk taking, and a self-managing workforce. It needed a culture that would continue to change and develop to meet a changing marketplace.

The Fibers Department began investigating variable pay systems in 1986. The corporation gave each business unit the option of introducing alternative pay systems as a way to increase flexibility and improve the businesses. The Fibers Department had recently reduced its total U.S. employees by 7,000 and created a strong spirit of change within the organization. It reduced layers of management, changed work structures, and invested in new technology. However, the existing pay system at that time was fundamentally inconsistent with the new desired corporate culture and its values. The Fibers Department wanted to consider the move away from traditional entitlement pay to variable pay.

Designing the Incentive Program

To begin the process, the Fibers senior executives selected a study team to investigate what other organizations were doing, discuss alternatives with leading academic and consulting practitioners, and determine the best strategy for the department. The team was composed of representatives from all major areas of the business, including manufacturing, marketing, research and development, business units, human resources, and corporate compensation. Twelve individuals were on the team. Robert P. McNutt, formerly a line manager in Fibers' business and marketing group, was selected to lead this team effort.

During the process of data collection, the team identified a basic philosophy and a set of beliefs and principles about pay systems that guided them in the development effort. They used focus groups of employees to test ideas; more than 1,000 people of the Fibers Department provided input and feedback to the team. This was one of the most involving activities the department had ever been engaged in.

The program they developed became known as "Achievement Sharing." It was a single program that would apply to all 20,000 employees in the U.S. Fibers Department. The design team believed that employees should not have their pay or wages reduced in order to participate in Achievement Sharing, but that a portion of future increases in pay would need to be "placed at risk." The payouts would be paid to everyone based on the success of the entire business.

Implementing Achievement Sharing

The implementation of Achievement Sharing was to be phased in over approximately a three-year period. Individuals would receive 2% less of an annual base pay increase than their counterparts in other departments of DuPont. This would be capped at 6%. In turn, if the department achieved its annual earnings objective, employees would receive 6% of their pay as a bonus. The minimum threshold, set at 80% of the earning objective, would earn a 3% bonus, and 150% of the earnings objective would earn an 18% bonus. This range of payout opportunities was deemed to be highly meaningful to the participants. Payouts were made annually.

The implementation of Achievement Sharing involved a great deal of communication and education. For example, each of the 20 site locations viewed a video on the new program and a brochure on the program was given to all participants. There were follow-up meetings at all plants and offices to help employees understand, question, and consider what they could do differently now that they were on a variable pay program. There were teams trained at each site location to answer questions and to promote the Achievement Sharing program. A year after the program was introduced, these teams provided refresher education to employees on key aspects of the program. They also assisted people in understanding the department's financial statements and the earnings objective in particular.

The initial response to the program was quite positive. Four of the five unions agreed to participate in Achievement Sharing. There was a strong statement of commitment by senior management to communicate frequently on the status of the department's performance. Each plant could choose its own methods of communicating specific results. Bob McNutt frequently stated that this program should touch every employee and reinforce the idea that they can make a difference.

The program generated payouts in the first two years. The average payout was between 2% and 3% each year. The payouts were related directly to the department's operating income. However, the program was disbanded at the beginning of the third year.

While one may consider this a major problem, there were important reasons for this decision.

Why and How Achievement Sharing Was Terminated

It is clear that the program made a major, positive impact on the culture of the Fibers Department, DuPont, and U.S. industry in general. This program was one of the most publicized programs in the national press during the late 1980s and has been the source for many discussions. An analysis of this program is essential to learn the critical factors of success and how such programs can support major organizational initiatives.

There were several important reasons for terminating the plan. First, when the impact of the program was assessed in year two, more people indicated that they wanted more choice in the payout opportunity levels. People wanted to make individual choices regarding the amount of money they would put at risk and opportunity to reward. It was important to DuPont's senior executives to support this request. When they reviewed the legal feasibility of this option, they discovered that the Securities and Exchange Commission (SEC) would treat the Achievement Sharing program as an investment opportunity. The SEC would then require DuPont to make public disclosures of detailed business information. While executives would easily make information available to employees, the risk of getting detailed information into the hands of competitors rendered the requirement unacceptable. Consequently, the Fibers executives faced a critical dilemma—disclose sensitive information and honor employee choice, or offer no employee choice and limit the amount of communication of financial information.

A second factor that contributed to the decision related to the design of the program. As stated earlier, the primary unit of the program was the Fibers Department. Employees in the department selected this payout method because it was important to create a common, shared fate. It would encourage teamwork within and across the department, as stated in one of their core values. The operating earnings objective was selected because it was the only basic common metric of performance for all units of the department.

The problem with this approach, however, is that individuals did not have a clear and compelling line-of-sight between their actions and their results that determined the payout. When structured in this manner, the program would have little impact on behavior but would create a common fate for all concerned. The design team considered these various options and decided that it was more important for the program to be fair and to unify people within the Fibers Department. If different units were to have different performance targets, how could one be assured that the efforts and opportunity to achieve payouts were comparable? If one area were to receive a payout because it had favorable market conditions and another were not successful because of business conditions, would the program be fair and credible? A common plan was deemed appropriate, even though it had this inherent line-of-sight problem.

The third reason for the Fibers Department decision to terminate the program was the concern that the overall market was heading into a recession and the plan would not make a payout. This business condition was not expected during the time of the program's design. The concern was that if the program did not make any payouts for several years due to declining markets, then it would not have any credibility with the workforce. Early successes are very important to any program's commitment. While it is often difficult to select the right time for a program of this nature, it was felt that forces that were clearly outside the control of individuals would adversely impact them. Furthermore, because the program was based on the overall Fibers business, there was little that individuals or small units could do to offset the decline of the overall business that would impact the payouts. There continues to be uncertainty about whether "riding out the recession" would have been better than discontinuing the program.

Prior to the decision to terminate the program, senior managers explored the option of restructuring the program to link more directly with the performance requirements of the 25 business lines. They were concerned with the line-of-sight issue and with modifying the program to reflect a major portion on unit performance and a small but significant portion on department-wide performance. This was then likely to increase the impact of the program on behaviors and performance. If adopted, managers wanted to create a "handicap" provision for different groups in order to ensure that performance targets would be comparable across the various lines of business.

The Impact Has Continued

Although this program did not endure, it made a lasting impact on the DuPont organization and on other companies seeking to implement variable pay programs. The development process clearly demonstrated how a large, stable organization could create involvement and build support for a controversial subject—pay at risk. It displayed critical values of employee involvement in the development of the program and effective communication once the program was approved. Finally, it identified all the critical issues one needs to consider in developing a variable pay program for a large, stable organization. However, there were fundamental conflicts in the need for choice and in the development of a better line-of-sight on performance and on understanding business conditions.

Many organizations have learned from DuPont's experience. They have modified variable pay programs to have a more direct impact on behaviors. They have used design teams and created statements of core beliefs and principles as part of their design efforts. They have decided to keep the program in place even in recessionary times. The Fibers Department experiment with variable pay has made an important contribution to changing how American industry thinks about variable compensation.

DuPont is now considering alternative models for variable pay throughout its lines of businesses. It has learned from the Achievement Sharing process and is implementing many other alternative methods for pay and rewards within the DuPont organization. In this way, experiments serve to create learning and clarify key principles. The investment made in Achievement Sharing continues to generate a favorable return.

SUSTAINING CONTINUOUS IMPROVEMENTS IN A HIGH-PERFORMANCE WORK SETTING
AT

Cummins Engine

How does an organization improve its competitiveness and performance? How does an organization that is known for its quality continue to create and improve? How does an organization that works in teams strengthen its collaboration across units and with the customer? These are challenges facing Cummins Engine. In particular, these were the tasks that Atlas Crankshaft, Inc., a division within the corporation, attempted to address with its variable compensation program.

Cummins Engine is the world's biggest maker of large diesel engines and power generators. They are used to power trucks, buses, and equipment for mining and construction. The company has annual sales of more than $5 billion and more than 26,000 employees worldwide. Atlas Crankshaft is a components manufacturing division with a specialty in crankshafts and related equipment. Most of Atlas's outputs are provided to other Cummins plants to be assembled and sold to major vehicle and equipment manufacturers.

Organizational Context

Historically, many employees at Cummins have participated in a companywide profit-sharing program. This program has sought to establish a stake in the success of the business for each employee. However, management felt that the program did not offer a strong line-of-sight relationship between individual actions and results. Therefore, they encouraged the divisions to create their own approach to reward systems that would provide a better focus on performance.

Atlas Crankshaft decided to develop a variable compensation program in 1993 for implementation in 1994 because it needed to create a connection between its employees and the requirements to improve the performance of the division. Atlas understood that it needed to continually improve its performance and capabilities.

Atlas Crankshaft, Inc., is located in Fostoria, Ohio, and has just under 300 employees. Many of the employees are represented by the United Auto Workers (UAW). Since 1993, the company has maintained a team-based work system where all employees are in teams and manage a strong process flow from rough manufacturing of products through to finished goods and shipping. The plant operates in a comfortable environment; in addition, there is continuous emphasis on safety and creating an attractive workplace. Although there is significant material fabrications, movement of large pieces around the plant, and a great deal of work in process, the plant's environment places a high degree of importance on safety and professionalism. People take a great deal of pride in their products, their workplace, and each other.

The Variable Compensation Program

The variable compensation program was developed, as stated earlier, to encourage and reward members of the plant for improving the performance of Atlas. It was developed by the plant operating team that now includes the local UAW president, but over time it has evolved to include more and more people to improve the program. They have realized that like any good system, the compensation program needs to continually change and be upgraded. However, the program has not changed fundamentally since its inception.

The program includes all members of the Atlas organization, including union and nonunion employees. Because the measures are set based on plantwide performance, they continue to struggle with bringing the line-of-sight closer to what the individual has control over. The number of measures ranges from four to six; the importance weighting and performance levels change each year. This is important so that people can see the continuity of the program over time and learn how each person affects the results.

The core measures of the program include the following:

- Safety incidence rate
- On-time delivery
- Productivity (i.e., number of pieces per person per day)
- Managed expenses (i.e., managed expenses as a percent of the budget)

The purpose of the safety incident rate is to reinforce a clean and healthy workplace environment. This is important to ensure employees work in a safe workplace that enhances their ability to produce high-quality products at the lowest possible cost. When an employee is injured, there are costs related to both healthcare and lost productivity, not to mention the impact in human terms. This is measured by calculating the number of recorded safety incidents as a percentage of the total hours worked by all employees.

They establish a range of performance for this measure and control the process through frequent safety inspections and training.

On-time delivery is measured by meeting the delivery date of their customers, usually other plants within Cummins. Atlas uses the receipt of the order as opposed to the shipment date because the most important consideration for customers is when they receive the product, not when it was shipped. This means that Atlas needs to consider the delivery vendor it uses for products and the extent to which they are reliable. Although delivery is less in one's control than the shipment dates, the receipt is critical to other plants that operate with a just-in-time materials management function.

Productivity of the plant is measured by determining the number of plant hours needed to produce a product. The ratio is the number of pieces per person per day. This factor perhaps has the greatest impact on the performance of the plant. All employees either work directly at producing the products or supporting those who do. This causes people to reflect on whether or not an individual needs to be replaced or added to the staff. This also gives credit to the plant if the employees are able to grow the volume without adding concomitantly to staff.

The final measure examines how well expenses are managed according to the company budget. These expenses do not include wages, as this is captured in the productivity measure. The expenses include controllable items such as maintenance supplies, operating supplies, scrap, utilities, freight, medical costs, and general expenses. Once the budget is set, the plant needs to produce expenditures that are less than the budget in order to achieve a payout. Specifically, they need to be 2% under budget to achieve their target performance. If expenses were 10% below budget, they would receive a high level of payouts.

How Payouts Are Determined

The payouts are determined by combining the performance in all measured areas. For each measure there is a payout schedule that ranges from minimum to target to high performance. Based on performance level achieved, a certain number of points are earned.

The range of points reflects the performance of the measure. Each measure is capped differently based on its performance factors. The points are totaled and averaged by the number of measures. The payout range then is applied to determine the percent of total earnings one receives. The calculated payout factor for each quarter is multiplied by the participation level of the employee, which ranges from 4% to 6%. The demonstrated performance payout has been from 0% to 11%, but the potential is there for that to be greater based on improved performance in the various categories. Everyone's payout is based on the same factor; payouts are not adjusted for individual performance. The payout is paid quarterly and payouts are typically made within 10 days of the end of the quarter. The target percent is between 4% and 6%, depending on your position. The payout factors can range from 0.25 to greater than 3.00—which, in turn, could lead to a payout greater than 18%.

In addition to these performance measures, the program has two "hurdles" that need to be met before the payouts are made available. This is important to ensure that the plan is self-funded— that is, the gains in performance would more than pay for the financial awards. The first hurdle is that sufficient savings need to be generated from the performance to fund the plan. Although managed expenses and productivity are the two measures clearly tied to financial performance, the delivery and safety incident rates can clearly be translated into financial impact gains.

The second hurdle is that the customer acceptance rate must equal or exceed 99.5% for each quarter. Customers have the ability to review the quality of the products and if they are not acceptable, they can return them to the company. If these returns exceed 0.5% of the products shipped, there will be no payout for the quarter. Fortunately, and reflective of the Atlas quality management process, in only one quarter in the history of the program has this threshold not been met.

At the end of each quarter, the Atlas plant operating team reviews the performance results and recommends the payout factor. The business unit that Atlas is part of is responsible for final approval. This Atlas leadership team is heavily invested in achieving the desired performance and making the associated payouts. As they make payouts, they realize that the company is improving its productivity, quality, and use of resources.

The Costs and the Return on Investments

Since the implementation of the program in 1994, Atlas has made a payout in all but one quarter (this was due to the quality of customer acceptance). The average payouts have ranged as follows:

Year	Payout %	Payout $
1994	1.34%	$686,556
1995	1.53	800,776
1996	0.78	418,880
1997	1.40	850,244
Total payouts over four years		$2,756,456

But the payouts need to be measured against the gains that have been achieved by Atlas Crankshaft. The savings generated from this program have exceeded $5 million. That is over a 2:1 savings ratio. Furthermore, the program has encouraged continual improvements in performance because the performance levels are increased or adjusted each year based on corporate requirements.

Over time many skeptics about the program have become supporters. Managers actively seek ways to encourage change that improves the performance of the plant. They see a direct relationship between the plant's performance and the individual variable compensation payout.

Continuing the Improvements

Each year managers seek to make improvements in the program. In 1997 they actively sought the involvement of the labor union leadership to improve the program. This has had a very positive impact. One of the most critical issues is educating people in how their actions impact the performance factors. Even though Atlas is a relatively cohesive organization, people need to see a line-of-sight between actions and results. The union leadership has been instrumental in building this educational process and encouraging people to find ways to improve the performance of the company. This partnership has led to strong improvements in safety and delivery performance.

The program will continue to develop in the future. It is not likely that the program's fundamental structure will change, but the measures and the process that supports the reinforcement of everyday activities will change. Managers understand how the program has affected behavior and have seen the potential of what it can truly do. Personal involvement, collaboration across teams, implementation of process improvements, and reinforcement of individual performance will be key drivers for the future.

Atlas has learned that the program cannot exist in a vacuum of leadership; managers and team leaders need to be involved. Union leadership support is critical as well. By working together, Atlas expects to continue to improve performance by linking individual performance to the plant's. They have the spirit to continue to make changes and learn new approaches that will enhance the ability to meet customer needs. In many ways, people feel that they have just begun.

LEARNING TO SOAR WITH THE EAGLE AWARD
AT

Blanchard Training & Development, Inc.

When it comes to rewards, many managers believe that the only thing that their employees want is more money. However, while money can be an important way of letting employees know their worth to the organization, it tends not to be a sustaining motivational factor to most individuals. That is to say, cash rewards such as salary, bonuses, and the like are nice, but seldom are they what motivate people to give their best efforts on the job.

Cash rewards have one more problem. In most organizations performance reviews—and corresponding salary increases—occur only once a year, whereas the things that cause someone to be motivated today are typically activities that have happened recently within the immediate workgroup. Things such as being thanked for doing a good job, involved in decision making, or supported by one's manager. To motivate employees, managers need to recognize and reward achievements and progress toward goals by employees on a daily basis.

When you ask employees what is most motivating to them, rarely is money listed first. In fact, in numerous studies money is ranked about fifth in importance. What is most important to employees are such intangibles as being appreciated for the work they've done, being kept informed about things that affect them, having interesting work, and having a sympathetic manager who takes time to listen to them. These intangibles cost little or nothing to implement, but they do take the time and thoughtfulness of a manager who cares. These principles have been put in place at Blanchard Training & Development, Inc. (BTD).

Company Background

BTD is a management training and consulting firm located in Escondido, California. It employs a particularly effective form of recognition to keep employees motivated. At BTD, specially designed "Eagle Awards" are presented to individuals who have gone above-and-beyond to assist a customer. The Eagle Award is part of an overall system of employee rewards and recognition at BTD that has helped to create a highly motivated workforce—and more satisfied customers. The company was founded in 1979 by Ken Blanchard, coauthor of *The One-Minute Manager* (New York: Berkeley Publishing Group, 1986), and his wife, Margie. Since its founding, BTD has grown to a workforce numbering some 150 employees and has operations throughout the United States and abroad. Some of the stated goals of the organization are to:

- ▸ Develop leadership at all levels.
- ▸ Empower employees to set goals and solve problems.
- ▸ Provide exemplary customer service.
- ▸ Implement learning through technology.
- ▸ Manage the organizational change process.
- ▸ Energize organizations around the world.

Reasons for the Program

The Eagle Award was established to recognize "legendary service" to customers—one of the organization's strategic objectives. Customer surveys conducted indicated that customer service was ranked seventh or eighth as an attribute by the company's customers. BTD's goal in designing the Eagle Award was specifically to increase the perception of customer service in the eyes of its customers.

How the Eagle Award Was Developed and How It Works

The first step in establishing the Eagle Award was to ask for volunteers to form a committee that would take charge of developing and implementing a customer service recognition program. This committee was given the sole goal of improving customer service, along with complete freedom to do whatever it took to get the job done. The only constraint was that the program was not intended to be a cash-based program. Since employees were already being paid salaries to do their jobs, bonuses and similar financial incentives would not be a part of the program. However, some funds were available to the committee to support recognition items and activities as needed.

The committee met to discuss the best ways to improve customer service at BTD. The result of these discussions was the Eagle Award program. Anyone caught providing exceptional service to customers could be acknowledged by any other member of the organization, who would complete a half-page "eagle-praising" form distributed to all employees and available in the company lunch room and mailroom. One side of the form contained the program's objectives; the other side was the application itself. The application asked for the nominee's name and a description of the behavior worthy of recognition. Typical examples of rewarded behavior included staying late to ship materials, helping a customer locate a cost order or resolve a billing problem, and rearranging training schedules to deliver a last-minute request by a customer.

Once completed, nomination forms could be submitted to any member of the Eagle committee, which was composed of five volunteers, including both managers and nonmanagers. The committee reviewed each submission and in general honored most with the Eagle Award, then made a surprise visit to the individual's work area for a picture of the person holding his or her Eagle Award, which was actually one of several eagle trophies that rotated around the company. The winner got to keep the eagle trophy on his or her desk until it was needed for a new recipient—typically a week or so. The presenters also gave the awardee a choice of a nominal reward that included restaurant discounts, zoo passes, car wash coupons, and so forth. Most of these rewards were obtained by bartering services with other businesses in the community.

To further recognize the efforts of each Eagle Award recipient, awardee photos were placed on a bulletin board in the front lobby of BTD's headquarters building around a picture of an eagle in flight, along with a couple of lines about what the employee had done to earn the award. In addition, a listing of "eagle sightings" was included in the employee monthly newsletter. At the end of the year, an Eagle of the Year award was selected by a vote of employees from a list of multiple Eagle Award winners. That person was presented an engraved clock at the company's annual celebration program.

The program was initially announced and explained at a companywide meeting, and it was open to any employee, with no limit on the number of awards given out each month. The Eagle Award program was run entirely by employee volunteers, with no intervention by management.

Primary Outcomes and Continuing Enhancements

The Eagle Award program was credited with making "legendary customer service" an established part of the company's culture. In the seven-month period following introduction of the Eagle Award, customer service came to be the number-one company attribute in the eyes of BTD's customers. Program costs were nominal at less than $200.

While the program was clearly successful, it was not without problems. Sometime after implementation, the Eagle Award program was reviewed to find out what worked well and what could be improved. Two findings were prominent:

▸ It was discovered that the majority of people who received the Eagle Award had direct customer contact as a part of their jobs. Since others without direct customer contact (over half the company) could have a great impact on the delivery of exceptional customer service, the program was expanded to focus on internal customers too.

▸ At the outset of the program, the committee accepted most nominations. However, as the program evolved over time, the committee became more and more evaluative, turning down an increasing number of nominations for a variety of reasons. For example, some questioned if you should receive an award if "that's that person's job!" This was not a desired outcome of the effort, and Ken Blanchard personally met with the committee and proclaimed, "Your job is to celebrate successes—we already have enough evaluations."

The result was that the program was modified to make it even easier to be acknowledged for helping others by shifting from the Eagle Award as the end-all, be-all, to a new form of recognition known as "Eagle Hatchlings." Every employee received an Eagle Hatchling card, each of which contained spaces for 16 hatchlings, nomination postcards, as well as a supply of Eagle Hatchling stickers. Whenever an employee felt that a coworker did something worthy of recognition, he or she could write it up and award an Eagle Hatchling sticker on the spot, without going through the Eagle Award committee. The date, performance, and nominator were listed on the back of the hatchling card for each occurrence.

A completed Eagle Hatchling card earned the employee an Eagle Award plaque, which was engraved with the recipient's name and inspiring words about Eagle behavior and then presented at a company meeting:

EAGLE BEHAVIOR
Eagle behavior is behavior that creates a story. It is doing something extra, unexpected, or special for someone else's benefit or the good of the company as a whole. Eagle behavior is going out of your way to satisfy a need that might otherwise have gone unsatisfied.

The plaque included spaces for nine Eagle chips, small-engraved brass plates of an eagle in flight given for subsequent completion of Eagle Hatchling cards. A "completed" plaque thus represented 144 instances of an employee going beyond his or her job requirements to help a coworker or customer. Employees who completed a plaque received a U.S. Savings Bond. Plaque recipients and their spouses were invited to attend a year-end dinner with Ken and Margie Blanchard, the company's owners.

Outstanding events could also merit bypassing Eagle chips with a committee nomination that a plaque be awarded. For example, BTD's chief financial officer once volunteered to fill in for the company's shipping manager, who was out on three months' disability leave, in addition to his own job. This earned him an Eagle plaque and a standing ovation from the company when it was presented.

Remembering the Purpose

This type of program is particularly effective because it starts with the employees you are trying to motivate to do something different; thus it is their program, not management's. It focuses on a grassroots level—namely, the daily interactions among employees—yet "rolls up" to include traditional recognition elements of plaques and public praise as well as social acceptance, communication, and visibility with top management. Participants learned that it's okay not to do a recognition program perfectly at first. It's more important to get it going by doing something that is timely and sincere and to make improvements and modifications along the way.

The Eagle Award was simple yet effective—driving specific behavior and performance and allowing employees to feel valued for doing so.

ALIGNING COMPENSATION WITH CORE VALUES AND STRATEGIES AT

K/P Corporation

Company Background

K/P Corporation (K/P) is a privately held company established in Salem, Oregon, in 1929. A single individual, Jim Knapp, has owned it since 1967. The corporation now does approximately $90 million in sales from 12 facilities in California, Oregon, Utah, and Washington. It is headquartered in San Ramon, California, and has approximately 650 employees.

K/P Corporation supplies graphic communication products and services. It serves corporations, not consumers. K/P Corporation is in a well-established industry as far as the core competencies of imaging paper with ink and mail distribution are concerned; however, there are other dynamics causing change. Computers have substantially changed the way the customer submits information for reproduction and distribution over the past 20 years—the input to K/P's processes. This has been most notable in the past 5 to 10 years. The personal computer and the Internet have now dramatically changed both the input and the output options available to the customer. In addition, there has been considerable consolidation among competitors, a need for global distribution by many customers, a request for outsource solutions by some customers, and a continual demand for faster turnaround and lower cost. Consequently K/P finds itself in a mature industry facing the same marketplace dynamics as high tech or fashion. These marketplace dynamics influence the career options and the development planning for each individual within the K/P organization.

A Vision for the Future

In 1967 Jim Knapp purchased the Salem, Oregon, commercial printing business from his father, Gardner Knapp. He then grew the company by acquisition of geographically dispersed, privately held companies. During the process of acquisition, Jim met and worked with many retiring business owners who had a strong love and passion for the organizations that they had built during their careers. From these associations a vision for the future was established. That vision, and the associated values, continues to guide the course for K/P Corporation. The vision remains to develop a special company made up of competent, ambitious people who direct their lives by a common sense of mission. The shared mission is to build an organization that enables people to experience that they are "doing something worth doing" with their business lives and feel that they are "being someone worth being." To practice this philosophy every day throughout the organization, K/P Corporation seeks to attract and retain people who strongly agree with these three shared beliefs:

HONESTY
We believe in the importance of searching always for
"intellectual honesty"; being honest with ourselves about
whether we are true to our own convictions.

RESPONSIBILITY
We believe each person in the organization must fully
accept responsibility for successfully completing the work
he or she is assigned or accepts.

LOVE
We believe the most important result of a successful
career is the love that develops over time among people
who work together. When all is said and done, our
relationships with each other are our most significant
and lasting possessions.

Facing Market Changes

K/P Corporation came face-to-face with two market realities in the late 1980s. First, many of its customers demanded that it become "quality literate" and actively participate in supplier certification programs that they intended to launch in order to achieve turnaround-time and cost-of-goods reduction targets. Second, the industry associations for print were predicting a significant reduction in number of surviving firms during the coming decade. The most vulnerable firm was predicted to be the medium-size community printer. At that time K/P Corporation was organized as a holding company of several midsize printing and mailing facilities. Each had its own president and operated autonomously within its business community.

The leaders decided to take action. First, they embraced an aggressive plan to learn, understand, and implement the quality teaching of the time—most specifically that of W. Edwards Deming. Second, they realized they could "beat the odds" being predicted by the industry associations by acting as one corporation. As one corporation it in fact ranked as the 87th largest in the United States in the early 1980s. There was potential synergy to be had in the implementation of these two activities. In fact, Jim Knapp and his leadership team felt that the vision and values of K/P Corporation could be experienced by a greater number of individuals within the organization by effectively acting upon these two initiatives.

Aligning Compensation

By mid-1990, K/P Corporation had been restructured as a single identity in the marketplace—all facilities used one name, one logo, and consistent graphic standards so that the customers, suppliers, and employees would recognize the multiple facilities as units of one corporation. The leadership had adopted consistent employee policies, procedures, and benefits across the corporation, which made it easier for individuals to consider transfer as a career option. However, compensation was not consistently administered, nor was there a plan in place to do so. This seemed a significant hurdle for continued evolution of the organization design and the business strategy. The CEO, Kim Wright, began a search for a solution. It was determined that an outside consulting company would be used to develop the compensation plan.

While at a conference on the topic of world-class manufacturing, Wright was introduced to a consulting firm that had helped other organizations with their compensation programs. He felt that he had found a solution for K/P. Wright gathered the leadership team together to review his findings. It was agreed that the material presented by this consultant was in philosophical alignment with K/P's vision and that there was consistency with previous work accomplished. Wright and his leadership team further agreed that there was an opportunity to leverage their actions on compensation to achieve both business initiatives and greater realization of the vision and values. Thus, a strategic "top-down" and a tactical "bottom-up" implementation process began. (See Figure 5-1.)

Developing the Strategy

The strategic top-down portion was led by CEO Kim Wright. The key strategic elements were to ensure that the outcome would em-

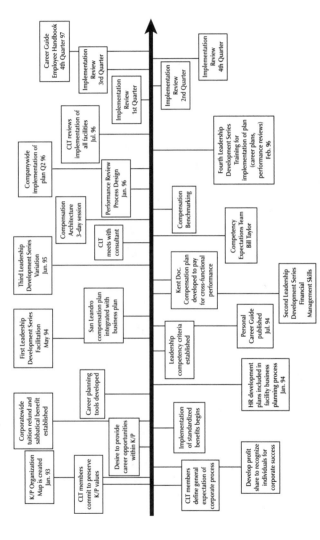

Figure 5-1. Evolution and foundation for base compensation plan "architecture."

brace the vision, be aimed at the business mission of the corporation, and remain consistent with the guiding principles and values of the organization. Wright also facilitated the process to provide stakeholder input on expectations of leadership roles within the company.

The bottom-up portion was led by Bill Taylor, general manager of the Northern California region. Taylor facilitated a process to provide input on skill competency. This input came from a team of people pulled together for this specific purpose. The team was made up of machine operators, administrative personnel, and frontline supervisors to document the expectations that team members have of each other in the workplace. Their input addressed all roles, from entry level to craftsperson or professional.

A three-day working session was scheduled with representatives from each of the two input groups, along with human resources personnel and the outside consulting company. Wright intended to be the facilitator—and essentially the consultant's "client" for this working session. It was a great plan that was put off track by Wright's coming down with pneumonia. Without access to the CEO, Chuck Parsons, general manager of the Northwest region, and Patricia Ellsworth, director of human resources for the Northern California region, determined that the process should proceed if possible. The team of individuals pulled together for the event were prepared; they had collected the appropriate information and they had clarity of purpose. In addition, all involved felt they had had sufficient direction from Wright to proceed. It was an intense three days. The task was accomplished—at the end of the three-day working session K/P Corporation had a company-wide compensation plan. The plan included a base compensation philosophy, a base compensation strategy, base compensation management guidelines, competency dimensions, competency measures by career band, and "benchmark jobs" identified by career band. The team was proud. Wright was especially proud!

The K/P Corporation base compensation plan consists of six competency dimensions. These include:

1. Knowledge and skills
2. Customer focus
3. Continuous improvement
4. Personal development

5. Business performance
6. Interpersonal skills

The plan includes eight career bands. Examples are: career band one includes entry level; career band four includes highly skilled professionals and craftspeople; career band five includes those beginning to assume leadership responsibilities; career band eight is the CEO. All six competency dimensions apply to each of the career bands. The competency measures (see Figure 5-2 for an example) vary considerably from one career band to the next.

Knowledge Skills	Customer Focus	Continuous Improvement	Personal Development	Business Performance	Interpersonal Skills
Interpret instructions and understand their effect on the customer Basic computer/ data entry skills High School Diploma or equivalent Track and plot CIC data Operational knowledge of mechanically controlled equipment within functional level Perform simple maintenance routines within functional areas Recognize need for corrective actions Perform according to SOPs	Identify internal/external customers Anticipate customer requirements Recognize/ communicate deviations from customer requirements	Actively participate in process improvement within functional teams Learn the Plan/Do/Study/Act cycle Suggest improvement tools Suggest improvements to SOPs as well as understand the effect on other internal/external customers Utilize R+ Board to acknowledge successes	Be willing to learn new skills Commit to a personal career/ development plan Seek and utilize training to enhance personal contribution Help others once personal job is done Demonstrate ability to work with people/teamwork	Work within established work schedules and standards Understand scope of responsibility Understand that assigned work will affect other areas Recognize a process problem or variation and communicate to appropriate team leader Knowledge of regulatory/ governmental compliance requirements	Display team member characteristics: ♦ commitment ♦ initiative ♦ extra effort ♦ work with some supervision Practice six Human actions Accept that K/P is a diverse community

Figure 5-2. K/P Corporation's career band two competency measures.

The plan also distinguishes performance levels within a job pay zone. There are four levels within a job pay zone. These include:

1. *The learner* (the lowest pay level for the individual who is developing the competency)
2. *The applier* (the individual whose competency is sufficient to fully meet customer expectations)

3. *The expander* (the individual who consistently shares knowledge with others for purposes of process improvement)
4. *The developer* (the individual who coaches and helps others to develop the competency)

Much has been stated about the base compensation. It needs to be emphasized that base compensation is a component of the K/P Corporation Behavior-Based Reward Strategy. This overall reward strategy also includes the components of variable compensation for sharing in positive company financial results, and performance management to both reinforce or correct behavior as appropriate. CEO Wright again facilitated the integration of the base compensation plan into the overall reward strategy.

Implementing the Compensation Plan

Next came implementation. K/P Corporation had previously initiated a leadership development series to accelerate the learning and implementation of both process improvement and business literacy. This provided an appropriate forum to roll out the K/P Corporation Behavior-Based Reward Strategy and to achieve consistent, simultaneous implementation of the base compensation plan. Wright, Parsons, Ellsworth, and selected team members of the three-day working session conducted the two-day training and launch meeting. The event became the fourth session of the Leadership Development Series. It included basic education materials so that the K/P leadership could understand the concepts behind the reward strategy and the specifics of the base compensation plan. The content of this leadership development session was aligned with K/P business initiatives. Role-play was heavily used so all leaders could experience the materials, and each facility leadership team completed their individual implementation plans before leaving. Ellsworth met with the facility leadership teams shortly after the session to answer any questions that arose as they began implementation back at their facility. Wright and his leadership team, which included both region managers, followed up on the implementation progress of each of these plans during the following year. Parsons and Ellsworth collaborated to incorporate the entire plan into the latest revision of the K/P employee handbook (career guide) released in late 1997. The compensation plan has now become an integral part of recruiting and career planning at K/P Corporation.

Having accomplished this program effectively removed the barrier perceived earlier by CEO Wright. More important, it established a foundation for further evolution within K/P Corporation. In 1997 the corporation launched an employee stock ownership plan (ESOP) to begin ownership transfer into the hands of the employees. This represents a whole new dimension for the concept of a total reward strategy—much stronger than base compensation alone can offer the individual.

Issues During Implementation

Two issues surfaced during implementation. The first requires corporate-level leadership to manage. There is a tendency for "career band creep." Job descriptions can be monitored to ensure that bands five, six, and seven are not excessively used. These bands have significant overlap in pay amount. The "creep" seems to be driven by perceived status.

The second issue is related to human resources development. In order to achieve the competency dimensions listed for each career band, all facilities must have rather aggressive human resources development plans in place. If not, the individuals will lack the knowledge necessary to achieve the competency measurements—and thus accomplishing the vision and values of K/P Corporation will be at risk. People will just not feel fulfilled when they know they are not measuring up to stated expectations.

The Future

The marketplace dynamics and the changing needs of the customer continue to evolve for K/P Corporation. It appears that the total reward strategy and, more specifically, the base compensation component will support and endure change. K/P has continued to make changes in organization design and leadership. New products and services have been added and unneeded ones discontinued. The organization has had to attract and retain new skills to keep pace with the information technology needs of its customers. All these rather dramatic changes have been accommodated without reworking the structure and process of the base compensation program.

The need for training and development in the six competency dimensions discussed earlier may be linked to an even more fundamental issue for businesses today. How does a facility leadership team, or an organization, provide continuous, repeating learning opportunities? Perhaps the answer lies in providing more structure and support for those individuals willing to participate at the "developer" level of their job pay zone. It's an idea. Consistent with K/P's core values, the company will continue to experiment, learn, and develop. By doing so, it strengthens its relationship with customers and its employees.

EVOLVING THE REWARDS FOCUS FROM ENTITLEMENT TO RESULTS AT

Baptist Health System, Inc.

Within the past decade, remarkable innovations in reward systems have taken place across all industries, in many cases unleashing powerful discretionary effort and strategic results that were previously unimaginable. Some industries, such as start-up technology companies, were natural incubators for rapid innovation in variable pay, and many valuable lessons were gained in employee stock options, team pay, and other incentives. However, more mature industries, such as healthcare, which built their very success on more traditional pay practices, faced the quite different obstacle of changing reward systems at exactly the right pace. The case study of Baptist Health System, Inc., in Birmingham, Alabama, shows how a series of smaller successes in reward systems can evolve a mature culture toward a pay-for-results philosophy.

An Overview of Baptist Health System

Baptist Health System (BHS), a not-for-profit company, is Alabama's largest integrated healthcare delivery system, providing quality healthcare to Alabamians through its 11 hospitals, primary care network, Birmingham-based Health Partners Southeast HMO, wellness/exercise facilities, and senior living communities. BHS was recently ranked in the top 50 of the *Integrated Health Care 100 Directory*. This listing was developed in cooperation with *Hospitals and Health Networks* magazine (March 20, 1998) to identify the top U.S. healthcare enterprises that are pioneering change and have gone the furthest in developing services for the coming millennium by building organizations that boast coordinated systems of care. Factors considered in the listing were types of managed care contracts for each system, whether management is centralized, the status of information technology innovations, and other markers of integration.

BHS traces its beginnings back to 1922, when a group of local Baptist congregations acquired a small infirmary in Birmingham's thriving West End. On the site of that original, historic facility is today's Princeton campus of Birmingham Baptist Medical Center (BMC). The center is complemented on Birmingham's east by its sister flagship hospital, Montclair Baptist Medical Center, and on the south by Shelby Baptist Medical Center, which is located in Shelby County and has experienced a 300% growth rate over the last 30 years. Corporate offices include centralized systemwide functions such as laundry operations, accounting, information technologies, compensation, an employee benefits service center, and patient accounting. Eight additional hospitals provide healthcare to smaller communities in north and north-central Alabama.

Baptist Health System's growth through acquisitions in Alabama has been breathtaking, with the system's size doubling since 1993. However, rapid growth has not compromised quality, with BHS recently being awarded the Alabama Quality Award, which is modeled after the Malcolm Baldrige National Quality Award. BHS is also recognized as an "employer of choice," earning the Wellness Council of America's highest honor, the Gold Well Workplace Award, and being named Employer of the Year in 1997 by the Alabama Career Development Association for its commitment to career development, literacy training, and family-friendly employment practices. These practices genuinely flow from BHS's long-standing mission values of compassionate care, innovation, performance, and teamwork.

One example of a recent BHS acquisition illustrates the importance of BHS's cultural values. In 1995, BHS acquired a 267-bed hospital facility in Walker County, 75 miles from Birmingham. BHS inherited a hospital that had been unionized in Licensed Practical Nurse (LPN) and lower-wage-level jobs for more than 20 years, in a county whose labor force was historically dominated by the United Mine Workers and other unions. BHS immediately implemented its compensation, benefit, and other HR practices for the nonbargaining RN and professional/management jobs. Within two years, by virtue of union employees seeing the fair treatment of the nonbargaining group, and through competitive total compensation practices, the hospital union employees moved to hold an election to decertify the union, voting unanimously to do so in 1997.

BHS, along with virtually every other healthcare system in the United States, faces unprecedented challenges to its business mission from multiple pressure points, including extreme Medicare reimbursement cuts by Congress and the President, continually declining inpatient utilization, intense competitive pressure, and a turbulent managed care environment. BHS is now in the fourth and by far most aggressive year of reengineering its operations through consolidation of services, cost cutting, and rightsizing. The latter, remarkably, has taken place thus far by "inplacing" more than 90% of staff members whose jobs were eliminated into jobs in the growth areas of the business. Any one of these business pressures would itself require a healthcare system to make significant business decisions; however, the convergence of numerous business pressures at once has forced performance improvement initiatives never before witnessed in the BHS culture. The plaque on the wall of BHS's CFO states the case succinctly—No Margin, No Mission. In a very real sense, the people who increasingly declare their preference for not-for-profit, community-based healthcare depend on BHS to be fiscally responsible.

Fortunately, an evolution toward more variable and results-based systems of pay had begun at BHS in the mid-1990s in the form of targeted variable pay plans. A review of three targeted incentive plan success stories will show how BHS has embraced a strategy to evolve toward a more results-based compensation philosophy that will serve organizational objectives into the coming millennium.

An Incentive Plan Whose Time Had Come

In a recent challenging fiscal year, the patient accounting area had become the focus of both financial and cash-flow scrutiny. Patient accounting has a major impact on critical financial measures, including days in accounts receivable for patient billing accounts and reduction in bad debt expense. The reward system had been base pay driven, was not tied to important business measures, and promoted a shallow employee understanding of the operation. The entitlement mentality and underperformance that typically accompanies base-only reward programs was quite evident in all the relevant performance measures of the patient accounting area.

Accounts receivable had crept up to 90 days, which was bringing the business to its knees through poor cash flow, exerting burdensome pressure on capital expenditures. For the casual reader, the financial impact of merely one day's delay in receiving payment on a patient account at only the Montclair BMC hospital is equivalent to $800,000 in delayed payment and the resulting lost time value of money. Problems were not limited to delayed accounts receivable, as baseline data quality had been measured at a disappointing 72%. A high-performing patient accounts area based on national benchmarks would include an average days in accounts receivable of 60 and a quality measure of 95%. The perspective of both operations management and their human resources business partners was that, without question, desperate times existed in patient accounting, and thus a far more leading-edge approach to pay practices was business justified. Out of this dire need for high performance, the first significant targeted variable pay plan at BHS was born.

Patient Accounting Incentive Plan Design

The objectives of the Patient Accounts Plan are as follows:

- ▸ Enhance teamwork within and among departments.
- ▸ Increase employee understanding of hospital economics and key business measures.
- ▸ Focus and reward employees for behaviors that support hospital goals.

▸ Serve as a pilot to assess the feasibility of variable pay programs elsewhere in the organization.

Measurements were selected that would support plan objectives, including quality of billing data collected and entered, days in accounts receivable, reduction of bad debt expense, and patient satisfaction. To emphasize quality in the strongest possible manner, plan design dictates a "winner's circle" for quality measures, such that no award will be payable if the specified quality threshold is not attained. This had a dramatic impact in improving quality as employees suddenly found the quality measure relevant due to reward opportunity.

Has the plan positively impacted patient account performance? Without question, as improvements over baseline performance show an astounding return on the compensation investment (ROCI) of 29 to 1:

Incentive Plan	Financial Gains*	Incentive Investment	ROCI
Patient Account Plan	$3,658,000	$125,800	29.8:1
Transcriptionist Plan	$384,000	$80,132	4.8:1
HMO Member Services	$224,838	$48,892	4.6:1
Combined (3) Plans	$4,209,238	$254,824	16.5:1

*Financial Gains result from increased productivity, reduced days in accounts receivable, increased quality, and error reduction. "Soft" gains such as improved customer satisfaction, though very real, are not captured as financial gains. Each plan's first-year results are shown.

When the ROCIs for incentive plans are this eye-popping, skepticism as to a direct cause and effect relationship is understandable, but the fact that the right results are happening is more important than proof of their multiple causes. One must remember that often other parameters are changing concurrently when redesigning incentive plans.

Through an entirely new way of working together in patient accounting, and focusing greater discretionary effort on quality, days in accounts receivable were dropped from 90 to 46 days over a two-year period. This compares to a national average of 60 gross days in accounts receivable, which most healthcare providers are happy to maintain. Employee turnover, which was at 20%, has been cut in half to 10%. Anecdotal evidence may be more compelling, as the Birmingham patient accounts department now holds two to three site visits per month, hosting consultants and health-care providers from across the United States who are interested in exactly how BHS achieved industry-leading performance measures. Mitzi Winters, vice president of patient accounting, observed that one recent visitor commented that "BHS should charge admission for the site visits."

This plan has placed patient accounting above national averages in days in accounts receivable, customer satisfaction, and bad debt collection. Yet proper courtesy and billing collection methods are ensured so that organizational values of compassionate care do not suffer.

In fact, customer satisfaction survey scores for patient accounting increased after the incentive plan installation. The efficiencies from accelerating collectible sources also benefit the community BHS serves in the form of the availability of greater resources to provide care to the most needy patients.

Teamwork has taken root as finger-pointing over errors between areas has disappeared and has been replaced by pride in quality. With quality at an impressive 98%, there are too few errors to even cause the "blame game." Employees understand their personal impact on days in accounts receivable and quality measures. For example, failing to verify insurance coverage of patients up front may disqualify the team from the quarterly payout. Veteran employees now help out new hires to teach fundamentals, ensure quality, and solve problems together.

The plan has paid out consistently, days in accounts receivable and bad debt expense are still continuing to decrease, and patient satisfaction continues to improve. The ROCI and the success of plans such as this clearly helped set the stage for broader-based pay-at-risk plans.

The Medical Transcriptionists Incentive Plan

A second incentive plan, which has been highly successful, is the Medical Transcriptionist Plan. The purpose of this plan is to reward each transcriptionist to develop productivity to peak levels of quality and quantity, thereby benefiting them as well as the hospital. Currently, medical transcriptionists are compensated under a mix of base and incentive pay designed to attract and retain peak performers, while encouraging low-performing candidates to "self-deselect" in the interview process. The incentive is paid out biweekly to ensure maximum reward immediacy, because the measurements lend themselves to this frequency. Transcriptionists are paid $0.05 per line for each line in excess of 520 lines. BHS transcriptionists in the plan are performing at an average production of 1,700 lines per day, which is 70% above national average production, which has allowed BHS to achieve lower than national average staffing ratios. In addition to the number of lines, quality measures ensure coding, medical records, and physician information is accurate. Although the basic incentive design pay for the transcriptionist plan is fairly common in the industry, recent plan innovations include moving transcriptionists to a pure production pay model concurrent with a time telecommuting implementation.

Complements to Variable Pay Strategies

BHS is in the second year of its telecommuting work option and is within six months of having all transcriptionists working out of their homes. The concept of telecommuting has created a flexible work option for employees that is superior to local competition, thereby dramatically reducing turnover. At a time of unprecedented short labor supply, qualified talent is actually seeking out BHS as an employer of choice due to its telecommuting policy. Continuous improvement in the areas of information technology has made this possible. Telecommuting has been a win-win strategy—improving productivity, creating fewer discipline problems, increasing employee morale, and relieving pressure on pay systems as base salary fixed costs were dropped in favor of a "100% at risk" pay model. The new plan is designed based on number of lines typed per day with quality as a modifier. It is graduated so that as the number of lines produced increases, the cents per line accelerates. The outcome has been slightly reduced compensation for underperformers and increased compensation for the very highest producers, but with a cost-neutral transition that has thus far caused zero turnover.

A Balanced Performance Scorecard for Health Partners Southeast HMO Member Services

The critical service link between any HMO or insurance provider and its members is a well-run member services area. The health insurance industry has faced particular challenges in rapidly training service center representatives to master systems, group plan benefits, provider networks, and other member information, let alone deliver accurate, timely answers to members with consistent quality. Health Partners Southeast HMO member services department was no exception. The 1996 performance baseline painted a bleak picture—14% member call-abandonment rate, 35% staff turnover rate (with most being lost to local competitors), and low member satisfaction scores. There was minimal teamwork, with training of new member services representatives left largely to their manager.

A design team of corporate compensation and member services management introduced an incentive plan with a monthly target payout opportunity of 8% of pay, which was aimed at driving individual performance levels higher while promoting new collaborative behaviors. The performance matrix established individual goals for productivity (calls per week) and quality (assessment of a sample of recorded calls for accuracy, courtesy, and other skills), weighting individual goals 60%. The performance scorecard was then balanced with 40% weighted team goals, including the month's call-abandonment rate and member satisfaction scores. Special care was given in communicating the plan mechanics, emphasizing the new behaviors that would create teamwork. Of equal importance were special celebrations that were held for monthly payouts so that incentives extended beyond mere financial to psychosocial rewards.

The first-year results (1997) for the member services incentive plan posted a 4.6 to 1 return on the incentive investment (refer back to the table) through increased productivity and quality. Perhaps the most unexpected outcome was the dramatic reduction of member services turnover from 35% to 5%, with the associated operational stability and improved quality. Other benefits include reduced pressure on management to train, as the 40% weighted team goals have created collaboration. Employees are working to bring a new hire rapidly up the learning curve as they share system shortcuts, communication skills, and coach fellow team members on Health Partners Southeast's service values. Employees feel a personal stake in sharing their best practices.

When Payouts Are Meaningful

It's all too easy for executives and compensation practitioners to become cynical about the size of incentive payouts and at what level they become meaningful. BHS has learned that payout size or meaningfulness is often in the eyes of the beholder. Jane, an accounts receivable employee, received a quarterly incentive payout of $205 for two successive quarters, which according to reward and motivational theory would be considered "undermotivating" as a reward. Some incentive plan designers would abandon such a plan's very implementation. But the truth was that both the recognition for performing and the reward were special to Jane. She said, "Every Monday night I thank God for BHS's incentive plan. For the past five years, I always had to go to the laundromat to wash clothes and never got to spend time with my husband. With the first two incentive checks, I was able to buy a washer and dryer, and now my husband and I look forward to Monday nights." The limited purchasing power that often exists with today's worker might help explain why even modest lump sum rewards can be motivational, producing better performance and stronger commitment to the organization.

The Foundation for a Results-Based Rewards Future

> "An invasion of armies can be resisted, but not an idea whose time has come."
>
> Victor Hugo
> *Histoire d'un Crime,* 1852

The three illustrated variable pay plans discussed in this case study, as well as five additional targeted variable pay plans that followed at BHS, have served as a springboard to an even broader-based pay for results philosophy. There was clear business risk in each plan's implementation, including perceived inequity by employees in adjacent areas who were not incentive eligible, and the risk that if performance improvements were not achieved, the incentive plan designers might be viewed as "throwing good money after bad." Perhaps the greatest risk was the possibility of a failed pilot program. Had these plans shown a disappointing return on the compensation investment, it might have signaled the commitment to a base-only pay strategy for years to come, despite national trends to greater pay at risk in every industry. Even in a faith-based organization, seeing is believing. It is difficult to argue the ROCI on each plan, and the minimal internal inequity that is attributable to using a targeted approach is offset by each plan's success in retaining staff in what were historically high turnover areas.

These variable pay successes have intersected in time with unprecedented business financial challenges. Even if it were desirable, healthcare organizations can no longer afford to protect employees from the company's financial variability. This is witnessed in the industry's shrinking, barely-at-inflation merit increase budgets, in the aggressive management of benefit plan utilization, and in unprecedented lean staffing. Yet organizational values and objectives remain the same: to provide faith-based, not-for-profit healthcare of the highest quality to the communities entrusted to BHS.

Reward systems are now understood properly for their role in driving peak performance toward results that are critical to the business. In recently approving a systemwide gainsharing plan, senior management has taken a bold step to create a sense of ownership and caring among employees at every level of the organization. Basic plan design will provide for system-level funding of a pool from financial gains over budgeted net income from operations. To drive intense focus on patient satisfaction, quality will be a gainsharing plan facility-level threshold. Finally, operating margin will be the performance modifier at each facility, focusing team efforts toward controllable expense reduction and continual process improvement. Despite an annual payout frequency, reward immediacy will be achieved through intensive communication of progress toward goals, recognition of key successes, and lively measurement feedback displays. Bob Roeder, of William M. Mercer, Inc., observes: "It is my opinion from working with healthcare systems that it is more a question of when than if they will adopt broad-based reward strategies such as gainsharing plans, because of the great potential to harness and focus efforts on the right results."

Heading Boldly Into an Uncertain Future

The healthcare industry in the United States is arguably the industry facing the greatest degree of uncertainty in the next millennium. BHS and other leading healthcare organizations are nonetheless confidently building reward systems that will help forge working America's "new deal," which rewards results that are important to the business and shares the gains created. It is precisely this reward strategy that will make business-critical measures relevant so that entitlement rapidly gives way to results.

6

Supporting a Business Turnaround

When an organization faces a major problem, one that means that it might not survive, fear runs deep in the culture. This occurs when the organization realizes that the conditions are not temporary abnormalities in the business. There are two possible responses—flight or fight. Those that deny the crisis compound their situation. Those that choose to fight at least have a chance of winning. Succeeding in a crisis requires a strong game plan and commitment of people to its implementation.

Each of the organizations in this chapter took on the task of turning themselves around. Some of the situations were more critical than others. They each developed a strategy and communicated it heavily throughout the organization. But what does one say to employees about their stake in this strategy? Is the opportunity to keep one's job the only benefit? These companies knew they needed to offer more. They knew that the turnaround strategy would be more meaningful and create more commitment if people could see a personal stake in the outcomes. The decisions and actions would be understood in the context of mutual interest. While the process of major change is not easy, successful implementation is essential if the organization is to survive.

The turnaround experience of Sears is perhaps the most significant in terms of the cultural change and the magnitude of the organization. Avid Technology was smaller in scope, but no less significant for those working for this video-technology company. Burke Customer Satisfaction Associates is a consulting firm that developed a strategy to recapture the leadership in its markets by restructuring key jobs, accountabilities, and rewards. OSRAM SYLVANIA needed to significantly improve its performance orientation in order to recapture its competitiveness in the market. It used a performance management process as one of the key drivers of this message. Finally, a division of SunLife was facing its sale or closure if it did not turn into a profit contributor. The company took an "all hands on deck" approach and used a variety of rewards to drive a substantial change. They all succeeded.

Crisis can provide an opportunity to galvanize people into a common mission. Some believe this is the easy part. Once the organization has become repositioned and has celebrated the victory, how do you not retreat back into past practices that led to the crisis in the first place? Each of these organizations is now facing that challenge of continual improvement when the pending crisis has past. Sometimes after winning, the elements of the old culture return because the pressure for change is diminished. These companies have a better chance of sustaining their change than those who treat the change efforts as a project. These companies at least have changed the way they pay people and the meaning they place on reward systems.

REGAINING MARKET LEADERSHIP AT

Sears, Roebuck and Company

There is perhaps no greater example of a turnaround of a business than was achieved at Sears. Much has been written about how Sears has achieved its critical turnaround. Here is a company that is huge and complex, facing a changing marketplace and changing customer values. In this case study we will focus on how a variety of reward systems, some formal and others informal, were integrated by a set of clear themes to support the change process. In this way, we can understand how Sears was able to be successful and build fundamental commitment of its people.

Discovering the Need for Fundamental Change

For decades Sears has been part of the American culture, growing along with the country from its founding in 1886. People had personal relationships with the company and found great value in buying from its stores and catalogs. The structure of the market remained basically unchanged year after year, through the 1950s and 1960s, though the sheer volume of retail outlets increased dramatically.

This long history of success and leadership may have blinded the executives, managers, and professionals about the crisis that awaited them. The problem with being successful, and being highly rewarded for it, is that a company may become oblivious to competitive change and deny the pressures growing around it. In the early 1970s, something fundamental began to change in the retail market. Sears started seeing companies like Kmart and specialty retailers providing customers with comparable products at lower costs, greater choice for items of special interest, or service levels that were qualitatively different from what people received from large department stores. People began to change their primary retail store as an unprecedented number of choices started presenting themselves.

For Sears, there was no single competitor. Instead, it started facing a variety of niche players, each one finding and fully meeting the needs of a particular set of customers. They provided services in a superior fashion and changed customers' traditional buying patterns. Sears did not rest during this time; it tried many strategies to regain prominence. It offered sales to compete on price and even changed pricing policies to "everyday fair pricing" in response to customer mistrust of sale prices (the customers stayed away). Sears opened stores in malls around the country and closed stores that were not showing signs of growth. It introduced many marketing and merchandising strategies, only to find that few of them worked for long. Sears was being attacked from all sides, and it was having trouble sustaining market leadership.

In 1992, Sears had sales of more than $33 billion and more than 300,000 employees. While this size enabled it to remain the major force in the retail industry, it wrote off $2.3 billion, more than the total revenues of most major companies in the United States. Sears hired Arthur C. Martinez as the new chairman and chief executive officer. His challenge was to turn this major enterprise around so that it could address the needs of a new marketplace and a new customer preference and do so predominately with the same people, store locations, and infrastructure. Time was not on his side.

Implementing a Strategy for Change

While much can be written about the renewal of Sears, there were several key strategies that emerged to guide these efforts. First, the company needed to reduce costs and align the cost structure to the revenues of the company. The actions to support this strategy led to the closing of the 101-year-old Sears catalog operations, as well as more than 100 stores, and downsizing thousands of employees. The financial and real estate companies Sears had acquired in the 1980s were divested so that the company could focus on its core business of merchandising.

Second, the company needed to regain the confidence of customers and employees that Sears was an attractive place to shop. Only active executive leadership, not restructuring activities or policies, could do this. In April 1993, the CEO took a group of more than 50 executives for an offsite meeting to review the business and set a new course for the company. He directed the meeting and engaged each executive in facing the new realities of the business. The output of the meeting was an articulation of five strategic imperatives for the company's turnaround:

1. Become a compelling place to shop.
2. Develop a local market focus.
3. Focus on core business.
4. Build a winning culture.
5. Seek continuous improvement in costs.

These goals persisted throughout the first five years of Sears's turnaround, but they were distilled into a simple, memorable vision statement: Sears wants to be a compelling place to shop, a compelling place to work, and a compelling place to invest. These "3Cs" formed the basis for major organizational change.

To implement these concepts, the executives began a process of engaging people from all corners of the organization to explore what could be done to improve the organization in these three areas. Through surveys, focus groups, and other intensive dialogues, thousands of people were brought into the process of change. As ideas came forward, they were not dismissed. Task forces were created and led by managers from all areas of the company. People who had been hidden from senior management had opportunities to demonstrate their leadership and commitment to reshaping the organization. Those who waited for the change to pass became evident as well.

Finally, as the process of change unfolded, two factors worked in Sears's favor. First, it did not need to convince people that change was needed or important. People were ready for new leadership and wanted to improve the performance of the company. Second, the marketplace still had a positive, trusting image of Sears as a good and honest place to shop. It still owned most of the "hearts" of the marketplace, though rapid change was needed to sustain that relationship.

Finding the Drivers to Focus Organizational Transformation

Throughout these change efforts and subsequent senior leadership meetings, a consensus was building on what was needed to be successful. The company had years of data on its financial operations, customer preferences and attitudes, and employee opinions—three data sources for which to measure progress on the 3Cs. It analyzed these factors to determine if there could be a connection, and if this could form the basis for renewing the organization. Through a yearlong process of statistical analysis, it was shown that there was indeed a strong correlation between the three factors of the business. The company observed the following:

> Employees who were valued for their contributions behaved in ways that would . . .
> Lead to improved customer satisfaction and retention, which would . . .
> Create attractive financial returns and make Sears a good place to invest.

These three factors—employees (a compelling place to work), customers (a compelling place to shop), and shareholder returns (a compelling place to invest)—would lead Sears into a strong leadership position in the market. The executives intuitively realized that the way people were treated would directly be manifested in customer relationships and that customers would determine the company's financial results, though the empirical connection took a good deal of work to conclusively demonstrate.

Following this logic, the company developed a balanced scorecard of performance measures and used these to link all reward systems into an integrated management process. These became known as the Total Performance Indicators (TPI). Over the years the company has continued to refine the measurement systems to capture employee/customer/financial results. It uses these factors to establish major "audacious" goals as well as integrate them into all incentive compensation plans.

To illustrate, this model, which is based on rigorous correlation analysis, determined that a 5-point improvement in certain employee attitudes would drive a 1.3-point improvement in customer satisfaction, which in turn would drive a 0.5% improvement in revenues. As applied to a typical store, a 5% improvement in employee satisfaction would result in a $150,000 to $200,000 increase in store revenues (and as model refinements are made, the bottom-line impact appears even stronger). Managers could apply this analytical framework to the overall company as well as at the store level. Hence, Sears found a clear, integrated tool to manage the performance of the company.

Changing Behavior

All the concepts and strategies, models and measures, would be of little value if they did not result in changing behaviors throughout the organization. The organization is composed of the actions that people take. If Sears was to ultimately be successful, people needed to embrace the changes and see a personal benefit for improving the results of the company. The payback needed to go beyond just keeping one's job. People would need to understand, be trained, and receive reinforcement continually for their contributions to improve performance.

Sears took a bold and multifaceted approach. In 1996 it made a truly revolutionary step of basing all long-term incentives on the three key measures of employee satisfaction, customer loyalty, and financial results. This involved more than 200 senior managers. Their three-year incentive plan awards were based on a balance of improvements—one-third on employees, one-third on customer measures, and one-third on investor measures. The board of directors took the leap of faith of supporting this plan even though the employee and customer metrics were still being refined.

Then, these metrics were cascaded down through the organization to every associate. A significant portion of the manager's variable pay was based on target improvements in these three areas. This carried down through the district managers responsible for a major area of stores. Each manager had accountability for improvements in these factors or sustaining them at high levels of performance.

In addition, initiatives were begun to engage all employees in the process of business planning and reaping the rewards of success. Sears had had a profit-sharing program since 1916. While stores had long been rewarded on their financial performance, the TPI measures expanded the focus to employees and customers as well.

Finally, all 15,000 salaried associates are participating in the company's stock option program. Sears is making "owners" of its managers and professionals and is expanding that ownership to all employees through a discounted stock purchase plan.

Charting the Future of Change

We have witnessed at Sears a process of discovering what drives the success of the business. The company has then implemented these processes throughout the organization. The results over the past five years can speak for themselves:

- ► Revenues have increased by more than 15% (to more than $42 billion).
- ► Net income has increased from a loss of $3 billion to a gain of $1.3 billion.
- ► Earnings per share have gone from a loss of $7.02 to a gain of $3.12.
- ► Customer satisfaction scores have increased 4% while the comparative industry data has remained flat; from 1995 to 1996, customer satisfaction jumped 5.6%, more than twice that of other retailers.

> ► Employee satisfaction, as surveyed, increased at comparable levels.

The involvement process has been key to Sears success. The strategy was simple, clear, and related well to the needs of the managers and associates. The reward systems have provided the personal stake for each individual to make contributions to the turnaround efforts. Sears has once again emerged as a leading retail company.

Now the efforts of change are focusing on continuous improvements. The process of change is an unending process; there is no finish line. In many competitive industries making change is not as important as the rate of change; one needs to continually stay ahead of the improvements made by one's competitors.

Sears is now facing the challenge of sustaining the momentum of change. They clearly have the building blocks and systems to implement a competitive strategy. And what has evolved is a company that is now ready for new market opportunities, as long as complacency does not emerge within the culture of the new Sears.

LINKING REWARD SYSTEMS TO A BUSINESS TURNAROUND AT

Avid Technology, Inc.

When companies primarily focus on revenue growth, they often make substantial reinvestments in the business or keep prices low to gain market share. The challenge is to sustain sufficient capital to invest and manage cash flow effectively until growth in both revenue and profitability can be sustained. This is a study of a unique technology company that achieved market dominance and faced a number of business issues. When new leaders were selected, they instituted an effective turnaround effort. Their reward systems were a critical link to the implementation of the strategy. The company is Avid Technology, Inc.

Company Background

Avid Technology was founded in 1987 and shipped its first product in 1989, with the dream of revolutionizing the film and video editing industry. Prior to Avid's formation, motion pictures, commercials, broadcast news, and TV shows were edited in a labor-intensive way by cutting and pasting film segments together. Avid created software that enabled this entire process to be done digitally, using the computer to edit the film and later to add graphics and special effects.

The company's growth was phenomenal as the market saw the clear advantages of digital, nonlinear, real-time editing of film and video. Revenues grew from $1 million in 1989 to more than $400 million in 1995. The number of employees grew from the starting founders to more than 1,500. In 1994 and 1995, six companies were acquired. Sales offices sprang up across the globe. In 1994, the company earned the distinction of being named in the top 10 of the Fortune 100 hot-growth companies and was later named to the Fortune list of "Cool Companies to Work For." The technology was so advanced that it became the standard for the industry. This was effective in driving out major competitors.

This growth, however, was not without its costs. In a concentrated effort to increase market share and dominate competitors, the company drove revenues with a passion. This strategy was highly successful and led to dramatic increases in sales. Yet it also resulted in minimal profitability. Avid focused on making major investments in technology development and sales and marketing. Investments in the infrastructure (e.g., human resources systems, financial reporting, information systems, manufacturing quality), so crucial to a rapidly growing company, were neglected. When problems surfaced, customer confidence and profitability eroded. There was little established protocol to address customer concerns and manage costs.

The compensation systems supported this drive for growth. Stock options were used extensively as an inexpensive way to attract and retain growth-oriented individuals. To retain the effectiveness of the options, the company needed continual growth in market value. If they were effective in growing share value, this would counteract any dilution effect of these options on the share price. When the growth started slipping, shareholders started placing increased pressure to improve the firm's profitability. Additionally, cash-based incentive plans began to cause additional problems as the company faced declining cash flow. Finally, a change in company strategy and performance orientation were key to the firm's future prosperity.

The board of directors decided to take several bold steps and put a new leadership team in place. Curt Rawley, the chief executive and technological visionary, became vice chairman of the board; Bill Miller, former CEO of Quantum, the multibillion-dollar disk-drive manufacturer, was appointed as CEO.

Reasons for Changes in the Compensation Programs

When Bill Miller took over the leadership of Avid in April 1996, the company was facing substantial difficulties. The company had an expenditure profile that would mean it would soon run out of cash. Employee turnover had climbed to 25% on an annualized basis. The declining share price made it difficult to use stock options for retention of top talent, and many of the outstanding options were below their exercise price. The company was facing significant losses, revenue growth was minimal, and an informal survey revealed that many critical employees were disillusioned. Direct industry competitors, as well as companies in the surrounding labor market, started attracting key talent away from Avid, further placing any recovery at risk.

Upon assuming control of the company, Miller knew that while he had taken over a company with outstanding technology and market leadership, it was a company facing incredible challenges. He had to make changes quickly and decisively. He formed three core strategies. First, he needed to address cash flow concerns and restore the company to profitability. Second, he wanted to return Avid to being a great place to work and stem employee turnover. Without key people, any comeback attempt would be very difficult. Finally, the company needed to retain its technological leadership and make significant investments in the infrastructure of the company.

Within several months of assuming control, Miller had assembled a new senior leadership team and crafted the details of his strategy for the company. He also worked with the vice president of human resources and the director of compensation and benefits to develop new compensation systems to support the changes he had initiated.

How the New Compensation Programs Work

The director of compensation and benefits developed the new compensation system, in conjunction with an internal compensation and benefits committee and an outside consulting firm. This committee was composed of vice presidents and directors within the company and was chartered to provide senior-level involvement in the design.

They developed several programs to better align the compensation system with new business objectives. First, the management incentive program, in which all directors and vice presidents in the company participated, was changed from a plan based on earnings-per-share to focus on return on invested capital (ROIC). This change was instituted to focus on both profitability and effective asset management, two areas the company desperately needed to improve.

Second, all other employees in the company became eligible for a profit-sharing program based on the same measure as the senior management incentive program—return on invested capital. This program was instituted in the company to ensure that everyone had a stake in the same goals—increasing profitability and effectively managing the assets of the company. All employees attended presentations that educated them on the ROIC concepts, and extensive written communication materials were developed to explain what actions would lead to improved performance. Each area of the company discussed the critical actions it could take to improve the profitability of the firm.

Third, the stock option program was completely redesigned to reward key performers and retain critical talent, while at the same time reducing share usage and concerns about dilution. These provisions were accomplished in several ways. First, the share distribution, which had been heavily weighted to grants for new hires, shifted more toward grants based on performance of existing staff. This would recognize exceptional contributions of existing employees and help retain critical talent. New hire grants continued to be given, but they went to a more limited population—those hired into key technical staff and major leadership roles.

To align employees with the new business strategy and increase retention efforts, a performance-accelerated restricted stock award plan was adopted. The program was applied to approximately 150 key executives, managers, and individual contributors. It used five-year vesting restrictions with an opportunity to accelerate vesting based on the corporation achieving certain stock price objectives and financial returns. Furthermore, if the company achieved specific stock price objectives, individuals would receive additional stock grants. This ensured that shareholders would realize exceptional gains in stock value before more shares were granted to executives and key employees.

Finally, a targeted cash compensation strategy was implemented for critical hardware and software development talent. It was imperative to meet new product development schedules, support the current customer base, and retain highly talented individuals. This strategy included adjustments to base salaries and instituting retention bonuses. For base salaries, pay levels for all positions were targeted at the market average in the technical community; however, individuals identified as critical performers were targeted at the 75th percentile of the competitive marketplace and special pay adjustments were made accordingly. Selected individuals were also granted substantial cash-based retention bonuses if they stayed through the completion of critical projects. If they left before the project completion, they would forfeit a significant amount of money.

Results of the Programs

The results of these programs have been dramatic. Overall corporate turnover has dropped from 25% to just over 12%, or slightly under the labor market average. More important, turnover of critical talent has virtually halted. In 1997, turnover of critical employees was a remarkable 3%.

From a business perspective, the company results have been even better. Until Q1 (first quarter) 1997, the company had reported five consecutive quarters of losses. In Q1 1997, the company returned to profitability, substantially beating analyst projections. This occurred again in Q2 of 1997. In Q3, while revenue growth fell short of expectations, profitability was at record levels. Return on invested capital also soared, due to intense management and employee actions. Inventories came under control, accounts receivable fell, duplicative capital spending was reduced, inventory turns increased, and days-of-sales-outstanding dropped markedly. As a result, the company's cash position quadrupled in 15 months.

After two years of no bonus payouts, the executive and senior management incentive plan anticipates making payouts well above target levels. Employee profit-sharing should also pay out over target, yielding an attractive reward for employees. Finally, the stock price has risen from a low of $9 per share in early 1997 to $45 per share in late 1997. These were remarkable performance achievements.

Lessons Learned for the Future

Several lessons were learned from the implementation of these change efforts. First, the compensation system provided tremendous support to changing the business and achieving key objectives. It was closely aligned with effectively executed strategies. Second, effective communication of the programs, along with continual reinforcement and reporting on progress, was critical to success. Avid managers were effective in providing strong rollout communications and continual updates and reinforcements of efforts. The CEO and other executives were actively engaged in these communication and recognition efforts.

Third, the company learned that using several levers at once and instituting significant changes at one time can work. If the business is undergoing major change, human resources and compensation systems must also undergo fundamental change. If Avid executives had limited their bold actions, who knows whether the turnaround goals would have been achieved.

Finally, Avid learned that taking big, carefully calculated risks is necessary in troubled times. Not having gone through similar change before, and having few positive examples in the marketplace, many uncharted waters were explored. The traditional measures were not working and substantive change was necessary. The company and the new executive team decided that taking risks was the only option they had—risk of upsetting internal equity, risk of shareholder backlash, and risk of infusing too much change in too short a time. The risks were carefully managed; communication on why these actions were being taken was open and often, and the executive team led many of the discussions within the company. Their involvement and ability to engage others led everyone to understand the importance of their tasks.

While the future is not completely clear, it is safe to say that the company has achieved a remarkable turnaround and that the compensation system played an important role in making it happen. It gave people a clear stake in the success of their efforts. While compensation is but one of the levers in helping achieve business change and the accomplishment of business objectives, it is a lever that should not be underestimated or overlooked.

RETAINING CRITICAL TALENT WITH CUSTOMER-FOCUSED REWARDS AT

Burke, Inc.

Burke, Inc., is a leading international business research and consulting firm. Since it was founded in 1931, Burke has been helping manufacturing and service companies understand and accurately predict marketplace behavior. Burke is known for its analytical capabilities, leading-edge research methods, and consultative ability that help companies drive improvements through a comprehensive understanding of their markets and clients.

Burke is among the 20-largest marketing research and consulting firms in the United States. Its partner, Infratest Burke AG of Munich, Germany, is the world's seventh-largest research-based consulting company.

Burke provides business solutions to its clients in four areas of expertise:

1. *Burke Marketing Research* (BMR) provides full-service custom marketing research, analysis, and consulting for consumer and business-to-business product and service companies to help them understand marketplace dynamics.

2. *Burke Customer Satisfaction Associates* (Burke CSA) offers specialized services in customer satisfaction measurement and

management to a wide range of business categories. Burke CSA's Secure Customer Index provides industry and "best in class" standards for assessing and improving customer-driven practices in order to improve customer retention and loyalty.

3. *Burke Strategic Consulting Group* (BSCG) offers services in implementing strategic change through service lines that include employee surveys and evaluation, work process reengineering, activity-based costing, selection systems, executive assessments, and coaching for top-level managers.

4. *The Training & Development Center* (Burke TDC) offers public seminars on marketing research, data analysis, customer satisfaction measurement, and qualitative research techniques.

The Role and Challenges of the Senior Consultant/ Account Executive

The employees purchased Burke from Control Data Corporation in 1989. Over the next few years, they began to understand that part of what they bought was an enormous amount of fixed costs—substantially beyond what was reasonable for a professional service business. In addition, the company had lost a number of senior staff members—not to entrenched competitors, but to small businesses that were starting up and that were becoming competitors. Also, during the year or so after the purchase, Burke began to install a customer focus program within the company, creating both a culture and specific mechanisms for better understanding customers' requirements and expectations and significantly increasing its ability to respond to them.

The senior consultant or account executive is a key role in Burke's business. This is a sales and consulting position with responsibility for overall account development and account management. Individuals in this role have the responsibility for selling and servicing all Burke products and services. They are organized into specific areas of expertise (e.g., customer satisfaction, strategic marketing research, and specialized consulting services). Regardless of the specific area of competency, senior consultants are responsible for proposal preparation, sales presentations, program design and management, oversight of analysis of results, responsibility for results presentations, and further consulting with clients as necessary. Overall, the responsibility of the senior consultant position is to develop and maintain a profitable consulting practice within the overall service and product lines of Burke. In many ways senior consultants are the link between Burke and its customers.

Because of the strategic changes, the company needed to gain the full support and effort of the senior consultants. If Burke were ever to achieve the desired strategic objectives, senior consultants would need to be close partners in this process. The company decided at that point to make fundamental changes in its compensation program and develop a performance-focused plan.

The new program had four principal objectives:

1. *Realign fixed and variable costs.* The senior consultant staff was the most expensive per-head asset, so "salary creep" occurred in the organization. That is, regardless of whether revenues and profits were increasing, it needed to increase compensation "at-market or better" to remain competitive. Thus, the company was increasing fixed costs with no guarantee that it was increasing profitability sufficiently to cover these costs. The new compensation plan needed to realign fixed and variable costs associated with these internal assets.

2. *Retain best performers.* When the company lost a top performer, it was almost always because he or she was starting a competing business, rather than going to a traditional competitor. The primary interests of those who left were the independence of running their own business and the higher compensation potential. The new performance compensation plan needed to offer senior consultants virtually the same opportunities that they might see in leaving Burke to start their own business. In addition, Burke would continue to provide attractive marketing, operational, and administrative support, resources they would have to develop themselves in starting their own businesses.

3. *Incorporate customer-focus measures into company operations.* Consultants and everyone else at Burke accepted the customer-focus program in concept, because it was the core business of Burke. To make it real to staff, the company needed to find ways to incorporate it into company operations. There appeared to be no more direct

statement of the importance of customer satisfaction to the company's success than to link that concept directly to compensation.

4. *Increase the company's market leadership, revenues, and profits.* The growth of the company had stalled, and yet the market was expanding. Burke needed to reposition itself as a market leader. The senior consultants were key to this strategy. Their compensation plan needed to emphasize revenue growth, with particular focus on growth in profits. In addition to these objectives, the development process identified a paradox of core values that needed to be resolved in the new program. The success of Burke depended on the collective success of the organization. If Burke were to grow the share value of the company substantially beyond the original investment of its shareholders, it would require a collective effort. It would have to take advantage of the diversity of skills and experience at Burke to market effectively to new customer segments, with new products and services. Burke would have to function as more than a collection of individuals; its whole would have to be greater than the sum of its parts.

But individual contributions would be expected and rewarded. Each individual would be expected to contribute to the company's overall success. Exceeding the minimum individual contribution would be recognized and rewarded. Without some truly outstanding individual performances, the company's overall results would invariably suffer. The new performance compensation program needed to balance collective success and individual rewards in order to implement Burke's strategy and strengthen its leadership in the market.

How the Program Works

The compensation program is composed of three parts—base salaries, performance pay, and referral commissions. Each of these elements is described below, with an expansion of the measures associated with the performance pay program.

Base pay for the senior consultant staff is considered a fixed annual cost and is set within relatively narrow ranges by level. It is reviewed annually for possible adjustment based on consumer price index (CPI). Base pay by individual may be supplemented through a "draw" (advance pay against projected future performance pay earnings) or through a "subsidy" (additional, nonpermanent supplemental pay typically for people moving into the senior consultant role from outside the firm).

Performance pay is the variable portion of compensation and will be driven by individual results for the year. Early in one's sales and consulting career, it is not expected that performance pay will be a substantial portion of total compensation. Initially, Burke will provide base salaries at a level that exceeds the short-term (annual) financial contribution of the individual, as it invests in skill development and business building. As individuals grow their financial contribution beyond the investment cost, they will receive performance pay commensurate with contributions beyond the individuals' cost. At the senior-most levels, performance pay will be expected to provide a substantial proportion of total compensation.

The variable pay program utilizes three core measures for determining payouts:

1. The level of individual financial contribution
2. The ratings on external customer feedback (external customer focus)
3. The ratings by internal teams (internal customer focus)

Financial Contribution

Senior consultants had their own profit and loss (P&L) statement generated by personal sales, the project delivery costs, and personal operating expenses. The financial contribution is measured on an individual P&L basis by "net contribution." The key elements of the senior consultant P&L used in the calculation of net contribution are shown here:

REVENUE	Revenue from all clients being served by the senior consultant's practice.
DIRECT JOB COSTS	The cost incurred directly on all client projects.
GROSS MARGIN	The difference between revenue and direct costs.
EXPENSES	Labor and other expenses. Base

	salary and benefits of senior consultants and direct reports' expenses (e.g., travel and living) needed to maintain practice.
OFFICE SUPPORT	Expenses for maintaining the consultant's office (e.g., rent, equipment leases).
PROFESSIONAL SUPPORT	Cost of support provided by other staff at Burke not directly charged to a client project.
NET OVERHEAD	Total expenses.
CONTRIBUTION	Gross margin minus net overhead.
CORPORATE OVERHEAD	Deducted from contribution to cover a portion of corporate overhead.
NET CONTRIBUTION	Contribution minus corporate overhead.
PERFORMANCE COMPENSATION	Percentage (significant) of net contribution; remainder goes to the company.

Senior consultants are responsible for generating revenues at sufficient levels and managing the associated costs so that a desired profitability is generated that ultimately results in corporate profitability. This encourages strong selling efforts, targeting of profitable and long-term clients, and efficient management of account servicing efforts.

Senior consultants can draw on company resources for support, but since these expenses are charged against their P&L, they are encouraged to use this support efficiently. Company resources (overhead) are "fixed" and all consultants need to share in ensuring that the costs of these resources are covered.

Furthermore, the plan has a "self-accelerating" feature: Once the costs are covered, senior consultants are personally rewarded with a significant split of each additional dollar earned by their projects. This encourages them to "think and act like they were running their own business." In almost all business decision-making cases, the correct decision is taken—one that serves the interests of the individual consultant, the customer, and the company.

External Customer Focus

Each senior consultant is measured with the Secure Customer Index (SCI). Through Burke's own customer satisfaction program, it monitors clients' satisfaction with the same type of monitoring program it developed for clients to monitor their customers' satisfaction. The minimum standard for each senior consultant is to achieve an SCI equal to the overall company target. Any performance pay earned will be reduced by the same percentage that a consultant's total SCI falls below the company target.

The SCI is made up of three critical ideas: The group of customers who (1) are very satisfied, (2) will definitely recommend you to others, and (3) will definitely repurchase from or continue to use your products and services in the future. Figure 6-1 illustrates the SCI concept.

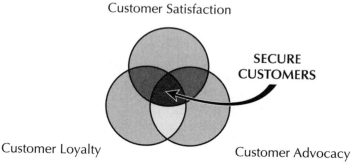

Figure 6-1. Secure Customer Index.

An index is computed based on the ratings in these three areas and compared to the overall company's standard.

The customer satisfaction program also emphasizes recovery with dissatisfied customers. This could involve working with internal staff members to correct a problem or working directly with the client to fix any problems. By documenting the problem and what was done to resolve the issues, the senior consultant can "recover" from any effect a dissatisfied customer might have on performance pay.

Internal Customer Focus

This is a survey of each senior consultant's performance by internal Burke staff members who have worked with the individual during the performance period. A minimum average overall rating is required, which indicates the consultant is adequately meeting the needs of the internal support staff and directing them to meet the needs of external clients. Consultants are evaluated up to three times during the fiscal year on this measure. Any performance pay earned is reduced by the same percentage that a consultant's overall rating falls below the minimum standard.

Business Development Referrals

In addition to their direct business development activities, senior consultants are encouraged to refer business to other areas or assist them in achieving new business. This directly supports Burke's culture of collaboration and improves the company's ability to grow. The performance compensation program rewards these results by providing additional compensation for referrals and sales assistance activities.

Referrals are any client opportunities or requests for proposals that business development leaders provide to other areas of the organization. Sales assistance includes any work a senior consultant may perform that enables another consultant to achieve the sale. When results are achieved by these actions, the "supporting" consultant will receive a royalty on any revenue generated by the "managing" consultant. The royalty will be charged as a cost to the managing consultant and applied to the net contribution of the supporting consultant.

Finally, the performance compensation program maintains several important provisions and special features. Performance incentive pay is paid out at the end of the fiscal year. Only members of the consultant staff who are employed by the company at the date of payment are eligible to receive the performance pay. The company can pay up to 20% of the performance pay in company stock rather than in cash. Any payments in company stock will be made at the time of fiscal year-end performance pay distributions and will be in compliance with all necessary legal requirements.

At the end of the first six months of the fiscal year, individual performance pay earned for that period will be reviewed, as well as the individual's business outlook for the remainder of the year. Up to one-third of the performance compensation earned through this period may be paid out. If consultants are unable to cover their midyear incentive compensation payment by the end of the fiscal year, the amount not covered will carry over into the following fiscal year and be shown as a decrease to their performance compensation.

Primary Outcomes of the Program

Burke's senior consultants have realized significant benefits from this program. Some are financial and others are qualitative, but all are strategic and have strengthened the firm's abilities to grow and be competitive. The results include:

1. Not a single senior consultant that the company has wanted to keep has been lost to a traditional competitor or to a start-up company in the five years since the plan was implemented.
2. Consultants have a much stronger understanding of the financial imperatives and operations of the company at a corporate level. They are better business managers.
3. Nonchargeable travel and living costs were reduced by 20% the first year and have been maintained at a substantially lower percentage of revenue than prior to implementation of the plan.
4. The first year of plan implementation was the first profitable year for the company following two unprofitable years since the company was purchased.
5. During the four years since the plan was implemented, performance compensation payments have increased by a factor of 6, and company profitability has increased by a factor of 9.5.

Key Lessons Learned From the Program

When an organization alters the compensation for one of its most critical positions, there is a strong sense of risk. When Burke assessed the opportunities versus the risk, it knew that there might be situations where the program would not achieve its objectives. However, the importance of the change was clearly worth the potential risks. The company learned several important principles necessary to the implementation of similar programs. First, the program could be set up as a win-win; as the consultants generated increased personal compensation, the company generated increased profitability (and it would not work in reverse order).

Second, performance-based compensation can be self-funding. Performance-based compensation can help to transfer some fixed costs to variable costs and create self-controlling mechanisms. The costs are variable and only need to be covered if sufficient profitability is generated to cover the costs of increased compensation. Performance-based compensation can increase overall company profitability.

Third, the program fulfilled its objectives because personal compensation was not tied to office, region, or company goals or performance. It was never considered "bonus" or dependent upon other performance metrics outside the control of the individual consultant. It was earned on the basis of individual performance metrics.

Fourth, the program required consultants to focus on being good business managers, not just on being good business developers and consultants. This has led to a better understanding of the costs to deliver projects and the corporate success factors as a whole. As a result, they make better business decisions that benefit not only their own practices, but the company as well. In the majority of situations, the best business decision for an individual consultant practice is also the best decision for the company.

This approach required risk-taking on the part of the consultant and the company; the consultant can no longer depend on consistently increasing compensation through standard base salary adjustments. High performance generates commensurately high compensation in a given year. However, average or below average performance in a given year generates lower compensation than one might have expected from a standard, annual increase in base salary. The risk for the company is that if only a small segment of the staff generates exceptional revenues and profits and the remainder of the staff is below average, a very high percentage of company profitability is returned to those few high-performing individuals. The system only works to the benefit of individual staff and the company if the majority of staff members are high performers.

This type of performance compensation system can appear overly directed to individual performance and not sufficiently concerned with teamwork among peers. Yet the royalty systems installed have encouraged team activity among consultants and made team-based incentives a more important part of the overall compensation system. In the future the company will continue to explore ways to reinforce teamwork with team incentives and other forms of special recognition. The issues that relate to retaining the senior consultants have diminished dramatically, enabling Burke to explore additional strategic drivers of the business and develop support systems for those drivers that directly contribute to the success of the organization.

BREAKING THE CHAINS OF ENTITLEMENT
AT
OSRAM SYLVANIA, Inc.

Times like these require bold action. After the organization underwent a change in ownership, OSRAM SYLVANIA, Inc., needed to take clear, demonstrable action to focus performance. For years, employees and managers had been shielded from making dramatic change. The company had been part of a large, bureaucratic organization with multiple lines of business. Now, with a new corporate parent focused on OSRAM SYLVANIA's lighting business, action was needed.

Perhaps it was the appointment of a new vice president of human resources, an individual who was a general manager and known for his criticism of the function. Perhaps it was a combination of factors, but OSRAM SYLVANIA began to find new ways to focus and encourage employees to make major improvements in product quality, costs, delivery performance, and development.

Company Background

OSRAM SYLVANIA (OSI) is a $1.8 billion manufacturer and marketer of precision materials, components, and lighting products.

It is the North American subsidiary of OSRAM GmbH, based in Germany, which is one of the leading parts of the Siemens family of companies. It operates 20 plants and has more than 12,000 employees; approximately 30% are exempt and 70% are hourly. The history of the company parallels the evolution of electric lighting. The company in its current form was created in January 1993, but many traditions and practices have been in place for years. A central challenge was that many aspects of the culture were inconsistent with the new performance requirements of the company.

OSI had a traditional compensation and performance management system for its salaried employees. Few employees were ever rated in the lowest category or were refused a pay increase. There was limited use of incentive compensation plans. Managers set all performance objectives and standards and judged people against these factors with little review or accountability. The performance review process was an annual event, and only the better managers used the process for constructive career coaching and development. During these review meetings, employees waited to hear about their pay increase and judged the fairness of the amount in relation to their expectations. Most managers did not complete the career development planning or take meaningful actions. Human resources conducted a periodic review and upgrade of the policies. No one was satisfied with the process.

During this time, OSI did not remain unchanged. It implemented an extensive quality management process and a variety of new structures and process improvements to increase productivity. But there was a clear need left unmet; employees wanted honest and timely feedback on performance, as well as rewards consistent with their achievements.

Time for a New Performance Management Process (PMP)

OSI's human resources leadership wanted to make a change. HR found significant support among OSI's senior executives. They did not want to continue with the inflation-driven salary increase process; they did not want to view pay increases as just a "cost of doing business." There was a strong commitment to make the new pay for performance philosophy work for OSI. This effort would be a major element of the organizational culture change process of the organization.

One of the first steps was to reconstitute a job evaluation committee into a Human Resources Advisory Committee (HRAC). The group was composed of senior managers from OSI and served the role of providing advice, feedback, and support to critical human resources initiatives. HRAC developed four new goals for the new performance management program:

1. Employees' performance measures need to support the objectives of the business.
2. Frequent and honest feedback needs to be provided to all managers and employees.
3. Performance ratings need to become equitable and be seen as equitable.
4. Employees should not feel entitled to receiving a fully standard performance rating.

These objectives then guided the reengineering effort of the entire process. While there were significant challenges as different elements were being implemented, the commitment to change by the senior managers did not waver. This was essential to the new program's ultimate success.

Performance Planning: A Process of Goal Alignment

A critical requirement of the PMP was that the performance and actions of employees would be assessed against the objectives of the business. There were two elements developed for this task.

First, job objectives were established for each salaried employee in the organization. These were developed by cascading the goals of the company to each business unit and each individual. Although employees often gave their input on their objectives or standards, this occurred after supervisors shared their own performance plans. This established a clear and direct relationship between the manager's and staff member's objectives for the year. This often resulted in a 70–30 split between top-down influence and bottom-up inputs. This ratio was intentional.

For jobs or units where there were common priorities, people shared the same objectives. Members of teams often shared the same objectives. It was important to align these joint accountabilities through the performance planning process. In this way the process was regarded as important and serious to everyone.

Second, OSI developed a set of competencies that were integrated into the performance management process. A set of core competencies was linked to the identified values of the company and outlined the desired behaviors by all staff members. Many of the departments went further to describe competency priorities that were unique to their specific roles in the organization. Employees received feedback on these competency dimensions as well as their performance on job objectives.

Performance Reviews: Not Just an Annual Event Anymore

Historically, employees learned how they were performing during the annual review cycle. Obviously, this was a counterproductive effort and led to needless arguments about events that could not be changed. The new PMP approach required midyear reviews by all managers. Employees could request more frequent performance dialogue with their supervisors, and many did. The documentation was also available on the company's intranet, and this encouraged frequent discussion of progress and data. This process helped the organization to update measures and standards as needed.

Ranking Employee Performance: Breaking the Entitlement Mind-Set

The company adjusted all reviews and merit pay decisions to a common date. This occurs three months after the end of the fiscal year. This permits sufficient time to review annual results, assess the performance of all staff members, and prepare performance reviews. But perhaps the most dramatic element was the process established to rank-order employees by their performance.

The ranking of employees by performance substituted for the traditional practice of a manager's rating employees on a one-to-five scale. The new program used this ranking process for allocating merit pay and development planning. To support this process, OSI identified a new role of the "merit manager." This is an individual who supervises 30 or more salaried employees through direct supervision or subordinate supervisors. In many cases this would be plant managers and their direct staff. Within a month after the end of the fiscal year, the merit managers would lead their staffs through a ranking process of their employees.

The ranking process was not an artificial ranking of 1 to 100 (or whatever the total number of employees). Instead, the merit managers and their staffs would rank all their employees into one of three groups:

- ▸ Clearly exceptional
- ▸ Successful/satisfactory
- ▸ Lowest contributors

These were ranking categories. The process was rolled up to provide the president and the senior staff with an assessment of the entire staff. Senior human resources staff members and the merit managers would lead the ranking meetings. In preparation, the managers would send to human resources their assessment of staff members against job objectives. The HR manager in turn would prepare the materials for review in the meeting. These meetings generally lasted a half-day; this was regarded as a minimum amount of investment for the subject and the critical nature of the discussions.

Employees were reviewed based on their performance to job objectives. Then they could be moved to a different level based on their assessment against the competencies. In other words, performance results would determine the preliminary ranking, but the competencies utilized would modify the results. Most of the discussions centered around "how" one achieved certain objectives and whether this demonstrated long-term value for the organization.

Formal distribution requirements were established for the ranking process. No more than 10% of the employees could be rated as "clearly exceptional." Initially, no less than 10% could be rated as "lowest contributor," but this was adjusted to 5% the following year. Over time, a fourth category ("successful plus") emerged to designate those who were strong performers but did not warrant being designated as clearly exceptional. Actual distribution of performance ratings at OSI has evolved to 10% clearly exceptional, 35% successful plus, 50% successful/satisfactory, and 5% lowest contributors.

This process enabled the merit managers and their teams to clearly identify employees consistent with their contributions. The "soft graders" became more consistent with the "hard graders," and all workers learned a great deal about their location's staff members. Although there was considerable rebellion about the ranking process early in the implementation of the program, top management used this as an opportunity to send a strong message that desired performance and the new culture necessitated new ways of managing performance.

Applying Merit Pay to the Rankings

The outcomes of the ranking meetings were used to distribute merit dollars and plan investments in people. The clearly exceptional performers received the highest merit pay increase, usually about two times the standard merit; the successful/satisfactory received a standard pay increase for the year; the lowest contributors did not receive any pay increase. When the successful plus category emerged, these individuals received a 2% value-added premium to the standard merit pay increase. Because managers were able to balance the ratings and the number of people who would receive merit increases, OSI was able to distribute merit pay dollars to the better performers and remain within desired cost parameters.

In addition, the ranking discussions strengthened the career management process. The managers identified individuals ready for promotions or transfers into key assignments. They were better able to determine the investment requirements and address potential retention issues before they became problems. These meetings also addressed performance issues in the open.

Primary Outcomes for the New PMP

Performance management systems have long been regarded as frustrating or wasted efforts in many organizations. At OSI, alignment between people and the objectives of the company has been achieved. There has been a successful shift in the culture from one characterized by entitlement to one based on performance. When employees realized that their performance would be assessed on a relative basis and that senior managers would do this through open discussions, they paid close attention to their actions. For some it produced a wake-up call; for others, it was a real affirmation of their contributions.

In the early stages of this new process, there was significant discomfort with ranking individual performers. Managers were uncomfortable and employees were highly skeptical. Managers were concerned that they would need to "do battle" for their best people, and employees felt the process was a popularity contest. Both expectations have been proved wrong. Managers now view the ranking process as an important quality assurance technique that allows honest and fair open dialogue to take place. They often learn new insights about their people, and they have an opportunity to express opinions about the staff of others in a constructive and helpful manner. While most employees still do not understand what happens in these meetings, most feel they are getting better feedback on their performance as well as an opportunity for their work to be discussed by the senior management team of their business unit. This has opened new career opportunities for some and has reassured others of their positive contribution to the company.

From a turnover perspective, some interesting results have been achieved. Over the first few years of the program, the average overall employee turnover was about 9%—similar to the rate under previous ownership. However, for the lowest contributors, turnover averaged about 30%. This was a desired outcome, because it meant that some of the poorer performers were deciding to leave the company. As units were able to achieve such terminations, they received a "credit" for these positions in meeting their lowest contributors' distribution allocation. This encouraged management action to address performance issues without having negative side effects for remaining employees.

For the first two years of the program, the business units exceeded their operating profit objectives. They achieved record profitability from the 1993 baseline year. Furthermore, over three-fourths of the performance plans demonstrated strong support to the company's business objectives, as compared to one-fourth several years before. While all this cannot be credited to the performance management process, actions to improve the performance of the company have increased dramatically. The results show the impact of these behaviors.

The Future Plans for Performance Management

The new PMP has clearly demonstrated its positive impact on the company. There are concerns about the ability to continue meeting the lowest contributor distribution standard as more and more of the lower performers leave the company. However, there is a constant need to continue to improve and grow the business. This means that people need to continue to grow and improve their abilities and contributions to OSI.

This process has created the foundation for incentive compensation plans and other forms of recognition. The company will continue to refine the process and make it more fair and effective. There is a major challenge of increasing employees' understanding and confidence in the system. The participants in ranking treat this as an important and objective process, but employees still do not fully trust the process. Communication and feedback will be key to addressing their concerns. Most important, the new PMP has enabled people to see how performance is recognized and valued by the organization. The entitlement culture, which had held the organization back from taking bold and significant actions, has receded into the corners of the organization.

THE ROLE OF INCENTIVES IN A TURNAROUND OPERATION
AT
SunLife of Canada

Insurance Risk

Characterizing the relationship between these two concepts presents a provocative challenge. The business of insurance, by its nature, attempts to mitigate risk. As the chief executive said to all employees, "Risk management is our business—and effective risk management rests on diversification." Actuaries are trained in the mathematical science of calculating morbidity and mortality tables and premium rates based on a multitude of "risk" factors. Underwriters determine the potential risk of insurance applicants to appropriately rate policies that balance potential loss with opportunity.

In recent years the insurance industry has gone through some major shifts. Business has become increasingly competitive, with lower interest rates spurring variable product purchases. The government has been scrutinizing sales practices to ensure compliance with regulatory requirements. And companies have been required to rein in expenses in order to create some competitive advantage. As a result, insurance companies have been forced to reexamine traditional compensation practices in order to reward employees for focusing on and achieving specific strategic results.

Background of SunLife

SunLife Assurance Company of Canada has been in existence for more than 125 years. It is a diversified financial services organization with total assets under management of more than $103 billion ($US) and operations in Canada, the United States, Great Britain, and the Philippines. The U.S. national office (USNO) is based in Wellesley Hills, Massachusetts, and is composed of the Individual Insurance Division, Group Insurance Division, and Retirement Products and Services Division (pensions and annuities). Altogether there are roughly 1,500 employees located in the U.S. home office.

> "As product areas began to report their preliminary profit numbers, my staff started asking me what our product could do to make more money in order to support the other products reaching their profit goals. I hadn't had a team of people pull together like that in such a long time."

SunLife had historically struggled with the concept of "putting pay at risk." For a variety of reasons, primarily culturally based, the organization resisted efforts to reward exceptional achievements with incentive pay—even at the officer level. It is not uncommon for an organization to fear the development of an "expectation" of incentive rewards, whether earned or not (the so-called entitlement mentality). Lots of questions surround incentive pay such as:

- Will there be an appropriate return on the investment?
- Is it fair or motivating to include some employees but not others?
- How do we deal with the external factors that are beyond anyone's control?

This is a story about how the Group Insurance Division moved from "out of the red and into the black" during the early to mid-1990s, and the role that risks and rewards played in helping to revitalize the division.

Facing the Challenges of a Changed Marketplace

Prior to 1990, the Group Insurance Division was in tough shape. The organization was losing money and James A. McNulty III (Jim) was hired to head the division and make it successful. He had his work cut out for him as he began to focus employees on emphasizing the following things: accountability (clear expectations of performance and how to measure), profit (number-one divisional priority), and growth (balanced with profit priority). He did this in several ways.

First, Jim invested in the field sales force and reorganized home office operations to align accountabilities consistent with this strategy.

Next, he focused managers and staff on attention to bottom-line results and the ways in which they impacted profitability.

Finally, Jim helped create a "stake in the business" by creating a profit-sharing incentive plan for the Stop/Loss Unit (i.e., excess risk), which was at risk of being discontinued due to repeated losses and poor performance.

Applying a Team Incentive Plan

The Stop/Loss Unit in the Group Insurance Division consisted of 14 people. For those unfamiliar with insurance lingo, Stop/Loss refers to a type of insurance policy designed to protect an employer from incurring catastrophic loss on either an individual employee or a group in aggregate. Its most typical application in the group insurance area is to reinsure companies that choose to self-insure medical benefits using a third-party administrator, to protect against claims exceeding a certain level, thereby "stopping the loss."

The first year, 1990, the profit-sharing plan was implemented for the Stop/Loss Unit only. Initially it included the underwriters, claims area, and marketing, with more than a dozen factors built in to measure profitability. It was a cumbersome and complicated program with a minimum threshold target that was bottom-line oriented.

Some of the performance measures first used were:

- Unit productivity
- Cases underwritten
- Claims processed
- Quotes issued
- Pricing of cases versus results one year hence
- Service levels (measured through surveys)
- Overall productivity of all product lines

One of the primary reasons the plan was approved was that it would be entirely self-funding, thereby costing the company nothing unless the unit produced results. The risks and the rewards were made quite clear and were quite high: Either the unit was going to make the threshold or it would be shut down. Pretty tough—and quite clear.

What happened next was remarkable. Jim convinced the group that they "owned" this challenge and could make it happen. He provided continual feedback and reinforcement so that the group believed it could make a difference. The plan was designed as a point system with various levels of performance paying up to a maximum percent of salary. Nothing about the plan was subjective or discretionary and the actual results relative to targets were published quarterly. In its first year, everyone "blew through their targets," receiving a significant payout.

Each year the plan was revised to be simpler and more closely aligned with corporate incentives so that the potential payout eventually reached a maximum of 10% of base pay. By 1994 the unit was turning a consistent profit and the plan was rolled out to all product areas. By 1995, it was inclusive of the entire division.

What is most exciting is that by the end of 1997, the Stop/Loss product line was one of the most profitable lines in the company, and SunLife ranked among the top three carriers in the country. While there are many factors contributing to this success, clearly the incentive compensation plan provided the burst of energy needed to get things moving in the right direction.

Widening the Participation

The expansion of the profit-sharing plan to all the divisional product lines was carried out with several key objectives in mind. First, a task force representing each of the product lines was brought together to design the program. One of the most valuable lessons learned from the previous program was the value of employee input and subsequent ownership. The parameters the group was given included an emphasis on profit, with payouts based on the incremental gain over plan or target, thus ensuring a positive ROI.

The areas of focus for the divisional plan included the following:

- Profitability (a threshold "triggered" the plan into effect)
- Efficiency gains/productivity
- Increased market share

In addition to divisional profitability goals, each of the product lines had its own profitability levels to achieve in the areas of:

- Long-term disability
- Short-term disability
- Life
- Dental
- Excess risk (i.e., Stop/Loss)

Another measure regarding progress on divisionwide projects was also included in the evaluation for plan payouts. Eligible employees have a bonus target of 6% of base pay for the plan year, with a maximum cap of 10% of base salary. In 1995, when the plan was expanded yet again to include all administrative and staff support functions within the division, different weights were applied to different objectives depending on the employee's role.

Jim McNulty has successfully moved this division to believe that results matter and that everyone can have a positive impact on the results. He continually reinforces the conceptualization of a "sense of ownership" and employee attitudes have improved dramatically in this regard. One of his staff cited:

> "There is a heightened awareness of profit considerations . . . there is a clearly understood connection between actions that result in savings and the opportunity to share in those savings as they contribute to profitability."

With the continued growth of the Group Insurance Division, bonus payouts have not only occurred for each plan year, but they have increased as a percentage of the annual regular rate of pay and improved performance levels of individual employees.

Key Lessons Learned

There have been several significant learnings as a result of the design and implementation of variable rewards in a traditionally risk-averse environment:

1. Involvement of employees in the process has been a critical component of the turnaround in the Group Insurance Division by focusing energy on the attainment of specific, challenging goals.
2. The increasing demands of the marketplace have put an emphasis on variable components of pay and enabled the organization to attract and keep high-performing people.
3. The self-funding component of the plan has continued to allow for the control of compensation expenses.
4. Frequent feedback, such as the quarterly progress reports, and senior management's reinforcement of achievements provided a fertile ground for the plan, and company results, to flourish.

These lessons have served to transform the design and management of variable pay plans in other areas of SunLife. The business is on a stronger footing, especially now that employees are involved.

7

Retaining Critical Talent

The competition for talent in most industries is intense. If one examines the population demographics and changing skill requirements, the trends for the supply of people within the United States is far less than the demand. So companies will be engaged in a continual struggle to attract and retain the talent they need for growth. More and more companies are realizing that their growth is being restricted by their inability to attract the talent they need. People are becoming the true competitive advantage.

Companies that offer exorbitant financial packages to people often find the loyalty and commitment only temporary. They get caught in a bidding war for individuals, and few organizations come out winners.

The companies that have been successful in addressing the "talent issue" have placed a great deal of importance on their reward systems, formal and informal. They use rewards to support a total workplace environment that is attractive to the individual and reinforces their importance to the organization. People feel valued.

Fleet Financial, after months of study and analysis, found the key to its ability to retain technical talent was to communicate that employees were important and back this up with reasonable compensation. CIGNA HealthCare needed to retain people in organizations that it acquired. By learning from past problems caused by not addressing this issue effectively, it developed a simple and highly effective process for retaining talent. Health Services Medical Corporation, a health maintenance organization, created a competency approach to pay that opened opportunities for career growth and personal development. Finally, Keane, a major software systems development company, has grown dramatically and uses its formal and informal rewards to support this growth. In each case, retention of key talent has been an essential element in success strategy.

There is no simple answer to retaining critical talent. But these companies, and many others like them, have used a strategic approach to address this complex concern and fully integrate rewards into the formula.

PREPARING FOR THE NEW MILLENNIUM: RETENTION FOR THE TECHNOLOGY SOLUTIONS GROUP
AT

Fleet Financial Group, Inc.

The advent of the new millennium is a cause of growing concern to corporations across the country and around the world. Exactly what will happen at the stroke of midnight on the last day of this century is largely unknown. What is certain, however, is that market demands for the technical personnel necessary to prepare companies for this event have already reached unprecedented heights. All computerized systems, whether used to monitor a Boeing 747's flight path, the federal government's payroll, or your own ATM card, must be Year 2000 compliant. For most companies, compliance extends beyond their own front door to include all systems of their vendors, suppliers, and customers, thus making the scope of the project enormous.

If the scope of Year 2000 compliance is enormous, then the cost is extreme. For many firms, total compliance will be measured in the tens of millions. Not the least of these costs is that of attracting and maintaining a stable, critically skilled workforce. With many organizations facing the choice of becoming Year 2000 compliant or closing their doors, an employer's technical (human) resources become pivotal to their continued success.

Fleet's retention plan was developed in response to the unique conditions precipitated by Year 2000 project demands. It is a three-pronged strategy aimed at retaining key technical personnel in the face of severely competitive market pressures.

The plan components are:

- ▸ A Merit Augmentation Program designed to provide highly competitive base salaries to all technical personnel

> ▸ An enhanced nonqualified stock option offering
> ▸ A retention bonus award for key contributors to be paid in March of the year 2000

Background of the Situation

Fleet Financial Group, Inc. (Fleet) is a diversified financial services corporation based in Boston, Massachusetts, with assets in excess of $85 billion and a rich history spanning more than 200 years. Fleet is the 11th largest commercial bank in the United States, employing more than 35,000 people in 36 states. As a financial services institution regulated by the Federal Reserve Board and the Office of the Comptroller of the Currency, Fleet is subject to an accelerated Year 2000 compliance deadline of December 31, 1998.

Fleet Technology Solutions (FTS) is the formal name for the technical services arm of Fleet. FTS includes all systems and programming personnel as well as related data processing, operations, and technical functions. This plan was developed to retain these highly skilled and specialized employees.

Reasons for the Program

By early 1997, competition for critically skilled technical employees was beginning to grow, causing increased turnover and recruiting difficulty. (It is important to note that since early 1996, New England has been experiencing its lowest unemployment rates in nearly two decades.) By midyear, Fleet's annualized turnover for key technical staff was tracking at more than 20%, an increase of nearly 150% from 1996. Consulting firms beckoned, with promises of increased salaries (some by as much as 500%), flexible work hours, and paid overtime. Recruiting costs skyrocketed due to the "seller's market" philosophy employed by individual candidates and search firms alike. Fleet was faced with three choices: continue to run on the "recruiting treadmill," hire consultants to fill open positions, or develop an aggressive retention plan.

The cost to fill positions as technical staff turned over was increasing. Market demands and the lowest unemployment rates the Northeast had seen in 20 years teamed up to inflate salaries at all levels. Sign-on bonuses, once a trump card used to attract key players, were becoming a standard part of most job offers. Relocation packages, usually reserved for high-level personnel, were now necessary to attract qualified candidates at all levels as local labor pools dried up. Search firm and headhunting fees grew along with market demand. Fee structures that normally capped at 20% to 25% of a candidate's first-year base salary began to climb to over 30%. In addition to the direct costs of the "recruiting treadmill," indirect costs (e.g., productivity downtime due to the learning curve and low morale due to increased workload of remaining staff) were also on the rise. However, of greatest concern was the largely unquantifiable opportunity cost of strategic initiatives not undertaken due to a lack of qualified staff.

A second option was to fill open positions with contract employees. In 1997, the average annual cost to hire a consultant was more than two and one-half times the position's average market salary. Add to this the indirect costs associated with the learning curve, low morale of existing staff due to consultants' higher salaries, and the mobile nature of the consultant, and it becomes an unattractive alternative.

After reviewing the options, the answer was clear; FTS needed to work quickly and aggressively to retain the staff it had, while positioning itself in the market to attract new talent. It had to do this, but the question was, how?

How the Retention Plan Was Developed

To say that the Fleet Technology Solutions Year 2000 Retention Plan (the Plan) was challenging to develop is an understatement. FTS was attempting to anticipate future market conditions caused by an as-yet-unprecedented event. Consulting and survey firms, usually excellent sources of information, were dry and asked their usual client companies, like Fleet, to let them know if they came up with a solution to what was becoming a widespread problem. Competitor companies were also seeking answers, and those who had been quick to develop retention strategies were hesitant to share their findings for fear of losing their competitive edge. This lack of hard data not only made the plan difficult to develop, but nearly impossible to sell to management.

As with any project of this scope, the Plan evolved over time. Each piece was developed and introduced separately, allowing for maximum impact while giving employees an opportunity to digest the information.

The first step was to collect competitive salary data and determine where the company stood in relation to the rest of the market. To do this, FTS relied on specialized information technology (IT) salary surveys. Upon reviewing the composite survey data, it was clear that many of employees' base salaries were not keeping pace with the rapidly rising market, making adjustments necessary. Using monies set aside in a corporate market equity pool, Fleet provided increases to more than 600 technical employees in September 1997. This effort was known as the Merit Augmentation Program.

Now that the company had created a level playing field, it was time to address the issue of retention. To accomplish this, Fleet first turned to a traditional long-term incentive strategy, the use of nonqualified stock options. Fleet has a three-year vesting schedule for stock options, so this time frame was appropriate (it surpassed the critical date of January 1, 2000). In October 1997, a pool of options, separate from the company's regular annual grant, was created for this initiative and distributed to recommended employees.

The Merit Augmentation Program and the stock option grant were both well received; however, Fleet continued to be plagued by high turnover and recruiting difficulties. The option grant, although an excellent long-term retention tool in theory, did not reach enough people or provide enough monetary reward to be effective. To be eligible for a grant, an employee's salary level and managerial responsibilities were heavily weighted. Many of the employees Fleet aimed to retain either fell below the salary threshold or were individual contributors. The company needed another retention tool that would significantly benefit a broader population.

This last piece, a retention bonus award, turned out to be the most difficult to create. The elaborate plan document had numerous schedules, attachments, and exhibits. The first attempt resulted in a complicated deferred compensation scheme with staggered contributions, interest calculations, and participant statements. Managers labored for months over eligibility requirements, award amounts, funding issues, payout schedules, and the treatment of new hires, terminations, retirees, and transfers. They wrote long-winded managers' tools and meeting agendas. In the end, the final product was surprisingly simple. In December 1997, a one-page letter was presented to each of 500 eligible employees. The letter, signed by Fleet's CIO, thanked them for their commitment to the company and indicated the award amount they would receive if they remained in their critical role until March 31, 2000. (Award amounts were roughly 50% of base salary.) A single page of terms and conditions accompanied the letter and addressed administrative issues. This brief, personalized correspondence said more than all of the elaborate documents that preceded it: "We appreciate you, we need you, we entrust our future to you."

Primary Outcomes Attributed to the Program

It is impossible to predict the outcome or overall success of this plan, as its term stretches two years into the future. However, the short-term successes of the plan are clear. Turnover is down, morale is up. FTS is attracting people (new hires receive competitive salaries and are eligible for a retention bonus award if hired before January 1, 1999) and is keeping the people it has. The week the retention bonus award program was announced, HR staff began leveraging it to salvage external job offers and enhance counteroffers to save existing employees. The greatest success, however, is the most difficult to calculate. How do you measure goodwill, employee satisfaction, and positive morale?

Looking ahead, Fleet realizes that continually escalating market pressures may make it necessary to repeat one or more of the initiatives of the FTS Year 2000 Retention Plan. If that happens, it will be ready.

Key Lessons Learned

The lessons learned from this project may seem fundamental, but had Fleet focused on them from the very beginning, it could have been more effective earlier in the process. The key lessons are:

1. Simple is best. People react more positively to things they understand.
2. When you give someone a monetary award, don't overshadow it with lots of verbiage. Remember, money talks.
3. If you appreciate someone's efforts, always say "Thank you."

Closing Comments

Few initiatives come along that are as closely linked to an organization's ultimate success or failure as the Year 2000 project. Many firms have already determined the cost of compliance is too burdensome, and they are choosing to close their doors. For those, like Fleet, that choose to remain viable, maintaining a stable, critically skilled technical workforce is the key to future success.

No one knows exactly what will happen at 12:01 A.M. on January 1, 2000, but at least now Fleet is confident that it has a strategy in place to handle whatever comes.

RETAINING EMPLOYEES WHEN FACED WITH CONSOLIDATIONS AT

CIGNA HealthCare

The decision to consolidate two operations meant that more than 100 people would lose their jobs. Yet if people left the company before the other operational areas could assume the additional workload, major customer implications would result. The employment market was relatively strong, so the risk of losing people, especially top performers, was high. Yet there was a strong viewpoint that retention packages do not work.

"These retention programs never work," expressed a frustrated senior operations director in a meeting with Mike Jaques, vice president of compensation and benefits for CIGNA HealthCare.

"What if we had offered them a full year's salary to stay with us? Would that have worked?" asked Jaques.

"Well, of course," the senior operations director responded. "But we can't afford that."

"Then, it's not that these programs don't work; we didn't offer them enough," Jaques countered. "How important is it for us to keep the operations going until we can make a smooth transition, and how much would it take to keep these people over this time?"

When the meeting concluded, Jaques and the local human resources managers agreed to develop a different approach than company practice. This time would be different.

Why Do Things Differently?

This was the Healthsource experience prior to its acquisition by CIGNA HealthCare in June 1997. As companies like CIGNA acquire others, it is often important to consolidate operations. This creates greater economies of scale for the operational areas and often increases customer service or reduces costs, hopefully both. The merger between CIGNA and Healthsource was a major move in the managed care industry; the challenge to CIGNA was to make the transition work.

One of the most critical areas impacted by this acquisition was in operations. This function creates patient accounts; processes healthcare claims; provides reimbursements to physicians, hospitals, and other care providers; handles member questions and needs; and makes a significant number of necessary transactions for patients and their employers. This is the informational backbone of the healthcare insurance organization.

After the acquisition by CIGNA, two Healthsource operational areas, one in Indiana and one in upstate New York, needed to be closed down and the records and service systems consolidated with other operational centers. While a few employees would be transferred, most of the more than 100 employees would lose their jobs.

To make this process more complicated, Healthsource had managed its business in a decentralized manner. Many of the customer managed-care contracts were unique and had to comply with different state regulations. This meant that the operational provisions of the contracts were different, known by the local centers, and needed to be processed in specialized ways. So transferring customer accounts to other centers was a major undertaking.

Furthermore, if people in these affected locations were to

leave prematurely, the company was likely to experience major customer problems. The consequences of these potential problems and many others like them could be catastrophic to CIGNA in its attempt to build market share in the areas served by Healthsource. These were very real and serious issues.

Background on Retention Programs

When companies seek to develop retention programs for employees of units that are targeted for closure, they traditionally first determine the prevalent practice in the marketplace and then determine what they can afford. They then develop a policy of providing employees X number of weeks of pay and benefits for Y number of years of employment. They often do this regardless of the employment market, the impact on the company and its customers if this program does not succeed, and the time of the year. They seldom consider what employees want.

In contrast, employees often know that their positions will be eliminated long before management makes the formal announcement. Because this situation poses a fundamental threat to their income and survival, each person assesses the situation and makes personal decisions on what to do. People will often start looking for jobs many weeks before they need to. The high performers or self-starters often do this without hesitation and can often find employment quickly. The "slow starters" may need to work through the emotional issues of job loss and fear of being unemployed before they begin their search for a new job. In both cases, the work of the organization suffers because people will do only the minimum level of work to retain their positions during this transition period and spend most of their energy on the job search. They see neither a future for their careers nor an opportunity for rewards; they no longer feel any commitment to the organization because the company has broken the ties. Each employee makes decisions based on what is best for him or her.

The potential impact on the company can be serious. As strong performers find employment elsewhere, a gradual implosion in performance occurs. The company does not seek to replace employees that leave. Because the work is often not diminished, the remaining employees become burdened with more to do.

However, they see little personal benefit for increasing productivity. The customer suffers and so does the company. Items take longer to be processed and errors increase. Improvements in the process are minimal and there is little concern by employees (and sometimes managers) about managing costs. This is simply a crisis that is building and building. This was the potential risk that CIGNA was facing.

The program CIGNA developed to retain employees in the two operations centers was relatively simple. The important point was the thinking process used to develop the program. Once the decision was made to consolidate the operations and the positions to be eliminated were selected, the task then focused on how to retain employees through this transition period. A team of human resources and operational managers assessed the impact on the company if the operational areas experienced premature terminations. So the retention plan was viewed as a "preventive investment" that would have significant benefits to the company—or serious business implications if it were not successful.

A New Approach to Retaining Employees

The decision process began in the fall of 1997 and the target date for consolidating the operations was set at November 15, 1997. Given past experiences with other organizations, Mike Jaques knew the more likely target date would be early to mid-December. This immediately surfaced a problem: Should they set the retention date in the middle of the holiday season? Even though this is a business, they did not want to have strong negative backlash by employees; timing is often a sensitive and critical issue in developing these programs.

The next decision was to determine the date through which CIGNA wanted employees to remain with the company. Until this was determined, CIGNA needed employees to stay focused on their current jobs. Then they should start job searches. December 31, 1997, was selected as the target date for closing the operations. People were assured that their jobs and responsibilities would continue until that date unless there were serious performance problems. It was critical to establish a firm date around which people could plan their lives and organize their activities. Then the severance pay should provide them with sufficient income during the "post target date" period until they found a new job.

Next, Jaques and his staff worked with the managers to determine how long it would likely take for these employees to find other jobs. They wanted to see the situation from the employees' viewpoint. They examined the marketplace in the existing cities and identified the potential employers of people with the skill sets similar to those at CIGNA. It was determined that people would most likely need approximately two to three months to find similar employment.

The next decision was to determine the length of the severance program. How long should people receive salary continuation? The corporate policy was the market-standard one week of pay and benefits for each year of employment, with a minimum of four weeks. For many employees, this policy would not fit the time needed to find new employment and the organization knew these people would begin looking during the performance period. This would likely disrupt the operations. Also, CIGNA knew that people would seek to find a job before the holidays if there was not sufficient incentive to stay with CIGNA. Through this analysis it determined that eight weeks should be added to the standard company policy. This was not a scientifically derived decision but was based on what the managers believed would reflect an effective incentive for people to remain until the target date.

The important consideration in this process is to determine when people will begin their job search and how long it will take them to find a good job. Obviously, high performers will move more quickly. The company also realized that once people started looking seriously, their job focus and performance would begin to decline, at least at the discretionary level—that extra level of performance that is above standard. CIGNA wanted to encourage people not to begin looking for new jobs until the operations were past the major transition period, in order for customers to experience no disruption in service levels or quality. Furthermore, it wanted people to feel that the organization was concerned about their personal circumstances and would be appropriately generous and supportive.

As a contingency if the closing target date needed to be extended beyond December 31, the company would provide additional bonuses to individuals who remained to complete the transition. This was to ensure that there was no interruption in the work. The bonus amount was set at between two and four additional weeks of pay.

In summary, the program provisions were these:

1. Employees would need to remain with the company until December 31, 1997, or release date, whichever occurred first. Anyone resigning before this date would not receive any of the benefits of the program.
2. CIGNA would pay the company's severance package of one week of pay for each year of employment, with a minimum of four weeks, with a continuation of healthcare benefits for the appropriate time period.
3. In addition, CIGNA would provide a special bonus of eight weeks of pay and continue with the healthcare benefits for this additional time.
4. If individuals were needed past the December 31 date, then CIGNA would provide an additional bonus of two to four weeks of pay and benefits, depending on the timing.
5. Employees were expected to continue their high level of performance and service to customers and help make the transition as smooth as possible.

What Really Happened

People were not surprised by the announcement of closing the operations. They were surprised that they were told about the severance program three months before the target date. CIGNA wanted to avoid the problem of people getting into the job market too early, especially their high performers. Because of rumors and uncertainty, it wanted people to have a firm date they could plan around. It also wanted people to understand that this program and this closure were not going to be rescinded.

When facing turbulent times, people will often seek security and certainty. Remaining with the company represented uncertainty; finding a new job represented certainty. Thus, it was critical for CIGNA to establish certainty and provide an attractive "bonus" that would encourage people to remain committed to providing their customers with services and assist in the transition. It was important for people to feel they had enough money to find a job before it ran out and to have a chance to get something extra.

The impact of this program was remarkable. The two operational groups experienced minimal turnover. People remained until the December 31 target date. The customers continued to receive the same level of high service, and the operational groups were able to make the transitions to the new systems. The company continued to increase renewals and retain credibility with healthcare providers. Most employees found new positions before their severance payments ran out and several used the extra income for something special for their families. By all accounts, the program was a success from the viewpoint of the customer, the employee, and CIGNA HealthCare.

Primary Lessons

There were several important lessons for CIGNA in this experience. First, it was important to understand the time of year, the employment environment, and how they would affect the employees' perspective on the situation they faced knowing that they were going to lose their jobs. For the program to be successful in retaining these individuals, people needed to see how they would be better off to remain with the company for the given time period, than to find employment elsewhere. From the organization's business perspective, it was essential that the high performers remain. Only by understanding the employees' perspective and addressing their primary concerns could a sound program be developed.

Second, it was important to communicate the program early to prevent rumors and uncertainty from forcing people into the job market while the company still needed their full work efforts. Some companies address this problem by delaying the communication; this often has a disastrous effect. CIGNA chose to communicate the date clearly and early. People appreciated knowing the situation, so they could plan their lives accordingly. CIGNA actually created certainty out of uncertainty.

Third, CIGNA learned that being conservative about spending money on retention can actually cost the organization a lot more. The return on investment of the program needs to be based on the total costs and impact on the business, not just the simple costs of the program. CIGNA's analysis included comparing the retention program costs with:

- Revenues from customer retention
- Costs of lost productivity and increased error rates

CIGNA would be prudently generous in order to maximize its return on investment.

Fourth, providing a "sweetener" to the standard program was a major benefit. People felt that if they remained they could actually come out ahead on the transition, and this incentive provided that extra-special component that persuaded people to make the mutually beneficial decision.

Finally, this was a one-time program with a clear end point. CIGNA did not need to change company policies, but it did need to be flexible. Each program needs to be custom designed. Each situation has unique issues, and the program needs to be structured, communicated, and managed to address them effectively. CIGNA learned the important value of customization.

Like other companies that consolidate operations, CIGNA found that retaining employees during the transition time is a critical business issue. Care and attention are needed to ensure the desired financial and customer objectives are realized. People make decisions about their employment circumstances and discretionary performance based on what they view as being in their best interests. Aligning employee interests with the business interest is the key to success.

This simple situation is rich in its demonstration of what can be done and what should be done to make major transitions successful.

BUILDING COMPETENCIES IN TURBULENT TIMES
AT

Health Services Medical Corporation

One of the complex challenges of the managed care sector is to develop and retain talent. Because the industry is relatively young, organizations often need to develop talent internally to meet unique requirements. Place this in the context of a marketplace that is undergoing fundamental change and one begins to see the nature of the issues. The environment is becoming more competitive, and customers are becoming more sophisticated and demanding. Employees often join these organizations out of a commitment to the healthcare industry, but find that new job opportunities emerge as they become more experienced. So a critical human resources task is to hire people with great potential, train them well, and retain them, all this while the pressures for survival are becoming more intense.

These are some of the challenges facing Health Services Medical Corporation (HSMC) of Central New York. Based in Syracuse, New York, HSMC—which is known as Prepaid Health Plan (PHP)—is a not-for-profit healthcare insurance company. Along with its related company, Health Services Association (HSA) of Central New York, HSMC provides healthcare services and insurance to more than 150,000 members and patients serviced by a total of 1,100 employees. The company was founded in 1972, when many similar start-up medical group practices were emerging on the scene. As managed care continues to be a highly cost-effective way for employers and the federal government to support healthcare services, these companies have established their mark on the broader healthcare industry.

Company Background

Upstate New York has not been a high growth market for employers or employees in the recent past. Nonetheless, it has become intensively competitive as new managed care companies enter the market and physician practices offer alternative healthcare service arrangements to area employers. HSMC and HSA need to continue to hire and retain talent within the context of improving their performance and competitiveness.

These companies are located close to each other and often act as one organization. Although they are separate legal entities, they share the same human resources, finance, and business planning functions. Both companies are facing a significant turnover of talent, both within and outside the organizations. To managers, the turnover to other internal departments can be just as painful as losing people to other companies. Turnover means the loss of trained staff, increased work pressure on existing staff, and continual efforts to hire and train new staff members. Furthermore, many of the changes in the marketplace require new skills by staff members and managers. There is a continual need to upgrade staff members' skills and productivity.

If they could reduce turnover and build stronger human resources capabilities, HSMC and HSA could improve their services and lower costs. The paradoxes surrounding this task were:

- Increasing the competitiveness of pay levels without increasing payroll costs
- Building new capabilities and improving performance
- Creating stability in the workforce and offering people clear career paths

How effectively the organizations addressed these issues would determine much of their future success.

In addition, HSMC and HSA had a complex compensation program. It was established several years earlier when the organization was smaller and simpler. There have been major revisions and modifications since then, resulting in a great number of levels, different pay scales, and an administrative process that had become politicized. Executive management and human resources (HR) staff decided to replace the entire system with one that would focus on competencies and how they were employed in the workplace.

How the Competency Management Process Was Developed

After an assessment of the current situation, a design team composed of senior managers developed a new concept for their compensation program. The purpose of the new program was to define and reward the key competencies within departments that enable them to improve services, productivity, and contribution to the overall organization.

This meant that the compensation system would be integrated into a comprehensive management process for people within the organization. Compensation would not stand as an independent program, but rather would support the organization's efforts to improve performance. Competencies would form the core foundation on which many human resources programs would be established and managed. This included hiring, training and development, planning staffing levels, and rewarding performance. Finally, the process would reflect overall organizational requirements, the unique needs of each major department, and skills/behaviors specific to each job family or career track (e.g., management, professional, service). It became known as the Competency-Based Management Program.

The program was developed with a group of senior managers with extensive guidance from the human resources leadership team, Jennifer Fulton-Vacco, director of human resources, and Ellen Wilson, vice president of human resources and communications. There were numerous reviews by department managers as ideas were developed and tested. Managers and other human resources staff members provided a lot of input and feedback, so the resulting program addressed many operational and administrative questions and was generally understood. Furthermore, the communication process was extensive and highly visible; this led the program to be viewed as quite comprehensive and robust.

Overview of the Competency-Based Management Program

This new approach has several important elements that are defined and described in the following sections.

Step 1. Definition of the Competencies

Competencies within the context of HSMC and HSA were simple statements that articulated key behaviors or actions needed for the organization to be successful. The design team, through a number of iterations, determined that they needed an overall set of competencies, as well as ones that were applied to different roles or units within the organization. Although much detail is behind each statement, the overall core competencies were:

- ▸ Functional or technical expertise
- ▸ Customer focus
- ▸ Action orientation

- ► Ability to deal with ambiguity
- ► Integrity and trust
- ► Organizational agility

Each of these statements was defined further by three to five behavioral action statements. These competency dimensions became the focus for much of the program design work.

Step 2. Establishment of the Key Career Tracks

The next step involved defining the primary career tracks (or roles) within the organization. These career tracks were:

► *Service.* These functions are important building blocks for the department and provide basic tasks and services for its customers, internal or external. These are usually standardized activities and generally encompass nonexempt positions.

► *Professional.* These functions are unique and require a complex array of tasks, capabilities, and experience. They are usually result- or outcome-oriented and most likely include exempt positions.

► *Managerial.* These functions are oriented to providing business or people leadership for the department or company. They are usually unique within a department or group (i.e., held by only one person) and require extensive experience in the management of people and work process to achieve desired results.

These three career tracks were helpful in sorting through the roles and jobs within a department and identifying their unique competency requirements. A set of salary ranges was established for each career track to support the attraction and retention of people with the desired competencies and performance.

Step 3. Development of Department-Specific Competencies

For the three career tracks indicated above, the line managers for each department were charged with the responsibility of developing the critical competencies for their own units. Each departmental manager worked with a senior human resources representative to identify and select the competencies that would be critical to their own unit. Managers were encouraged to go beyond the core competency list that applies to the whole company and identify their special requirements. Additional competencies included those listed below:

Managerial Track:	Managing for results
	Building team spirit
	Measuring performance
Professional Track:	Planning
	Perseverance
	Understanding others
Service Track:	Setting priorities
	Informing others
	Organizing tasks

As with the core corporate competencies, these were defined and behavioral indicators were developed for each dimension. The process was open and involved a high degree of reflection by the unit's managers and senior staff members. This again became a clear focal point for developing and managing the key human resources programs.

Step 4. The Assessment Framework

While the competencies were useful in focusing on the fundamental requirements, the most challenging task was to assess each person within the departments. The managers and human resources representatives were involved in defining the competencies, so they understood the principal meanings of each dimension. Managers then reviewed the performance history and other relevant background of each person and used this data to compile an inventory of abilities. To aid this process, a four-level assessment scale was used. Each person was given a rating for each competency dimension using the following levels:

1. *Developer.* This individual has only basic-level skills in this area and should work at improving how he or she performs the particular competency.

2. *Applier.* This individual performs the competency in a fully competent or proficient manner; the manager can always count on these people to do what is needed to make the department successful.
3. *Expander.* This individual goes beyond the standard expectations and is innovative or creative in how the competency is applied; expanders are the individuals that work "outside the box" and exceed normally expected levels.
4. *Leader.* This individual is a role model for the competency dimensions and provides training, coaching, or unique guidance to others.

These levels were easily interpreted and applied to the competency dimensions. They enabled managers to gain a full perspective of their staffing talent, and then plan the overall development efforts for the department. These assessment levels would be used later when integrating goal accomplishments with competencies.

Step 5. Building the Supporting Compensation Plan

Independent of these competency development and people assessment activities, the human resources team and overall design team developed a new compensation plan that would integrate with and support the development of competencies. To summarize the tasks briefly, they identified a large number of positions where current compensation levels could be compared to valid and reliable market data. In many cases, several compensation surveys were used for each position. From this data, they were able to establish a target market range for each position, consistent with an overall compensation strategy that is sufficiently competitive and affordable by the organization.

The next task was to construct a set of broad salary ranges and to place all positions into the new pay ranges. HSMC and HSA used six progressive salary ranges, with a spread of 75% from minimum to maximum. Positions were slotted into the new salary ranges based on a combination of market rates and current compensation levels, and in relation to comparable positions within the organization. This enabled the company to eliminate the complex array of salary ranges and job evaluation controls, and provide people with significant upside pay opportunities.

Once the salary ranges were established, they were divided into four competency zones. These correlated precisely to the assessment criteria—Developer, Applier, Expander, and Leader. These zones reflected appropriate pay parameters for individuals performing at the associated overall competency level. These pay zones represented desired or target pay ranges; a specific target rate was not necessary. It was felt the range within each zone was an acceptable variance from an internally equitable or externally competitive standpoint. When there was a gap between the amount a staff member "should" receive and "did" receive in terms of a pay change, the manager could address this issue as a special adjustment (to be discussed later).

Step 6. Integration of the Elements With Salary Management Policies

At this point all the critical program elements were developed. A set of competencies was defined for the entire organization, for each specific department, and for each career track; people were assessed against these competencies; a salary structure was created to link pay to the market and to internal practices. The task now was to integrate them into a common system. That was the purpose of the salary management policies. The human resources group, in collaboration with the design team, developed a set of policies that would serve to integrate these elements into a process for managing people. The policies covered such topics as hiring, transfers, promotions, demotions, and salary actions.

The salary action policies had the most unique features. First, the company moved all salary increases to a common review date. This was established at three months after the end of the fiscal year. The organization addressed the transitional pay issues so people would not experience a significant windfall or loss of salary adjustments. Second, managers were required to assess their staff on two dimensions—performance against goals or standards and competencies applied (see Figure 7-1). The performance dimension included three levels: fully meets standards, falls short of established standards, and exceeds expectations. The competency levels were the same as discussed above—Developer, Applier, Expander, and Leader. A new form was devised to assist managers with documenting their competency assessments to be used in ad-

Name: *Mr. Black*	Developer	Applier	Expander	Leader
Professional Track:	Basic Requirements 1　2	Fully Competent 3　4　5	Innovative Application 6　7　8	Role Model and Coach 9　10
Core Competencies:				
Action Orientation		X		
Functional/Technical Expertise		X		
Customer Focus			X	
Dealing with Ambiguity			X	
Organizational Agility	X			
Integrity and Trust		X		
Additional Target Competencies:				
Teamwork			X	
Business Acumen		X		
Understanding Others		X		
Planning		X		

Figure 7-1. Performance assessment form.

dition to the traditional performance appraisal. There were no salary increase guidelines at this time. The performance ratings and competency assessments were furnished to human resources by a specified date after the end of the fiscal year, one month before the common review date.

Third, human resources staff reviewed the ratings and merit increase budget. They examined the market data and identified cases where a special market adjustment or internal equity adjustment was needed. Then they prepared the salary increase amount that each manager could give to staff members. Fourth, these amounts were reviewed with the managers individually, so they could discuss any concerns about the amounts. If managers rated most of their staff members at the highest levels and this was not justified by unit performance, then each member received the average increase. If a department's reviews reflected performance at all levels of the rating scale, then there was a wide variation of pay increases. This ensured that the top performers would receive the highest pay increases and that rater bias was minimized. This process also ensured that the pay increases were within budget guidelines and integrated with the performance and competency assessments of the managers, and that internal or market pay issues were addressed.

This process is conducted annually. If, however, managers have particular "special pay adjustment" needs in their departments, the design team devised a way to fund these solutions. If during the year managers are able to reduce headcount through voluntary or involuntary terminations, they can use some of these dollars for midyear salary adjustments.

The principle of this policy is simple and represents a major delegation of responsibility to the managers. When a member of the staff leaves for whatever reason and the work is picked up by other members, then the manager can use up to 50% of the budgeted but unused portion of the salary for special adjustments in pay to those that took on the extra responsibility. HR staff reviews each recommendation for equity and legal purposes before they are approved. The position created by the termination is then "eliminated" and cannot be refilled the next year. But if process improvement continues or enhances the high performance of the unit, these actions are well worth the investment. This encourages the departments to improve their work process, develop their competencies, and share the benefits of these efforts.

The process is coordinated closely with human resources and divisional senior management. Furthermore, if there are departments that significantly increase their productivity without staff additions, they can receive additional "special adjustment investments" for their people. These funds come from a portion of the company's share of the cost reductions and the performance improvements.

Impact of These Policies

HSMC and HSA continue to undergo change and development in response to a dynamic marketplace. Fundamentally, the new compensation program served as a catalyst for encouraging and rewarding improvements needed in the organization. In essence, the pay levels provided the reward opportunity; the competencies applied and the performance achieved defined the pay levels.

This is a long-term development process. The results will

build over time. The immediate impact has been in several critical areas:

- ► Turnover within and external to the company has begun to decrease. The company was able to provide both a sense of new career opportunities within departments and improve the competitiveness of pay in at-risk areas.
- ► Managers and employees are discussing and embracing the competencies, which have been used to focus hiring, staffing, and development efforts.
- ► Several departments, including human resources, have used special adjustments and reduced their payroll expenses while increasing salaries above limited merit budgets.
- ► The compensation system is no longer seen as a drag on the company's change efforts or as an impediment to the ability to recruit people from the market; it has become an important and unique feature of the organization.
- ► Managers are excited, executives are supportive, and the human resources group has become an active partner with line managers. This has changed the mood of the organization in many profound ways.

This process has enabled the focus to shift from job structures to employee contributions and organizational performance. This has changed the pay program from a highly controlled, misunderstood structure to one that is in the hands of managers and is well understood. The needed controls are addressed through financial decisions, not salary increase guidelines. This has given managers the responsibility and empowerment to make changes in their organizations that will improve performance, then benefit from the results. Hence, the emphasis is on increasing capabilities and productivity. Over time, executives expect that more dollars will be going to fewer people and the organization will be better able to attract, retain, and develop talent for the new marketplace.

Perhaps the most important shift in mind-set was expressed by a manager during the rollout process. She indicated that the program moved from a philosophy of complexity and compliance to one that brought opportunity and responsibility. Managers need to coordinate their efforts with each other and with human resources; managers were given the responsibility to improve the performance of their organizations and the opportunity to benefit from it. Those who understood the true messages have made many important changes; those who sat back and complained became evident. This process is clearly making HSMC and HSA a very special organization at which to work and build a career.

UTILIZING VALUES TO ACHIEVE COMPETITIVE ADVANTAGE AT

Keane, Inc.

In today's world of complex markets and changing competitors, the effectiveness of an organization's information technology (IT) can often determine the difference in success or failure of its strategy. This function can provide the company with information, transactions, and customer service that create (or fail to create) competitive advantage.

Yet many companies are mired in supporting a complex accumulation of software applications. Many of the applications are incompatible with business needs and fail to provide an easy way to link information to different functional needs. Furthermore, as of this writing, the inability of internal computer clocks to recognize the Year 2000 problem may lead to tremendous operating breakdowns. Finally, as technology continues to change and progress at ever-faster rates, a company needs to stay abreast of these advances and determine the right new technology, then implement and maintain it with tremendous effort. These conditions often exist in mission-critical areas of organizations in many industries. Few organizations have addressed these issues to their satisfaction.

This situation opens the opportunity for a company like Keane, Inc., to provide organizations with meaningful solutions. Keane is a software consulting firm based in Boston, Massachusetts. Its purpose is to help clients build and manage high-performance information technology systems. It has grown to become one of the largest firms in this industry and a major contributor to IT solutions. Since its beginnings in the mid-1960s, the company has expanded its office network and service offerings greatly. Keane will achieve revenues in 1998 in excess of $900 million, supported by 40 offices throughout the United States and

Canada. It has been recognized by *The Wall Street Journal* as the number-one company for creating shareholder value over the last 10 years, and by the Gartner Group, an IT industry research firm, as one of the industry's top three consulting firms for addressing Year 2000 issues. Finally, Keane has received the Software Engineering Institute (SEI) level-three certification for its software maintenance capabilities. Each of these achievements—shareholder return, reputation, and quality—has positioned Keane as a leading company in the IT industry.

Keane's Keys to Success

Keane has been able to achieve this growth and market leadership position while staying true to its mission and values. Keane is often regarded as a "shirt sleeve" consulting firm, because consultants work with their clients to make IT changes. While they provide assessment services, the staff are often seen as more of a partner to their clients than other major IT consulting firms. Furthermore, they truly embrace and foster the concept that the only sustainable competitive advantage is to learn faster than one's competitors.

Keane demonstrates its commitment to building high-performance IT organizations by utilizing a service offering framework in three areas:

1. Formulating a strategic information plan and assessing a client's current capabilities and performance against these requirements
2. Developing program management competencies to manage risk and ensure alignment between information systems and the client's business imperatives
3. Delivering IT applications development and maintenance projects, outsourcing services, and Year 2000 compliance upgrades that enhance the client's ability to compete

There have been several key elements to Keane's success. First, Keane has developed the ability to replicate successes from project to project and client to client through its project management methodology. This is a quality assurance framework for planning and controlling the IT development work. Second, it has built offices from acquisitions or investments to serve companies in local markets. There are three issues in considering any company for an acquisition. These are:

- Financial strength and potential
- Compatibility with the company culture
- Due diligence for legal and accounting records

Concern with any one of these factors can stop an acquisition. Furthermore, Keane strongly invests in the communities it serves and the companies based in these locations. This has also enabled Keane to offer a workplace environment where full-time travel is not an employment requirement (as found in many large IT consulting firms).

Third, it invests heavily in training and development. It regularly invests more than 5% of its revenues in the development and delivery of training curricula. In 1997, Keane built a multimillion-dollar Learning Center in Boston. It uses training for multiple purposes. For Keane, training is a way to enhance the skills of staff members and encourage its desired culture. It uses the training process to foster sharing of information, learning what works and doesn't work in its client projects, and to drive continuous improvements. The investment in training is also reflected in each of the branch offices and is an important element is assessing the performance of branch managers.

Finally, many of the conventional human resources functions are decentralized into line operations. For example, recruitment is handled at a local branch level. Professional recruiters report directly to senior line operating managers, and they are responsible for finding and recommending attractive candidates for the organization. The screening of candidates relates to both technical skills and "style," or those attributes and competencies Keane wants to be known by with its customers. People are what Keane offers to its clients, and the process and methodologies are how these people add value to their clients.

These elements to success are a reflection of the company's core values. These values include a commitment to:

- Learn from experiences of all kinds
- Drive for continuous improvement

- ▸ Teamwork and collaboration
- ▸ Respect ideas and people
- ▸ The success of its clients

Reward Systems That Reflect Corporate Values

The major force driving the Keane culture is the desire to learn and use this learning to support clients and the company's competitiveness. Reward systems serve as a process to support this philosophy with a meaningful stake in the outcomes. They are not overly sophisticated; the value of the reward systems is in their simplicity and flexibility.

There are several layers of reward systems that form a fabric of reinforcement for corporate values. First, they seek to provide salaries that are competitive to the marketplace for talent. Because Keane offers many other advantages for working with the firm, it does not attempt to lead the market when it comes to salary or fixed compensation. Furthermore, it seeks to find people who are new or at emerging stages of their technical careers. Then it invests in developing and retaining them to be meaningful contributors. Because the branch office network is focused on local markets, the lack of excessive travel is another competitive advantage to attracting and retaining desired talent.

Those involved in recruiting for Keane have a special bonus program. These individuals support the applications development and outsourcing staffing needs. This is regarded as a team effort within the local branch. Consequently, for each person who is hired, a specified amount is contributed to a common pool. The pool is distributed to all recruiters evenly at the end of each month. The recruiters have personal goals to achieve, and if they exceed them, they receive a personal bonus in addition to the pooled bonuses. This encourages both individual performance to meet or exceed one's personal goals and collaboration to assist others in meeting their goals.

For those involved in sales, Keane offers a special compensation program. This program has evolved over time and continues to reflect corporate strategies and priorities. These sales staff members support the business development efforts of each branch, and they refer business leads to other branches. They receive a two-tiered bonus. They receive an acquisition bonus when they acquire a client project contract. This recognizes the immediate achievement of a piece of business. The amount varies based on the size and business type of the contract. Then, they receive a percent of the revenues from the projects sold over their quota. Sales representatives have a quota that relates to their market and their salary. When revenues exceed this level, then they are eligible for the revenue commission.

There are several qualifications to these contracts. First, each practice area (e.g., applications development, outsourcing) has a minimum contract value that must be exceeded before bonuses can be earned. Second, the contracted work must use Keane's project management methodologies. This ensures that the project is consistent with Keane's quality standards and type of desired business. Finally, the commission rate varies based on the desired business work—higher rates are paid for desired business mix. Consequently, Keane uses a sales plan to address future year's business needs.

In each branch and within the corporation there are practice managers. These are individuals whose responsibility is to develop methodologies and ensure that quality standards are applied to the capabilities Keane provides its customers. They also serve as the primary resource to support learning and innovation across the corporation within their practice area. They are associated with each branch office as well as corporatewide functions. They directly support the sales representatives and other project managers in the delivery of high-quality services. Their incentive compensation relates to three areas: the profitability of their branch, the revenues from one's practice area in the branch (or corporation), and the quality of services received by the client. The quality is measured by both external technical standards (i.e., SEI certification) and customer satisfaction. They receive credit in their practice areas for both sales and implementation results.

The branch managers have profit and loss accountability for their area. A given branch may vary in size, depending on the market opportunity. Their success is assessed according to similar criteria as the practice managers'—profits, revenues, and quality. Goals are set in relation to market opportunities, desired project mix, and corporate requirements. As sales representatives develop new business, practice managers promote quality performance, and project leaders implement client projects; everyone gains. The branch managers' role is to lead these efforts within their markets and assist other branches in achieving profitable growth.

Integrating Stock Options and Special Recognition

In addition to cash compensation, Keane utilizes a targeted approach to stock options and employee recognition. The stock options have been a source of substantial opportunity in capital appreciation. As the stock value has grown over the years, the company has been able to provide a substantial amount of options to managers and technical leaders. The stock option program has supported the growth of the business so that there has been minimum dilution in shareholder value. As highlighted by *The Wall Street Journal,* Keane has been able to create substantial shareholder wealth over the last 10 years.

The stock options program has been used to reflect two priorities: The number of options one receives is based on individual performance and the value is established through the gain in the share price. This performance relates to the core factors of profitability, revenue growth, and quality. Senior executives review the revenue, profit, and leadership performance of branch managers each year and determine who have been the strongest contributors to the company. An individual may receive options in one year and none in the next. There are no rules that restrict how or who receives stock options. The symbolic value of the awards is achieved by being selected to receive an option award. The value of the options is based on the growth in market value of the company. They are not discounted and they need to be turned into stock in a relatively short period of time—reinforcing the idea that individuals "buy into" the company. Furthermore, there are restrictions to when an individual can exercise the options and sell the stock. This reinforces the principle of retention, but the growth opportunity has been the true value. Fortunately, the growth in value of the shares has contributed to a significant gain for many individuals.

In addition to stock options, the branch organizations have been highly active with creative special recognition programs. Each branch has an employee committee that has the responsibility of developing and managing a recognition program. The basis for these awards links back to the overall corporate values. Many provide strong peer recognition and celebrations for branch-level achievements.

For example, one of the branches has a recognition program with three levels. These levels and the awards are described below.

1. *Special contributions.* There are awards that are given for completing a special education program, serving on selected committees, participating in special community service activities, or contributing to recruiting staff. Individuals receive special thank-you letters from executives, mentions of their efforts in the branch newsletters, and discussion of their efforts in management and branch team meetings.

2. *Great achievements.* This level of contribution is based on receiving a client quality or service award, making a special contribution to sales efforts, or fulfilling a major responsibility that was not in one's standard job. These are given to individuals and teams. They may receive group dinners, membership in technical organizations, subscriptions to high-preference journals, or other awards of particular value.

3. *Grand contributions.* This level of award is for making a major contribution to the success of the branch and the clients it serves. It may include making a special "breakthrough" contribution to a client project that improves the impact of the IT project on the client or reduces the time or costs of major efforts, publishing papers that promotes Keane's reputation as a thought leader in the industry, and similar large-scope impacts. Individuals or teams may receive cash awards, paid time off, or certificates for new software or hardware of their choosing.

In each of these recognition programs, employees are highly involved in the selection as well as the awards. The recognition team and/or branch or corporate senior executives are involved in many award ceremonies. These events happen throughout the year and are tied to the project management culture of the organization. All individuals are eligible (excluding senior managers), and many of the award recipients and ceremonies are communicated throughout the corporation. They have served as an important process for reinforcing the corporate culture and values. In this way, Keane is able to sustain a culture even though it is spread throughout a broad network of offices, projects, and client locations.

The Future in an Increasingly Competitive World

The future for IT consulting is indeed great. Companies are making major investments in development or are considering outsourcing the entire operations. In each case, Keane is there to help. The challenge of attracting and retaining critical talent is a major issue for Keane as it is for all organizations where IT is an important function.

Keane has made a policy not to offer hiring bonuses or retention packages for remaining with the company. So far, it doesn't need to. The compensation program is so flexible that if branch offices want to offer a different package, as long as they are within corporate guidelines they are free to do so. Executives want to pay for performance, not just retention. If individuals perform well, they will receive meaningful incentive payouts in cash and stock options, as well as special recognition for their accomplishments.

Keane experienced a recent challenge to this policy. A major client in a large metropolitan area wanted to offer retention bonuses to retain certain key individuals who had become instrumental to the client's conversion process. Keane executives did not allow this to proceed. They felt this would compromise their commitment to integrity, would be difficult to manage internally, and might change the focus of the work from Keane to the client. They wanted employees to be committed to Keane, not to the client. While they did not approve the retention program, they did work with the company to prepare a performance-based retention program (i.e., a project bonus program) consistent with the needs of the client. This demonstration of flexibility and responsiveness has been a hallmark of Keane's success.

Retaining this level of integrity in a marketplace where talent is scarce and expensive will be difficult. Keane is about sustaining its unique culture and reflecting its values in every decision and investment made by the company. It keeps the focus on the client, not chasing talented individuals. Consultants have fun, contribute to their client's ability to compete, and learn from the process. This builds confidence and ensures that Keane continues to have a bright future.

8

Reinforcing the Quality Process

Retaining competitive leadership depends on many elements. One of the most important is a quality process that engages the entire organization to produce superior products and services. High quality has become a basic requirement for existence in most markets. Organizations that have made this an essential element of their culture have found that they are able to respond effectively to changes in the marketplace. They have also found ways to eliminate waste, increase the speed to market, and build greater customer loyalty.

The quality management movement has made a major impact on all industries. It has taught organizations many things. Those that treat quality as a project or an objective to be achieved have found little sustaining value. Organizations that use the key principles in everyday life continue to find significant benefits. Quality has become a process and an essential dimension of their organization. But the key is not achieving some predetermined level of quality, but improving at a rate that is better than one's competitors. If an organization can provide the market with products and services of greater value to its customers, and do this on a continual basis, it will succeed. Those organizations that forget this basic concept of competitiveness often fail to live up to expectations.

In this chapter you will see how several companies have integrated a variety of quality management processes into their organizations. They found their use of rewards accelerated and enhanced the change process. AlliedSignal has used a unique measurement and reward system to drive the points of continuous improvement home. Techneglas has achieved remarkable results. Its unique approach to a gainsharing program served as a catalyst to change, and its process for recognition is what has given it "everyday" benefits. Corning Incorporated started its goal-sharing program as a pilot, and its success has spread to all corners of the organization. Finally, there are two examples of physician incentive programs that encourage change. The focus of each has been on the quality of care, satisfaction of patients, and financial benefits from a better use of resources. Although there is considerable controversy with physician-based incentives, Community Health Plan and Harvard University Health Services have found that improving the quality and management of care yields important financial and community benefits.

CREATING A PROCESS FOR WINNING TOGETHER AT AlliedSignal

Even the most successful teams continue to improve and strengthen their competitiveness. Successful organizations know that they need to continually take actions to make themselves more competitive and attractive to customers. One of the most important elements of continuous improvement is the alignment between the strategy of an organization and the actions of its people. By getting people to understand and feel a vested interest in the success of the organization, one can create a more competitive and successful organization. Without this connection, it is difficult for success to endure.

AlliedSignal's Engineering Materials businesses created such an alignment. They developed a program called "Winning Together" to build a process of goal alignment, communication, and rewards that would impact every employee in the organization. It has become an important support to the corporation's continuing efforts to drive growth and productivity.

Company Background

AlliedSignal is a $15 billion worldwide company that develops and manufactures components and systems for the aerospace, automotive, chemical, fibers, and plastics industries. It is a highly diversified manufacturer with more than 70,000 people in 300 facilities around the world. It has maintained an intense commitment to total quality, with a particular emphasis on customer satisfaction, product and process quality, and time to market.

The commitment to quality resulted in an analysis of the company's manufacturing processes and recognition that there were substantial opportunities in moving these to world-class levels. As part of the efforts to improve manufacturing, AlliedSignal developed and trained people in process improvement, then implemented a wide variety of total quality management tools in measurement and process analysis. In addition, management realized that for the high-performance orientation to endure, people in the company needed to have a personal stake in the success. They needed to understand key goals, receive training and support to address opportunities, and answer the burning question: "What's in it for me?"

In 1995, AlliedSignal formally launched an operational excellence effort to focus on accelerating the implementation of improvements including yield, costs, lead-time to manufacture products, and customer satisfaction. The goals were quite aggressive, and businesses within AlliedSignal needed to implement their own approach to achieve planned results.

A number of specialty chemical businesses within AlliedSignal developed a unique and powerful supporting process to operational excellence. The businesses represented more than $3 billion in sales through the production of an array of specialty materials with applications in automotive, refrigeration, carpeting, construction, electronics, computers, and utilities. They manufactured products in more than 30 plants worldwide with a workforce of more than 10,000 people. To get this group of people committed to a single purpose was a significant challenge.

Realizing the complexity of this task, Frederic M. Poses, president of this group of specialty chemical businesses, brought together representatives from each facility, including plant managers and other leaders from quality, finance, human resources, and communication to develop a framework to implement operational excellence.

To make its operational excellence goals, Engineering Materials believed there were three critical factors:

1. Set clear goals that enable the units to focus on what is important.

2. Help all individuals to see how they can contribute to those plant/business goals.
3. Provide rewards and recognition for achievements.

Challenged with the task of implementing this process quickly, the businesses set up design teams to address each critical factor: metrics, communication, and recognition. Each team included six to eight representatives from across the businesses. A core leadership team coordinated these efforts. From this process they developed the Winning Together approach.

Winning Together: How It Works

Winning Together became an organizing framework for the operational improvements that would ultimately touch every person in the businesses. The framework was implemented in each plant as a standalone unit and tailored to the requirements of each setting within a set of guidelines. The businesses implemented an integrated approach that included the following:

▸ *Metrics.* Each plant established priorities and goals in safety, customer satisfaction, operational excellence, and business goals related to revenue and income. Each plant had five goals to focus its improvement efforts. The plants set annual and quarterly targets in each area and implemented or utilized systems to track progress.

▸ *Communication.* Each plant created scoreboards to display the goals and track the progress throughout the performance period. The Winning Together concept needed a theme to reflect speed, continuous improvement, and progress to achieve goals. The plants developed and incorporated race car and traffic signal images into the description of the program and the feedback mechanism so that everyone could see at a glance the performance in each goal area:

• Green light meant performance was at or above goal.
• Yellow light meant that results were just below goal.
• Red light meant that they missed the target.

However, the colorful feedback charts were only one component; employees were taught what each measurement meant and how the scoring system worked. They translated plantwide goals into each department or area within the plant. And they set monthly meetings to review progress, discuss issues, and give ideas for improvements.

▸ *Recognition.* The third element focused on recognizing employees' efforts to achieve the desired results. During monthly meetings the plant and area leaders recognized individuals and teams who made a particular contribution during the period. In addition, there were numerous informal ways in which people were recognized and appreciated for their contributions. Finally, they developed a system that provided a tangible award to all individuals in the plant.

The recognition component of the Winning Together program was the way in which people received special rewards for their achievements. In developing the program, Frederic Poses wanted employees to receive something they could keep over time, to create a "trophy" rather than provide money, which would quickly be spent. This would then symbolize the success and serve as a reminder to individuals of what they had done.

The goal-setting, performance management, and reward process for each plant was established around the quarterly time frame. The award was determined by the number of "green lights" the plant received for its performance. As stated earlier, the green light indicated the plant was either at or above the goal. For example, if during a quarter the plant achieved or exceeded four of its five goals, each member of the plant would receive four green lights. At year-end, there were also awards for meeting annual goals. After green lights had been awarded, individuals could trade them in for gifts at the end of the quarter or save them to build up green lights and redeem them for an even greater prize later.

The Awards for Winning Together

Employees' choice as to what they received and when they would receive an award was a major feature of the program. The program's prizes were tiered into four levels, with increasing value from levels one to four. They initially used electronics (e.g., cordless phones, CD players, VCRs, televisions, camcorders). Each plant monitored its own redemption records and would work with a corporate vendor who provided the items to employees at a discounted price to the corporation. The administrative system was quite simple and easily integrated into the operations of the plant.

The process of aligning goals was one of the most important aspects of the program. The overall business goals of sales, income, and customer delight were translated into the plant's performance measures. Income could be translated into cost drivers of the plant, such as waste, unit costs, and safety. Sales could be translated into productivity units or revenues associated with production or delivery. Customer delight was reflected in such customer satisfaction indicators as on-time delivery, survey responses, or problem resolution time. Each plant, depending on its business, would translate business goals into those measures on which they had the greatest impact.

The results from this program have been remarkable. The performance yielded major improvements in safety, product costs and quality, and on-time delivery. After the first year, 23 of the 25 sites achieved sufficient goals to provide awards. On average the plants gave out 19 green lights from a possible total of 30. Plants achieved a variety of performance levels, as follows:

4 plants achieved between 8 and 11 green lights
4 plants achieved between 12 and 16 green lights
6 plants achieved between 17 and 21 green lights
6 plants achieved between 22 and 25 green lights
3 plants achieved greater than 26 green lights

Understanding Why It Was Successful

Consistent with a total quality approach, AlliedSignal analyzed the activity and approach of the high-performing plants to identify best practices that could be shared and replicated in other sites. A study team was developed and identified the following differences between the high- and low-performing plants:

1. *Leadership was a key determinant in the plants' results.* In the plants with a high number of awards, leaders were active in com-

municating progress and reinforcing actions people took to improve the process.

2. *Employee satisfaction was very strong in specific areas for the plants with the most awards.* Employee opinion surveys indicated these comments, which were significantly different from the comments of the low-performing plants:

"I receive information on plant performance."
"I have the information I need to do my job well."
"My manager keeps me informed."
"My contribution is often recognized."
"I understand my site's goals."

3. *Education was emphasized.* People received significant education on how their activities support or distract from achieving the goals of the plant.

4. *Feedback on progress was displayed in many ways.* The high-award plants went beyond the plant scoreboard and developed visual feedback in all major areas of the plant. Many of these displays were developed and kept up to date by the work team members.

5. *Managers and other employees listened and responded frequently to ideas people had to improve the operations.* The ideas were not in the form of a suggestion system, but came through dialogue and discussions with people on a real-time basis.

Hence, the plants with the greatest number of awards, as reflected in the highest performance, placed a particular emphasis on goal alignment, communication on the progress, and frequent and meaningful appreciation of the contributions of people. They found the keys to their success through information, education, involvement, and reinforcement.

During the second year of the program, many of the principles and practices of the Winning Together program were communicated and adopted by many of the other businesses of AlliedSignal. Additional items were added to the rewards based on input from employee focus groups. Two additional award levels were established. The award items in these levels included personal computers, large-screen televisions, mountain bikes, fitness equipment, camping gear, and travel packages. Furthermore, individuals who had accumulated "lights" sufficient for level-four and above awards could select to receive AlliedSignal stock. They could receive 10 or 20 shares, depending on the level. This sent a powerful message of sharing ownership in the company to those who help make AlliedSignal successful. They continued the partnership theme in their awards and the process of the program. These additional award opportunities were developed again through discussions with employees and managers.

The accomplishments of the Winning Together program have created an important linkage between people and the organization. More than 80% of the employees have cashed in "lights" for a total of 5,000 awards. The redemptions at the sites run as high as 95% of the employees.

At more than 20 sites, employees have been eligible for stock awards. Approximately one-third have selected stock over the prizes, for a total of more than 50,000 shares.

This program has been expanded to more plants within the business. The total costs of the program to date have been between $6 million and $7 million. The Winning Together program has helped to generate process improvements that have resulted in savings in excess of $250 million. This is a return of more than 40 times the dollars spent on the program.

The Future of Winning Together

The challenge to AlliedSignal for the future is to continue to set the bar higher and sustain success in productivity and growth. What do managers and other leaders need to do so that more employees can achieve awards and the businesses continue to improve their operations and services to customers? What do employees need to do to achieve these improved results? What is the benefit to the organization of these results, and what return on investment do they provide?

It is quite clear that the Winning Together program has created a truly winning partnership. Employees have clearly benefited from participation in this program and realized a tangible return from their efforts to make their plant more productive, efficient, and competitive. Management and senior leaders have received the benefits of a more successful and competitive company and a workforce that better understands and acts on the strategy of the company. Customers have clearly benefited from working with a company that cares about their satisfaction and has implemented demonstrable programs to meet their needs. Only the competitors have been left behind.

GAINING COMPETITIVENESS WITH PRODUCTIVITY IMPROVEMENTS AT

Techneglas, Inc.

Perhaps one of the greatest business challenges is faced when a competitor decides to build a state-of-the-art manufacturing facility that competes directly with you. The implication of this action is that the competitor will be able to reduce prices because of lower costs, produce higher-quality products, and go after greater market share with the enhanced capabilities. Unless one is ready to match the technology investments, the only offensive strategy is to improve productivity and quality of products, or lower costs such that the competitor decides it is not cost-effective to go ahead with the expansion plans.

This was the issue facing Techneglas, Inc., several years ago. Techneglas is one of the world's leading producers of glass used in the production of television tubes and the largest such manufacturer in the United States. The company, headquartered in Columbus, Ohio, employs more than 3,000 people and operates three manufacturing plants. The company is a wholly owned subsidiary of Nippon Electric Glass, Ltd. (NEG). Prior to the complete acquisition in 1993, Techneglas was a 50% joint venture between NEG and Owens-Illinois, a strategic alliance that began in 1960.

The manufacturing of glass components for color televisions is a highly complex technology. The glass is subjected to precise variances in temperature and pressure and molded to exact requirements. The forming process uses molten glass that is manipulated by centrifugal force and presses, cooled in highly controlled environments, finished with various polishing steps, and inspected for defects in material, size, shape, and form. Products are made in two components, the front panel and the funnel. The television manufacturer will then assemble these parts with electronics. If a structural integrity problem in the product emerges during the electronics assembly stage, the costs can be significant. Quality is crucial.

The market demand for the products is usually established a year or two in advance, based on the forecast of the major manufacturing companies. Then Techneglas and its competitors battle over contracts and demands fulfillment. If Techneglas is able to maintain a high level of productivity, competitive prices, and high quality, it will continue market dominance. If it slips in any of these relative to competitors, it will face negative implications for years to come. This is the story of how its manufacturing facility in Pittston, Pennsylvania, took on this competitive challenge.

Background of the Situation

The Pittston plant of Techneglas currently employs more than 1,800 people and is a major employer in the northeast Pennsylvania region. Its primary products are the faceplates or glass panels for color television sets with screens ranging from 19 to 36 diagonal inches. The plant produces more than 13 million glass panels per year. It continues to make investments in plant and equipment to meet the demand for larger glass components as well as high-definition television (HDTV) products. However, capital investment alone would not allow the plant to meet its full potential. Also, there was the perception by its owners that the plant was not maximizing its return on investment.

In the late 1980s and early 1990s, Techneglas was facing increasing competition and cost pressures. The parent companies questioned whether continued investments in the Pittston plant were justified, given the difficult challenges it faced to remain competitive. If the plant could demonstrate improved capacity and sustained high quality, then the investments needed to retain market leadership would be made. The leadership team at the plant knew of these pending decisions and took on the challenge to dramatically improve the plant's performance.

One of the first strategies was to implement a variety of quality management initiatives to improve the manufacturing process. They implemented statistical process controls (SPC), created performance improvement teams (PITs) to engage employees in problem solving, and trained managers in performance management, a process for providing measurements, feedback, and behavioral reinforcement. Each of these actions made important strides in improving the performance of the plant. But soon after the initial gains, performance would return to near previous levels. The task was to sustain and increase the positive impact of these changes.

The plant manager, Bob Reynolds, and his staff, in conjunction with local labor union leadership, discussed the challenges they faced in common. They wanted to improve the productivity of the plant to make it an attractive place for investments and to retain full employment. They determined that a missing element was an incentive for each member of the organization to feel part of the process of change and to create a stake in the success of the organization. In the past, the new programs to improve quality or productivity were viewed as just more work or a troublesome change to one's routine. There was little self-interest in making the changes last.

The Development of PRIDE+

Once the decision was made to move forward with an incentive plan, management had to overcome the usual skepticism. Some felt this would be just another management fad, a program du jour. However, Reynolds and Ron Drennan, the administrative manager, remained committed and focused their efforts on getting others involved. Their sponsorship was key to gaining support for the development of the incentive plan at multiple levels of the organization.

They selected an outside consultant to guide and facilitate the process, but they clearly wanted the program to be owned by the organization. They selected a design team composed of a cross section of the organization, including production supervisors, the controller, labor leaders, and direct labor employees. Their assignment was to review all the various approaches and to recommend an incentive pay program that would support the goals of the plant. The program needed to be acceptable to both labor and management, to direct factory employees and the owners of the company.

The team became known as the Performance Reward Design

Team and was composed of 12 members. They met periodically for over four months to learn, discuss, and debate the issues of variable pay. They selected to approach the program with a gainsharing theme—that is, if the plant were able to improve its productivity, they would share the gains with all members of the plant. The program was named during the process by one of the members of the team, Bernie Nerbecki, then a direct labor selector in the final selecting process. He coined the acronym PRIDE+ (Performance-Related Incentives Distributed Equally). This title captured the essential theme and purpose of the new program.

How the Program Works

PRIDE+ involves the entire plant in a single incentive program. Although unit or team-based incentive plan options were explored extensively by the design team, it was felt that a common plan for all members would better reflect the work structure and values of the organization. The primary concern was how to keep people engaged in making a difference when the results are based on the combined efforts of more than 1,600 employees (which number has now grown to more than 1,800).

The program was essentially structured with several components. First, the plant needed to produce high-quality glass panels in excess of a historical baseline performance level. If it did so, then an incentive pool would be created. The pool would be in proportion to the number of panels that exceeded the baseline, based on a portion of the unit price of the panel.

Second, the formula to determine the portion of the unit price that went into the pool was dependent on the financial health of the organization. Due to a number of previous events, the plant was not highly profitable and needed to pay down a significant debt burden. If the financial health remained unchanged, the formula for the incentive pool would be 30% of each unit's price going to the pool, with 70% remaining with the company. If the company improved its performance to a specific level, then the split would change to 40% pool, 60% company. And if the financial performance was even greater, then the pool could be based on a 50% even split in the price of the products. This then established the gainsharing pool.

Third, because the company's price and customer demand have a strong influence on the value of the units, employees could earn a large gainsharing payout for doing little to improve the process of the plant. The pool had to be be modified based on other performance factors of the plant. These performance measures became additional focal points for corrective actions by different departments not tied directly to the production function. The combined performance of these measures would modify the pool by plus or minus 25%.

These measures were:

- Product quality
- Employee safety
- Customer satisfaction
- Gross profit contribution

Each of these measures was assessed and displayed to the entire plant, along with the productivity to baseline performance, on a monthly basis. The results were displayed on a matrix to show current results versus predetermined levels. This is shown in Figure 8-1. The score at the end of the performance period would determine the "modifier" to the pool.

Finally, the gainsharing program included all full-time employees and managers in the plant. It was based on annual goals and regarded as an annual plan. However, "progress" payouts would be made quarterly. Based on the results of each quarter, 75% of the earned amount would be paid out and 25% held in reserve. This reserve covered for any unforeseen loses that might occur during the year. If the productivity pool remained above the baseline level, then the balance would be paid out at the end of the year. The pool would then be distributed as a percentage of the employee's earnings (base wage plus overtime and vacation pay, excluding shift differentials or other bonuses or premiums) during the period. These steps are shown in Figure 8-2.

Making PRIDE+ Personal

Once the program was developed and reviewed by managers, labor representatives, and employees, it was approved by senior

Measures	How Measured	7	8	9	10	11	12	13	Weight	Points
Visual Quality	Defect rate for visual quality at our customer, parts per million	2900	2700	2600	2500	2400	2300	2200	30	
Customer Satisfaction	Total score of number of incidents weighted by level of priority	44	40	38	36	34	33	32	20	
Employee Safety	Rate of OSHA recordable claims by man-hours	18.69	17.80	17.35	16.91	16.61	16.31	16.02	20	
Plant Gross Profits	Gross profits as a percentage of net sales	7%	8%	9%	10%	12%	14%	15%	30	

Pool Modifier Factor

Total Score	Modified
Below 470	No Pool
471–699	75%
700–799	80%
800–899	85%
900–999	90%
1000–1099	100%
1100–1199	115%
1200–1300	125%

Total Score

Figure 8-1. Techneglas performance matrix (illustrative).

Number of Available Panels	4,068,609
Acceptable Panels Over Goal	× 3.2%
Additional Panels over Goal	130,195
Panel Value for Pool (40/60 split)	× $8.69
Total Value of Additional Panels	$1,131,395
Performance Matrix Score	× 100%
Final Pool	$1,131,395
Reserve (25%)	− $282,849
PRIDE+ Payout	$848,546

Figure 8-2. PRIDE+ payout formula.

management. Not only did the communication sessions describe the program in detail, they included questions and answers on what individuals could do to improve performance. A critical feature of the program was to use it to influence behavior, and this meant the program needed to be personalized.

To further support the implementation and management of the program, the design team was reconstituted into the PRIDE+ council. This group had responsibility for communicating the results, coordinating the information, and promoting the gainsharing program. Charts were displayed throughout the facility to highlight monthly and quarterly progress. Furthermore, the council advised senior management on actions within the departments that enhanced or detracted from the support of the program. The council served in important advisory, communication, and administrative roles for the program.

One of the important features of the program has been how department managers have translated the overall PRIDE+ performance measures into responsibilities of their own units. Many set up charts and made weekly and monthly progress reports to their departments. When departments exceeded their goals, they did not receive any additional payouts, but they did receive significant recognition by other members of the plant. One reward for exceeding monthly goals was the option to take the department out to lunch on a given day or for the department to "buy lunch" for everyone in the plant for a given day in the cafeteria. The department employees could decide which they preferred. If they provided lunch to all employees, then a special sign was displayed in the cafeteria on what the department achieved. This has always been an exciting celebration day for the plant.

In addition to feedback and recognition, the organization continued to increase the SPC and PIT teams' improvement process. They further implemented special employee safety improvement programs that measured and reinforced employees using safe behaviors. A wide variety of programs were renewed or implemented, but this time employees felt things were different. When the program could make a difference to the PRIDE+ measures, directly or indirectly, it got people's attention. Employees wanted to learn the tool or procedures well, and implement them in their workplace. The enthusiasm for change became strong.

The Dramatic Results Achieved by This Organization

The program was implemented at the beginning of 1993. The results that the Techneglas Pittston plant achieved were nothing but dramatic. There were financial, operational, and service enhancements. But more important, the spirit of the organization has increased remarkably. People from all sectors of the organization have been working together to make changes, improve processes, hold others accountable, and drive success. The PRIDE+ program has served as a significant catalyst and support to this change, but it was leadership from many levels that has made the difference.

Some of the achievements between 1993 and 1998 are as follows:

- ▸ Productivity has increased by 41%.
- ▸ Product quality has increased by more than 60%.
- ▸ Customer satisfaction has increased by more than 60%.

- Employee grievances have been reduced by 54%.
- There has been a 250% increase in the number of PIT teams, with a 400% increase in the number of participants to more than 1,000 people involved.
- Employee safety has increased by 21%.
- Costs for workers' compensation and healthcare have declined by $11 million.
- Gross profit contribution has stayed at levels acceptable to owners, even though there has been substantial price erosion.
- The labor contract was approved with a 95% yes vote.
- There has been a PRIDE+ payout in 20 of the 22 quarters.

Based on these results, the parent company has invested millions of dollars to upgrade the plant and equipment to state-of-the-art technology. It has increased and expanded the products provided by this plant. And, most important, the competitor decided not to build the new plant!

The Future Is Easy to See

At the Pittston plant, they have a saying: WE ARE WHAT YOU SEE. This has multiple meanings. The products require the consumer to see the broadcast television signal without obstructions or distortions. Clarity of picture is critical. When you walk through the plant, you can quickly see what measures are important and how they are doing, as an overall organization and as individual units. Finally, the investments in new technology are enabling the company to provide more, better, and lower-cost products to customers. The impact is all around—customers, employees, managers, and the owners.

Techneglas continues to make improvements and take actions to remain highly competitive. The challenge of success is now to remain the market leader. It has created an environment where achievement focuses on continual improvements and is rewarded in a variety of ways. People share in the success they help create. The future is clearly looking bright.

THE CASE OF CONTINUOUS IMPROVEMENT
AT
·Corning Incorporated

The challenge to those at the "top of their game" is remaining there. Corning Incorporated (formerly Corning Glass Works) is facing such a challenge. Its ability to retain market leadership in an increasingly competitive marketplace takes a full effort. It is able to achieve this leadership position in the market because of many fundamental operating systems. Every employee is engaged, makes a contribution in different ways, and is rewarded for achievements.

Performance, as stated by James R. Houghton, chairman and chief executive officer (1983 to 1996, currently retired), is a result of putting people and customers first. People make decisions and take actions that need to reflect the core values of the corporation—quality, integrity, performance, leadership, innovation, independence, and the individual. The outcomes are superior performance and an organization that continues to improve and be innovative. A centerpiece of this management philosophy is a simple, but powerful team-based incentive plan: goal sharing.

The Goal-Sharing Philosophy

Goal sharing as a concept was not developed overnight. One needs to understand the context and development process that has made the goal-sharing program what it is today. This has become not just a compensation program, but has stimulated a way of managing people and performance that reflects Corning's core values. In this way, one can appreciate the significant impact goal sharing has had on the company.

Often good ideas are spawned from problems. In 1987 Corning implemented a companywide profit-sharing program. It was quite simple: When the company achieved a certain level of ROE (return on equity), a portion of the profits would be paid to all salaried employees in relation to their salary. But soon Corning executives realized that there was little line-of-sight between the drivers of the profit-sharing plan (ROE) and what people perceived as their actions. Individuals in poorly performing units received the same amount of profit sharing as those in high-performing units. While ROE remains critical to Corning's performance today, metrics needed to be established at lower levels so that people could see a relationship between their performance and their pay.

In 1989 the goal-sharing program was pilot tested in a manufacturing plant in Blacksburg, Virginia. This plant was being restarted for a third time and represented an opportunity to develop the program at a "Greenfield Start-up"–type location. The program would not need to address existing work rules, culture, or expectations. It was an ideal situation for developing ideas that were new to the Corning culture.

A team of 12 to 14 members of the new organization developed the goal-sharing program. They represented a cross section of the organization; the union executives and management selected the individuals. Labor union representatives were on the team as well as engineering, production, finance, and human resources. An external consultant was used to provide education about alternatives and served as a periodic resource to the team. The team developed all aspects of the program.

The Application of Goal Sharing

The primary unit of focus for the initial program was the Blacksburg plant. There were approximately 100 jobs in the new organization and they produced a new product for Corning, a substrate for catalytic converters. They identified critical performance measures based on an assessment of the requirements for success in the plant. The model program has developed and been modified slightly over the years to improve the program's impact on performance.

Today the primary goal-sharing "team" may be a business unit, plant, or functional department (e.g., research and development, financial services). As part of the process, each group that has a goal-sharing program needs to utilize a team to develop the measures and oversee the program's implementation. The basic structure is the same for all plans throughout the company.

Since each unit may develop its own program within a basic framework, some of the measures include:

- ▶ *Quality* (as measured by the volume of scrap and rework)
- ▶ *Revenues* (as measured by sales per person)
- ▶ *Delivery* (as measured by the actual delivery to the promised date)
- ▶ *Productivity* (as measured by the cost management system)
- ▶ *Customer service* (as measured by surveys or other reliable indicators of service)
- ▶ *Financial* (as typically measured by cost per unit of service/products)

Each group should have no more than three to five measures in addition to the corporate ROE measure. The balance of financial, operational, and customer-oriented measures is an important feature of the goal-sharing program. This flexibility enables each unit to establish what is within its line-of-sight and what is critical for the unit to accomplish for the corporation.

To integrate these measures into a simple incentive system, a goal-sharing matrix was devised. See Figure 8-3. Each measure is weighted based on its importance and reliability. The corporate ROE measure needs to be weighted by 25% for all goal-sharing matrices. The remaining 75% is allocated to measures based on the priorities of the business unit. Then a range of performance levels is established from 20% to 200%. This range of levels reflects a continuous improvement philosophy.

The payout opportunity ranges from 0% to 10% of one's total earnings for the performance period. A payout level is established for each performance level of each measure. Payout is determined by multiplying the performance level achieved by the weight for the measure and then multiplying this by the overall target. In this way, if an above threshold level of performance is achieved on any one of the measures, individuals would receive an incentive payout. Even though the payout may be small, the design team felt it was important to have some payouts for achievement and to keep the focus on continuous improvements over the previous year's average.

Setting goals for the goal-sharing process is one of the most important aspects of the program. As indicated earlier, the goal-

SYSTEM _XYZ Plant_

LOCATION _____

Measures	X Weight	\u200b					PERFORMANCE PERIOD						Bonus
		0	20	40	60	80	100	120	140	160	180	200	
Product Quality	10%	0	0.1	0.2	0.3	0.4	0.5	0.6	0.7	0.8	0.9	1.0	0.7
		85	87	89	91	93	95	96	97	98	99	100	
Scrap/ Rework	15%	0	0.15	0.30	0.45	0.60	0.75	0.90	1.05	1.20	1.35	1.50	0.9
		.50	.48	.46	.44	.42	.40	.38	.36	.34	.32	.30	
Total Cost/ Unit	30%	0	0.30	0.60	0.90	1.20	1.50	1.8	2.1	2.4	2.7	3.0	1.5
		50	49	48	47	46	45	44.5	44	43.5	43	42.5	
Customer Service	10%	0	0.1	0.2	0.3	0.4	0.5	0.6	0.7	0.8	0.9	1.0	0.5
		96	96.4	96.8	97.2	97.6	98	98.2	98.4	98.6	98.8	99	
Customer Satisfaction	10%	0	0.1	0.2	0.3	0.4	0.5	0.6	0.7	0.8	0.9	1.0	0.4
		88	89	90	91	92	93	94	95	96	97	98	
Blended ROE	25%	0	0.25	.05	0.75	1.0	1.25	1.5	1.75	2.0	2.25	2.50	1.25
		10%	10.8%	11.6%	12.4%	13.2%	14%	14.8%	15.6%	16.4%	17.2%	18%	

5% Target (at 100)   10% Maximum (at 200)

Payout Opportunity: 0   Previous Year's Average Performance

TOTAL PAYOUT 5.25%

Key: 0.5 Payout as % of pay

    400M Performance level for measure

Figure 8-3. Corning goal-sharing matrix.

sharing oversight team for the business unit sets the goal levels in concert with the senior managers of the group. Then these plans are presented to one of two corporate review committees. The review committees are composed of senior executives of the area that ensure there is an alignment between the unit's goals and the corporation's priorities. This is a positive feature and one that provides increased visibility for individuals and teams. It also enables senior executives to communicate directly with the workforce at all levels. Hence, the goal-sharing process facilitates the alignment of goals and communication throughout the organization.

The program provides payouts annually. Although there was and continues to be considerable discussion about the timing of payouts, it was concluded that the program should provide meaningful payouts. The bonus is cash and is counted as income for 401(k) matching purposes. The reason is simple: They want people to use the payouts for something special.

Developing the Pilot Site

During the initial pilot run of the program at the Blacksburg plant, the payout was not in the form of money. The company was not sure at that time whether the program would have the desired impact on performance. It had not had a successful experience with the profit-sharing program, and there was considerable concern that linking pay too early would lock management into a formal program even after only a trial period. Instead, it used symbolic awards instead of cash. These awards included a jacket printed with the company's name, a watch, or dinner for two, depending on the level of results achieved. This applied to the first six months, since the program was implemented in mid-fiscal year. These awards were sufficiently attractive to get the attention of the plant's workforce, but financial payouts would be needed to sustain the program.

Since its inception in the Virginia plant in 1988, the program has spread to all units within the Corning organization. Even the chief executive officer and senior managers participate in the program. The process of goal setting involves numerous groups throughout the company and has become an important performance alignment process. Furthermore, there is considerable interest in the ROE results that are published and distributed quarterly to everyone in the company.

The program has become an integral element in managing the organization. Since its inception, the overall goal-sharing program has met or exceeded its goals. While some units may not have achieved full payouts, a great percentage has been successful. The payback to the corporation has increased over the years; the savings to cost ratio was 3.6 in 1993 and 4.6 in 1994. The corporation has realized strong revenue growth and has achieved a top quartile rating of ROE among other Fortune 500 companies. New products are being released and costs are better managed.

How Goal Sharing Impacts Performance

These achievements did not just happen. There has been considerable effort to use the goal-sharing process to stimulate growth and improvements in performance. Several units have used it to lead major turnaround efforts, and they have seen considerable improvements in quality, service, and productivity measures. Goal sharing has become a driver for change and is viewed not as a compensation plan, but more as an organizational unifying process within the company. Because the levels of performance increase each year, continuous improvement has become a core principle of the program and of the Corning culture.

The company has learned and institutionalized several critical aspects of the program. First, the goal-setting process has become an important hallmark of the program. This increases employee involvement and communication across many levels of the organization. Second, continuous communication of progress has become a necessity. The measures are important to the organization and tracking results in the selected areas is not seen as an administrative burden; it is the way the business is run.

Third, feedback is inexorably linked to the measurement process. In virtually every business unit there is an "eye chart." This is a chart that displays the primary measures and the current standing. It also tracks the current payout calculation but is a moving target based on performance. Furthermore, every other month Corning produces a videotape called "Corning Live." This provides a status report on the company's performance and describes critical events impacting the company. These programs are also used to highlight business units that have made a particularly important contribution either by improving their own performance or assisting others to achieve greater results. This creates a strong sense of community within the organization and clearly keeps the spirit of the goal-sharing program alive.

Fourth, initially the program required considerable education. The focus of this education was in translating performance measures of the business unit with the actions needed by people to be successful. Rather than letting people figure out for themselves what was needed, the education and discussion sessions were seen as instrumental to achieving a jump-start to the program. As measures change for the business unit, people often need to be educated about the key performance drivers. This once again supports the corporate values of people and business development.

Finally, Corning has learned that competitive advantage is sustained by the involvement of their people. It seeks opportunities to get employees involved in the improvement process and implementation of change. This supports the continuous improvement process and allows people to see how they can make a greater contribution to the company. While the degree and effectiveness of employee involvement varies across units, there is clearly a high standard within the corporation. Goal sharing answers the fundamental question often associated with employee involvement efforts—"What's in it for me?"—before it needs to be asked.

Continuing the Improvements to Goal Sharing

One of the recent enhancements to the program has been to offer employees the option of taking the goal-sharing awards in cash or in company stock. Individuals are able to purchase stock with their payouts at 85% of the market value through the company's employee stock purchase plan. This has the added benefit of linking individuals into the long-term success of the company. It was important, however, to introduce this feature only after goal sharing had become integrated into the business. That was achieved approximately three years after the program was introduced beyond the Blacksburg plant.

Corning continues to change. Business units are being divested and new ones are being created. The marketplace for their breadth of products is changing rapidly, and Corning is attempting to do what is necessary to remain the leader. Many of the groups that spin off from the corporation retain a similar version to the goal-sharing program. This alone is a statement of how positive the impact has been on the organization.

The program has changed and developed over time. Corning has maintained the core principles of the plan and applied the process to a wide range of organizational units. While at times the process is difficult, few would be willing to return to straight salaries and limited bonus opportunities. They have seen the power of this program and continue to move forward. Managing the process of change and seeking solutions to perplexing problems of market leadership continues to be a major challenge.

ENGAGING PHYSICIANS IN THE PROCESS OF CHANGE AT

Community Health Plan

The healthcare industry is undergoing such fundamental change that few can agree on its direction. Hospitals are no longer the primary providers of healthcare services, physicians no longer exclusively control the provision of services, reimbursement organizations are seeking to manage costs and services aggressively, and managed care organizations are no longer boutiques in the marketplace.

Patient care has become multidimensional, including access to services, disease prevention, clinical treatment, and interpersonal effectiveness. Accountability for the costs of providing care and the access to the delivery of care are being influenced by a complex array of groups. At the vortex of the whirlwind of change is the physician. The physician's role is changing from a primary focus on caring for patients to managing a complex array of resources to achieve desired clinical outcomes. Yet the basic framework on which physicians are compensated has not changed in most organizations.

Background of Community Health Plan: The Vermont Region

The Vermont region of the Community Health Plan (CHP) has taken the bold step of changing the way it compensates physicians. This organization is the medical group that serves the needs of member patients in Vermont and nearby New York communities. It included approximately 70 physicians in pediatrics, adult medicine, and family practice. They were located in 16 health centers in Vermont.

There were several factors that led to this decision. First, the organization was facing increasing competition from group practices and other managed care organizations. It needed to improve effectiveness in delivering services as well as the pay levels for clinical practitioners. Second, it had completed several important reorganizations that changed staffing levels within the health centers and developed new care management programs. Finally, it was increasingly difficult to reduce certain major costs that were attributed directly to the physicians. These included hospital utilization, referrals and consults with external specialists, and other related costs. The challenge was to retain a high level of patient care while reducing the associated costs.

To this end, Vermont Regional Medical Director Paul Jarris, M.D., M.B.A., and Bruce Nash, M.D., the vice president of medical affairs for Community Health Plan, decided to develop an incentive compensation program for the physicians. The Vermont region would serve as a pilot site for the new program. If the plan were successful, it would contribute to their ability to grow the practice and invest in the capabilities of the organization.

Developing the Physician Incentive Program

To design the program, Dr. Jarris and his staff selected a design team of full-time practicing physicians and physician managers. There were 10 people on the team. They met for a series of sessions over five months and worked with an external consultant who planned and guided the meetings. The plan was approved by management and was implemented in the fall of 1995.

In developing the program, the design team had to address several critical issues. First, there needed to be a compelling reason for the program so that it would be appealing to physicians. The group discussed at length the issues facing the organization and came to realize that physicians needed to take more accountability over the care of the patients and the resources of the organization. A key outcome of this discussion was to identify a set of characteristics that defined the "ideal practice" of the organization. This process identified the conditions that should exist if the organization were practicing medical care in an "ideal" fashion. Some of these factors included:

- ► Meet or exceed that patient's expectation for service.
- ► Create valuable healthcare services for our patients and payers.
- ► Improve the health status of the population we serve.
- ► Deliver services in innovative ways that anticipate changes in the marketplace.
- ► Work as a team throughout the organization.
- ► Be respected as active participants in community programs.

Second, the question of ethics in healthcare and the role of physician incentives was the single most important topic for discussion. Although an exploration of the ethical issues is beyond the scope of this case study, the fundamental conclusion was that incentives would indeed be appropriate if they were balanced and measured improvements in care. For example, measures of productivity must be balanced with patient satisfaction and quality of care measures to avoid the churning of patients. The design team addressed this issue at numerous times throughout the design process, in particular when identifying performance measures and establishing the emphasis between individual and team rewards.

Third, selecting the performance measures was perhaps the most important and challenging aspect of the design process. Not only did the team need to identify the "right" measures and achieve a desired balance, they needed to ensure that the systems were in place and the measures provided effective feedback on performance. The group identified five areas that would be important to the physicians and the organization:

1. *Patient satisfaction.* A survey of patients was conducted by an external public opinion survey company, with measures based on the satisfaction with health center and clinical care providers.
2. *Clinical quality.* These specific department measures (e.g., pediatrics) were selected from priorities identified by CHP, and were among those measured by the National Committee for Quality Assurance and HEDIS (the Health Employers Data Information Set).
3. *Resource management.* This entailed how well the health center utilized its resources for hospitals, emergency room visits, specialty referrals, and other associated costs of providing high-quality care.
4. *Personal productivity.* Relative value units (RVUs), a method developed by the U.S. Healthcare Financing Agency (HCFA), was used to measure the amount, intensity, and complexity of the services provided by individual clinicians.
5. *Teamwork effectiveness.* An internal survey of peers was conducted by regional administration to determine the degree to which clinical providers worked in a collaborative and supportive manner.

Three of these measures were captured at the team level—clinical quality for the department, resource management, and patient satisfaction for the health centers. Only the personal productivity and teamwork effectiveness were linked to the individual physician. This therefore achieved a desired balance between individual and team, health center, and the clinical discipline. Performance improvements in these areas would reflect a positive impact on the patient, the reputation of the organization, and the overall effectiveness of the Vermont region.

The program included physicians, nurse practitioners, and physician assistants. A performance score from the incentive plan "scorecard" would determine the payouts. See Figure 8-4 for an illustration of the CHP performance scorecard. The payouts were determined by multiplying the performance score by a percent of the individual's income over the performance period. This enabled adjustments for individuals who were not working a full-time schedule. Payouts were planned for every six months.

Measures	X Weight	50	60	70	80	90	100	110	120	130	140	Points
Patient satisfaction by health center	25%	80	82	84	86	87	88	(89)	90	91	92	**28**
Quality indicator by department (HEDIS target)	25%	50–59	60–69	70–79	80–89	90–99	100–109	110–119	(120–129)	130–139	140	30
Resource measurement by health center	15%	110%	105%	100%	97%	94%	(92%)	90%	88%	86%	82%	15
RVUs by provider	25%	4200	4300	4400	4500	4600	4800	(4900)	5000	5100	5200	28
Teamwork survey average score by provider	10%	82	84	86	88	(90)	92	93	94	95	96	9

Total Score
110

Points: Performance level achieved (50–140) × the weight assigned to the measure

Figure 8-4. The performance scorecard used at CHP.

Implementing the Incentive Compensation

The implementation process proved to be as critical as the design process. During the design meetings, team members frequently discussed the questions and concerns that were voiced to them by their peers. This was highly beneficial to manage any issues about the program and build support during the development period. The rollout of the plan included a presentation of the plan to all physicians. This was intended so everyone understood how the plan worked and all heard the same message. Members of the design team who were clinical peers attended the session and answered many of the providers' questions; this enhanced the credibility of the program. Second, each physician received a brochure that described the program and addressed the most frequently asked questions. This brochure served as a reminder and to update new physicians on the program. Third, all physicians met as a team with other department members or one-on-one with their managers to review specific goals and questions. They used this time to develop strategies and specific action plans to improve performance in the critical areas. The goal of these meetings was to provide the needed guidance on the desired actions.

What became very clear was that the program provided an important mechanism to guide actions and reward the gains that were realized. No one was placed in a situation where they received less income; instead the program was added to existing salaries. The region had not provided pay increases for several years due to its overall financial performance. The program provided a mechanism for the group to catch up to the market and go beyond it if high levels of performance were achieved. It was anticipated that over time the payout levels would increase as the people gained confidence in the program and the program was supported by stronger information systems.

Assessing the Impact

The results of the program have been quite remarkable. The most significant improvements in performance occurred in the quality of care and physician productivity areas. In particular, the group developed and implemented a greater number of asthma treatment plans and significantly increased the use of peak flow meters. It also increased the number of women receiving mammography tests and children being fully immunized. These preventative actions paralleled a decrease in use of emergency room services.

The median performance in personal productivity (i.e., RVUs) increased by close to 10%. This was achieved by physicians increasing their panel size with new members, opening appointments for fee-for-service patients, and assuming patients of physicians who terminated employment.

The Vermont region of CHP experienced an important improvement in quality of care and a strong overall rise in financial performance. Although the program was not dependent on financial results, the achievements realized from this program clearly increased the financial strength of the organization. Over the several performance periods, an increasing number of physicians received payouts. Dr. Jarris indicated that "the program did not really become operational until the providers received their first payouts. Then they knew we were serious and they could make a difference."

The distribution of payouts to providers over the first year of the plan were:

No payout:	15%
Between $500 and $1,000:	5%
Between $1,000 and $3,000:	20%
Between $3,000 and $5,000:	19%
More than $5,000:	41%

The medical group was able to demonstrate approximately a 4:1 return on investment from the program. This meant that if the group paid out $350,000 in incentives, it realized $1.4 million in increased income and savings. The funding of the program was built into the measures and performance levels. During the design process, the design team examined the payout opportunities and associated these to the measures. They realized that they did not need an additional funding mechanism for the program. This technique proved to be an important confidence-building process for the physicians and kept the program focused on quality of care (not financial) issues.

Going Forward

The program has achieved its primary objective of improving performance and building a strong sense of commitment by the providers. This program has enabled physicians to realize personal benefit from the actions they take to improve the quality of care, being more responsive to patients and improving the overall organization. One physician indicated that the program was a useful mechanism to measure and recognize contributions, and that physicians seldom received such feedback. It gave them an opportunity to share in the improvements they help create.

BRIDGING THE GAP BETWEEN PHYSICIANS AND THE ORGANIZATION AT

Harvard University Health Services

There are those who believe there is an inherent conflict between physician incentives and the quality of care. The argument suggests that if physicians are more interested in the financial aspects of the organization, they will pay less attention to caring for patients and providing sound quality of care. Organizations that have established quality- and patient-based physician incentive plans have experienced just the opposite. When physicians have a portion of their compensation linked to the effective management of care, the patient and the employing organization benefit. This has been the experience of Harvard University Health Services.

There is much controversy about physician compensation. As managed care organizations or private physician groups employ more and more physicians, the issue of designing a fair compensation program is of paramount importance. The reason is simple: They need to encourage and reinforce the right behaviors. The development of a compensation program needs to consider a variety of personal, healthcare, and business factors. It involves more than just providing competitive salaries and pay increases based on seniority.

Traditionally, physicians joined managed care organizations for lifestyle reasons. They made trade-off decisions of compensation opportunity for the ability to have more free time, operate with greater autonomy, and be free of the business responsibilities of managing a practice. However, pressures of the marketplace have caused many of these employing organizations to change these role expectations. Physicians need to consider the resource utilization necessary to provide the highest quality of care, and they need to coordinate care across a wide array of groups, including nursing and specialties, and participate actively in many organizational committees and programs. The confluence of the different requirements has created significant conflict in these healthcare organizations.

Dealing With Change

Harvard University Health Services (HUHS) has faced these issues and made significant progress. HUHS is owned by Harvard University. It serves the faculty, students, and staff members of the university and operates as an independent managed care organization. Faculty and staff members have several choices for healthcare insurance, so HUHS needs to "compete" for patients like any private health maintenance organization (HMO). Fortunately, it has achieved the distinctive reputation of providing excellent care and is the lowest-cost provider of these services.

HUHS faces the same marketplace and service pressures as most managed care companies. It primarily employs internist and pediatric physicians, as well as a strong nurse-practitioner staff and a network of health centers and administrative services. It has service contracts with specialty physician groups (e.g., surgeons, obstetricians) and two major Boston teaching hospitals.

HUHS continually develops and implements programs to improve its ability to manage disease and care for patients. In 1994, it decided to take a bold step to change the compensation arrangement for its physicians. The actions that resulted from this decision have made fundamental changes in the culture and performance systems of the organization.

The Task of Designing a New Compensation Program

HUHS decided to change the physician compensation program for several reasons. First, it was having increasing difficulty in attracting and retaining new talent. While long-service physicians continued to earn above market pay levels, other organizations were offering more attractive pay packages to new physicians. HUHS needed to compete for talent.

Second, the organization had never fully clarified the work expectations for its physicians. What is an acceptable level of clinical time? How should physicians participate in organizational committees? How many patients should they have in their panel (or assigned to them)? Should physicians be responsible for hospital rounding? What about being on call or covering for other physicians? The performance requirements for the organization were changing, and it needed a "new deal" with the physicians.

To begin this process, Director of Health Services David Rosenthal, M.D., and Associate Director of Administration Mary Hennings, along with several chiefs of clinical services, agreed that the compensation program needed to be clarified and changed. For the next several months they conducted meetings with many of the formal and informal leaders to create support for change. While HUHS did not experience the same major competitive pressures of the other Boston-area HMOs, it did need a reason for change. Through these discussions the focus became creating a program that would enable them to attract and retain new talent and provide a compensation program that was fair and reflective of the contributions made by the physicians.

Once a general consensus had been achieved, the senior managers selected a design team to work with administration and an outside consultant to review the current compensation plan and recommend a new primary care compensation plan. They were charged specifically with the responsibility of developing guidelines for the work expectation and a variable pay program for physicians.

The group met biweekly for more than 15 months. There were several status report meetings with the general physician population, and they solicited input and consensus from many sectors of the organization. The group included physicians as well as administrators. While many of the discussions were quite protracted, the group ultimately developed a workable plan and achieved approval of its recommendations.

The primary objectives of the physician compensation plan included the following:

1. Motivate and reward achievement of strategic goals.
2. Ensure the quality of care.
3. Attract and retain excellent physicians.
4. Encourage teamwork.
5. Foster organizational commitment.

Work Expectations and Base Salary

The first task the design group tackled was defining work expectations. They wanted to relate salaries to the basic performance requirements to ensure pay was internally equitable and externally competitive. The basic work expectations describe the baseline level of responsibilities for the physician. They are expected to evolve and develop over time as roles and organizational needs change. The expectations needed to relate to the desired level of compensation that was comparable to other organizations. This was a simple principle of "market work for market pay." If individuals achieved the desired level of basic work expectation, they would be able to participate in the variable compensation plan.

The work expectations define the following key accountabilities:

1. Provide primary care to members of the University Health Services.
2. Serve the patient's medical and psychosocial issues, which includes the number of clinical hours, collaboration with other care team members, educating and advising patients, referring patients to the appropriate specialists when necessary, and other care responsibilities.
3. Fulfill one's responsibility for acute treatment services at HUHS.
4. Admit patients to the infirmary network hospitals or other appropriate continuous care provider organizations.
5. Oversee patients' inpatient care.
6. Participate in departmental and organizational activities, such as committees, workgroups, and teaching and continuous medical education programs.

Each of these expectation statements is defined more fully than presented here. They were discussed with the physicians and clarified. They are calibrated based on the full-time equivalent (FTE) status of employment. The physicians are evaluated annually on each of these expectation factors and receive up to a maximum of 100 points. This provides the physician with a performance score.

The score translates into base pay increases and variable compensation eligibility. Physicians receiving a score of less than 80 will not receive a pay increase. If the performance is not improved beyond this point over three years, these are grounds for dismissal. Individuals receiving between 80 and 84 points will receive a pay step increase, but will not be eligible for variable pay. If the score is 85 or higher, the physician will receive the pay step increase and be eligible for variable pay. Individuals at the top of the salary range who receive a performance score of 85 or greater will be eligible for variable pay but not a salary increase. This links the work expectations directly to the pay base step increase system of HUHS.

The Physician Variable Pay Plan

The purpose of the variable pay plan is to recognize and reward physicians who demonstrate significant contributions as team members. The goals are established each year based on the strategic priorities of the organization. They are communicated to all members of the organization, and discussed in depth with the physicians.

Prior to making any payout the HUHS organization needs to reach or surpass its targeted budget. The payouts will be suspended if this overall financial level of performance is not achieved. The percentage payout is based on the correct step rate for the physicians regardless of current actual pay; this is adjusted for FTE status.

The variable pay plan uses five independent measures and a maximum payout of 3% for each. A payout can be earned on any or all of the measures. There is a point score for each measure based on performance in specific dimensions. The total performance determines the total payout.

The measures include the following:

1. *Excellence of care.* This measure incorporates HEDIS measures, NCQA (National Council for Quality Assurance) medical records standards, and the chief's rating of quality decision making.

2. *Collaboration.* This measures how well the physicians coordinate the care of patients with other members of the care delivery team, including fellow physicians, nurses, specialty clinics, and workgroups. This is measured through a survey feedback process.

3. *Patient satisfaction.* HUHS conducts periodic patient satisfaction surveys, and these responses are applied to each physician. This measure also examines the growth in the physician's panel size and the number of patients who seek a midyear change in primary care physician.

4. *Practice management.* This involves the use of resources internal or external to HUHS. Practice management includes hospitalization and home care services, laboratory and other tests, and the rate of referrals to specialists. It also includes a variety of activity measures.

5. *Overall contribution.* This measure involves the degree to which the physician makes a meaningful and significant contribution to improving the quality of care, the delivery system, and the annual goals of the department. The payout of this measure is restricted to only 10% of the physicians and is a full or no amount for payout (i.e., no proration).

As stated earlier, these five areas represent important performance factors of the organization and support its mission and strategic goals. Improvements are needed in each area. Physicians have a high degree of influence in each of these areas. There are a variety of tools and systems needed to support these measures. The important concept for HUHS is that it is developing measures because it is important to have information on these areas, not to support the variable pay plan per se. The compensation program became a catalyst to focusing on the most important factors of the organization.

The Impact of the New Compensation Plan

When the design team first met with the physicians to discuss the work expectations and compensation program, there was significant negative reaction. The physicians had been used to having little control over their activities and few positive or negative consequences as long as they worked within broad parameters. This program represented the organization's efforts to clarify accountabilities and performance requirements. There would be clear consequences for performing or not performing to these standards. Over the next several weeks, most of the strong performing physicians appreciated the effort and started supporting the objectives. The resistance diminished, and in some areas the opportunity to be recognized for their contributions became an important benefit of the program.

The measures that use peer feedback became the most valued by the physicians. Performance assessments provided by peer physicians and specialists in specific dimensions are very valuable. It not only became credible, but it provided important information about what behavior is important. This information has become a major force for influencing physician behavior.

Performance in many of the quality of care measures increased, and the costs associated with them have decreased. This was achieved by the physicians' taking a more proactive approach to managing care. Rather than letting the "system" care for the patients, many of the physicians increased their efforts to support the care delivery system. The patient satisfaction survey score increased slightly. HUHS exists in a highly demanding environment because many of the members are faculty and students of Harvard University. They tend to be well read and will challenge the physician's judgment regarding prescriptions and treatment methods. Yet patient satisfaction remains strong.

One additional area of improvement has been in the patient assignments. Physicians are seeking to add patients to their panels and to formalize the relationships. This establishes an important connection between the member and the health services organization. People now clearly understand whom they need to go to for healthcare, and the continuity of care has been enhanced.

When asked if the results were worth the effort, Mary Hennings said, "Absolutely. The program has given us what we needed to focus and talk about the key issues. We have created a sense of common goals and accountability. We have much to do to improve, but the change has been dramatic."

The Future of Physician Incentives

There are two key areas of desired change in the physician incentive plans. First, the feedback on the measures needs to be provided to the physicians in a faster and easier-to-understand format. It is essential for the physicians to understand the data during the performance period so they can have the chance to adjust and modify their actions. This involves both systems tasks and simplifications of the measures.

Second, physicians need coaching in how to maximize their performance. In the past, it was an informal process by which a physician learned about different programs, how to handle difficult patients, and how to support the health centers. Some found an effective means to achieve strong results; other floundered. HUHS is identifying best practices and then creating information and coaching sessions for the physicians on how to dramatically improve their contributions. Most of the areas will not be in clinical tasks, but in handling patients, educating them, and managing the resources of the broad network of healthcare resources. If the physicians excel in their performance, everyone wins.

The change process is clearly under way at HUHS. The threats from external competitors are no longer very effective. Instead, the organization is looking to focus the physicians and all providers with a vision of what the organization can become. It wants to create a foundation from which to make major advances in promoting health and managing disease. The tasks will be to improve many of the things HUHS does very well and to enhance the collaboration and coordination of efforts. One point is clear: If it is successful in achieving these important developments, the physicians and all members of the organization will share in these gains.

9

Matching Rewards to a Changing Strategy

Strategies change because companies, and the markets they serve, change. A change in strategy can be inspired by a new chief executive officer, a loss in market share, a new business opportunity, or an innovation within the firm. A new strategy may be necessary because the old one failed or was no longer relevant to the new organization.

Organizations need to continue to renew and develop themselves, just as people do. Those that fail to do this often die or become acquired and integrated into another organization. Strength comes from having a strategy that fits with the marketplace, the capabilities to implement it well, and a personal commitment by all members of the organization. Reward systems, when aligned with the strategy and effectively managed, enhance commitment and enable organizations to implement their strategy in a superior fashion.

This chapter looks at how companies have changed their reward systems to support new business strategies. As companies change, they eventually need to reexamine how they compensate and recognize people. Reward systems send powerful messages about what is important in an organization. The more the rewards support the organization's key success factors, the better people will understand and value its strategy.

Each of these organizations has made a change in strategy as well as their rewards. Harvard Pilgrim Health Care is integrating a merger and addressing the needs of a changing marketplace. Its executive compensation plan provides a leadership agenda for the organization. W. W. Grainger engaged a large group of people to examine a wide variety of reward systems and develop changes that created a better alignment between the company and their people. Genzyme is transforming itself from a biotechnology company to a pharmaceutical company, but with the qualities of a high-growth, development-focused organization. Its compensation plans made the adjustment and contributed to the transformation of the company's culture. Key Private Bank developed a specialized incentive plan for the business that services the affluent customer. This approach refocused staff members on the essential elements of success. Finally, Levi Strauss has built an organization based on its founding values. Though the garment market and organization have changed dramatically, Levi has retained a focus on its core values and reinforced this commitment with a variety of reward systems. They are all unique stories with powerful messages.

While markets change due to a wide variety of forces, changes within organizations don't just happen. To be effective, change needs to be focused, driven, and reinforced. Reward systems perform a crucial role and should not be overlooked. These companies are in a continuous process of change, and their process of rewards supports them. People are decidedly part of the process.

ALIGNING EXECUTIVE COMPENSATION WITH CORPORATE BUSINESS OBJECTIVES
AT

Harvard Pilgrim Health Care

In the 1970s and 1980s, managed care organizations were regarded as boutiques. Many thought they would not last. History continues to prove them wrong. Robert Ebert, M.D., former dean of the Harvard Medical School, had a very simple concept when he founded Harvard Community Health Plan: If people could receive high-quality, easily accessible healthcare services, we could reduce the cost of healthcare and enhance people's lives.

So, in 1969 Dr. Ebert founded Harvard Community Health Plan, and it has grown to be the largest managed care organization in New England. It is a not-for-profit organization with more than 1.3 million members and more than 20,000 physicians and 110 hospitals in its network of providers. It is recognized throughout the world as a leading provider of quality healthcare. But the challenges of growth and market change continue to be formidable. This case study will examine the dynamics facing a successful managed care organization and how its executives have aligned with the strategy and values of the organization.

Overview of the Context for Leadership in Managed Care

There is perhaps no industry that has faced such complex changes as the healthcare industry. While historically it has been an industry focused on service at whatever the cost, the economic pressures on the industry have created major change. While organizations have traditionally focused on the quality of care, they now need to integrate the cost and management of care into their operations. The managed care segment of the healthcare industry has responded to growing opportunities and pressures from both employer groups and healthcare providers (e.g., hospitals, specialty physician practices) in a variety of ways. The landscape has become intensely competitive as both well-funded companies enter various markets and attractive start-up organizations steal market niches. Success depends on satisfying a variety of conflicting constituencies—patients, employers, physicians, provider groups, and government regulatory agencies. In some areas, suppliers have become competitors (e.g., when hospitals enter the managed care market) and customers have established competitor organizations (e.g., when employer groups form new physician-based care networks). Furthermore, companies in this industry face the same pressures for access to people, capital, and technology as in other industries. But many of their challenges are quite unique.

Companies in the managed care industry are facing erosion of their already slim profit margins. Competitors and pressures from employer groups have restrained their ability to increase premium rates. Costs related to medical services, especially for hospital and pharmaceutical services, are growing more rapidly than revenues. In fact, Joe Dorsey, M.D. and medical director for Harvard Pilgrim Health Care, projects that in the next few years, the costs related to drugs will be greater than the costs associated with hospitalization. The ability to create value (quality of care as a function of its costs) for the employer customer and patient will likely be the primary determinant of success for these organizations in the future.

The movement of patients to managed care continues to remain strong; however, the medical costs associated with these populations are greater than historical standards. Individuals and companies like the ease of access and financial arrangement these plans offer over the indemnity-type health insurance plans. Many also favor the proactive emphasis on health and disease management, rather than paying for costs after services have been incurred. Acquisitions are increasing as the once cottage-like industry is consolidating. The larger organizations are able to provide greater resource investments and a stronger ability to influence the rates charged by healthcare providers. Consequently, the path to long-term growth and success is uncertain.

Background of Harvard Pilgrim Health Care

The Harvard Pilgrim Health Care organization has grown through a combination of gains in market share and from mergers and acquisitions. The most significant merger was with Pilgrim Health Care. The new organization changed its name from Harvard Community Health Plan and Pilgrim Health Care to Harvard Pilgrim Health Care (HPHC). But the changes went far beyond the corporate name and image.

Fundamental to the new organization was a commitment to continue to grow in the New England marketplace. Harvard Community Health Plan (HCHP) grew to become the largest managed care organization in the region, and Pilgrim Health Care (PHC) was emerging to challenge this leadership. While they operated in somewhat different markets in the Boston area, there was a clear advantage to both organizations if they could implement the merger successfully. The organizations agreed to join forces effective in January 1995.

The new organization created a broad and attractive delivery system for healthcare. First, HCHP owned and operated a broad series of health centers, throughout the Boston area and the northern and western suburbs. PHC utilized a network of independent physicians and joint-venture provider relationships to deliver patient care primarily in communities south and southwest of Boston. The integration of their operations and organizational cultures became a major challenge to the success of the new enterprise.

At the time the organization was undergoing significant integration, elements within were seeking to separate. Seeing a trend occurring in other large managed care organizations, staff physicians within HCHP desired to establish an independent medical group. From this platform they believed they could provide more cost-effective care to patients and have more control over their future. They were also viewing the uncertainties of the marketplace and wanted to establish a new relationship with the organization. The physicians formed the Harvard Vanguard Medical Group in 1997 and established an exclusive contractual capitated relationship with HPHC.

Finally, the complexion of the Boston market was changing. The diversity of the population was growing rapidly. People with different cultural values and approaches to medical care (other than Western medical practices) were becoming members of HPHC. If the organization was going to be able to serve the market fully, it needed to broaden its view of patient needs and values.

A Multidimensional Approach to Executive Compensation

For many years, HPHC had operated with an executive compensation plan that emphasized both organizational and personal objectives. It used a set of annual objectives, with a financial "circuit breaker" that needed to be exceeded to fund the plan. The actual payouts were based on the accomplishment of the organizational objectives and the individual's personal objectives. The payout could range from 50% to 150% of target.

Pilgrim's executive compensation plan utilized a team approach to executive compensation. If the organization achieved a specified operating income level, a pool was generated. From this pool the chief executive and senior management staff were awarded payouts that were a common percentage of their salary.

Their emphasis was on reinforcing a common commitment to achieving organizational objectives.

With the merger between the two organizations, issues in medical cost management, changing patient requirements, and many other organizational integration factors, the executive compensation plan needed to change. Larry Gibson, senior vice president for human resources, quality management, and information systems, led the executive compensation program redesign effort. He was assisted by a consultant. It was clear that adopting one organization's incentive plan would not reflect the spirit of the merger and focus the executives on the major challenges of the new organization. Instead, the organization needed a balanced set of measures that reflected the strategy and desired values of the newly merged organization.

To that end, the new executive compensation program was developed based on four primary measures:

1. *Financial results (i.e., meeting and exceeding the net surplus target).* For the organization to survive and continue to grow, it needs the financial resources created when revenues are greater than expenses.

2. *Membership (i.e., net growth in the number of members of the organization).* Members are individuals who are subscribers and patients of HPHC; net growth means that the organization has increased the number of members beyond the normal turnover.

3. *Customer satisfaction, as reflected in both purchaser and member satisfaction.* When people feel they are receiving quality of care, the services they want from the organization, and the intent to reenroll, this is a strong reflection of the organization's performance. This is measured by a professionally conducted set of surveys of key decision makers in employer groups and patients/members of the organization.

4. *Staff initiatives (i.e., achievement of employee satisfaction, as measured in voluntary turnover, and diversity goals).* The leadership of the organization is accountable to build an environment where people remain with the company and perceive there are opportunities for career fulfillment. Furthermore, diversity was also defined in hiring and retaining an employee base that reflects the marketplace HPHC serves.

Performance in these four measurement areas determines the incentive compensation of all managers and executives of the organization. There are at this time no individual discretionary-based incentives. The rationale for this bold statement is that HPHC needed to unify the leadership team around a common set of performance measures. Everyone who participates in the incentive plan would have a direct impact on one or several of the measurement areas. However, the amount of payout opportunity differed by level and degree of impact on the performance of the organization.

Each of the measurement areas were weighted the same—25% each. There was a range of performance levels for each measure, and the combined results would determine the payout. The payout would be expressed as a percent of one's target incentive opportunity. If the organization achieved above target financial performance, then the individual could receive above target payouts if all other measures were at least at target.

Finally, the organization maintained a financial "circuit breaker." This was a predetermined net surplus number that needed to be exceeded before any of the incentive payouts were made. Although this placed the incentive payouts at greater risk, the circuit breaker ensured that the organization was not placed in a fiscally difficult situation because of the incentive payouts. Furthermore, individuals could receive a payout that was twice their personal target incentive based on doubling the net surplus target. The financial measure was both a measure of success and a modifier to the overall payout. However, it was only one component of the overall program.

The Impact of the Executive Compensation Program

The importance of this program cannot be underestimated. First, if the newly merged organization was to be successful, it needed to align and allocate the resources to meet the needs of the marketplace. This meant that operating costs needed to be reduced in some areas and increased in others. Taking action was critical. The program served to encourage a faster consolidation of the organization than had been anticipated.

Second, the transition needed to not only assure the members of the two former organizations—Harvard Community Health Plan and Pilgrim Health Care—that they would be better off; the new organization also needed to be attractive to acquire new members. Many companies often experience major disaffections of their customers during a major merger. The competitors were seeking to acquire their employer and employee customers. A successful transition in products, services, and customer relationships was key to HPHC's continued success.

Third, customer satisfaction is critical to this organization. Customers in this industry are both employers (who purchase the services) and employees (who use the services). Once again, a successful transition was key to their ability to hold on to the existing customer base and perhaps grow it. Finally, the people in the new organization needed to see it as an attractive place to work. If turnover increased significantly, then providing high-quality services would be nearly impossible. If the organization was not able to attract a diverse workforce, including physicians, nurses, and customer service professionals, it would not be able to serve a changing and diverse marketplace. Simply stated, diversity of the workforce was viewed as an executive top priority and a core business imperative.

These were the challenges facing the executives of the new organization. The executive incentive plan provided the focus on the organization's critical priorities. It was supported by frequent feedback on progress and action plans where individuals were accountable for specific results. The program served to bring the people into alignment, from both a performance and a psychological perspective. Their success depended on the combined efforts of each individual member of the executive and management team.

The program made a payout for the first year. Although the achievements were slightly below target, this reflected performance given the complexity of merging the two organizations. The team did exceed the minimum financial performance requirement. For the second year, the organization did not surpass the circuit breaker. However, performance in each of the other three areas showed a dramatic improvement. The financial shortfall was primarily due to competitive rates that could not support higher medical expenses to serve the patients.

One of the critical issues now facing the board was to determine whether they should make a payout. If they did, then the integrity of the program could be compromised. Allan Greenburg, the chief executive officer, Larry Gibson, and the board of directors decided that the plan should reinforce its principles and not make a payout. Although people were disappointed, they understood why. As the executives face the next year, there is an even greater focus on improving performance in each of the key measurement areas. The executives have shown their commitment to the organization by remaining with and focused on the key drivers of the organization's future.

Trends for the Future

There is one obvious and profound statement for HPHC: The future will become more competitive and turbulent. It is clear that the future of managed care organizations will depend heavily on their ability to influence the delivery of healthcare services that promote wellness, disease management, and effective use of resources. Holding back on healthcare services has clearly been shown to have major long-term cost implications—the long-term negative effects clearly outweigh any immediate benefit. Instead, proactive treatment of diseases has been shown to provide substantial benefits to both the individual and the medical insurance company. So the role will be to provide physicians and other providers with information, support, and resources to do what they do best—manage the healthcare of their patients.

There are several strategies companies in this industry can and will employ to achieve leadership positions. At Harvard Pilgrim Health Care, the measures reflect business objectives regarding high-quality service, customer satisfaction, organizational development, and financial results. HPHC continues to examine how to provide information and services to its physicians and other provider network so it can achieve the highest level of quality of care. HPHC's role will be indirect, but it will have a major impact on the capabilities and behaviors of the provider network. The executive compensation plan has created the integration across all areas of the organization and will be altered as needed to reflect the organization's strategies and values. In this way, HPHC integrates its founding philosophy into measures of success and the rewards associated with achievements.

RESHAPING REWARDS TO ACHIEVE ALIGNMENT AT

W.W. Grainger, Inc.

When a business moves through a period of rapid change, the reward and recognition programs are usually left far behind. W. W. Grainger, Inc. (Grainger) took the initiative to avoid the confusion that occurs when business direction is changing and employees are being rewarded for behaviors and achievement of results that were effective in the previous environment.

Grainger is the leading distributor of maintenance, repair, and operating (MRO) supplies and related information to the commercial, industrial, and institutional markets in North America. With a 70-year record of success, the company continued a winning formula of a focus on customers and how best to meet their changing needs.

An emphasis on the total cost of the acquisition, possession, and use of MRO products and new technologies led Grainger customers to expect different alternatives to better suit their needs. This shift in expectations meant offering more than a "one size fits all" approach. While many customers continued to value Grainger's product breadth, speed of delivery, and ease of doing business, other customers required a more customized approach. Some customers began to ask for consulting support on inventory management or even asked Grainger to take over on-site day-to-day management of their MRO supplies. New alternative solutions often required employees to change their approach. The Internet gave customers access to product information 24 hours a day, 7 days a week.

"To be successful in today's marketplace," according to CEO Dick Keyser, "our employee goals must be aligned with the business goals. Employees are accountable for getting results. Getting results requires having the required tools and freedom to succeed." Keyser believed a necessary first step was to examine every reward and recognition program in the company.

The Redesign Project

"Initially, it was believed that our compensation programs were broken. But an examination of our competitive position, turnover rates and trends, and hiring experiences didn't support this assertion. Performance management seemed to be the leverage point," according to Jackie Barry, compensation director. The reward and recognition redesign project started with the establishment of a steering committee to develop an overall Reward and Recognition Philosophy and Policy Statement. The development of the statement began with an examination of the company's strategy and challenges and the identification of people requirements. The steering committee identified five major people requirements:

1. The linkage between business strategy, performance expectations, and reward and recognition were crucial to the success of the business.
2. Both depth and breadth of competence would be needed.
3. Encouraging and recognizing teamwork would support a results-driven process orientation.
4. Innovation would require a willingness to accept a few mistakes as employees search for improvements.
5. Flexibility in design would be necessary to accommodate the differing needs of the company.

Once the statement was developed, current programs were reviewed for alignment. It was decided that eight design teams would be created. Each design team was to address the major issues in aligning the programs with the desired reward and recognition philosophy.

Design teams were assigned to: base pay, benefits, companywide competencies, performance management, premium pay, profit sharing and ownership, recognition and variable pay. These teams developed objectives, current state analysis, desired state, and critical success factors as well as deliverables specific to their assigned area. An integration team was then formed to consider all of the recommendations and create an integrated approach to implementing the design team recommendations.

Early on, the design teams identified critical culture issues that had to be addressed for the entire redesign effort to be successful. They were:

- ▸ The role of the manager would have to change from administration to ownership for the success of the reward and recognition programs. Managers would now be held accountable for employee performance and employee development.
- ▸ Employees were also expected to assume greater accountability for managing their performance, developing and guiding their careers, and coaching and recognizing teammates and other coworkers.
- ▸ Communication, education, and training on all aspects of reward and recognition would need to be significantly increased and be ongoing. The tools provided would need to be simple to use and understand.

The eight design teams got to work quickly. The steering committee decided it would be more effective for the design teams to stay focused on the subject by dedicating a solid week of uninterrupted effort instead of taking the traditional approach of regular short meetings over a longer period of time. The results were impressive and the process moved quickly.

Recommendations of the Teams

Each of the teams developed a set of recommendations. They are described throughout this case study.

Recognition would have to become a way of life within Grainger. Everyone, not just managers, would be responsible for recognition. Service recognition, attendance awards, and similar programs were to complement company values. New programs/actions would have to support these values. Recognition guidelines were developed for use by managers, and the communication of these guidelines focused on creating a recognition-rich environment rather than a variety of formal programs.

Companywide competencies were identified based on business requirements. The Novations model of competencies describes four stages of increased contribution: laying a foundation, contributing independently, contributing through others, and leading through vision. Competencies were to serve as an integrator of the major human resources systems, with employee development being the lead system implemented. Where appropriate, supplemental competencies (bolt-ons) would be developed for specific business units or processes (not functions).

The performance management system would include both performance evaluation and performance development. The new performance excellence process (PEP) would consist of three phases: setting and aligning objectives and expectations, performing/coaching and counseling, and summarizing results. Setting objectives and expectations would begin at the company or business-unit level and cascade down through the organization. Employees were to have performance objectives as well as personal development objectives. Employee development, career planning, and succession planning would be critical links to the PEP.

The performance cycle would be based on the relevant business cycle and would be separate from the compensation review cycle. An overall summary rating would not be developed. Instead, employees would be assessed on achieving goals/results (e.g., does not meet/meets/exceeds), developing competencies, and living the values (e.g., progressing/not progressing). Multisource feedback would be used to provide additional insight to determine development needs.

Because of the emphasis on flexibility and employee development, the base pay structure would be based on a career banding concept, with jobs being placed into bands based on the band descriptors/roles. Career bands are characterized by fewer bands with wider ranges of pay opportunity. Jobs would be assigned to a market reference point within the relevant band based on the market value of the position. Career banding would be implemented after successful implementation of a competency-based employee development process and a performance management process. Rather than using merit increase guidelines based on the employee's performance rating and range position, a merit pool concept with general increase criteria would be used. Salary reviews would no longer occur on an employee's anniversary date but on a common review date. Using a common review date, along with having the performance management cycle coincide with the business cycle, serves to separate these discussions.

The premium pay team developed recommendations that provide greater flexibility to managing work schedules. These recommendations included: paying weekly overtime unless business needs dictated otherwise, converting all full-time nonexempt employees to a 40-hour workweek, and providing for alternate work schedules (i.e., flexible hours, compressed workweeks). In addition, shift differential, on-call pay, and call-in pay policies were recommended.

The 1998 Recognition Award program would provide managers with the ability to recognize exceptional contribution by individuals or teams. This program is aligned with the Recognition Guidelines. Rather than designing a companywide incentive program, a design guide would be used by managers to develop incentive programs.

The existing profit-sharing plan (PST) was a strong retirement vehicle, and increased communication reinforced the value of this program. An employee survey would be done to determine each employee's sense of ownership and what changes needed to be made to the PST to increase this sense.

Finally, employee time off would be made more flexible by establishing a paid time-off bank and a managed short-term disability (STD) program. New benefits, some of which were voluntary and would be provided on an after-tax basis, included: life cycle savings accounts, resource and referral programs, adoption assistance, dependent life insurance, long-term-care insurance, vision care, and travel services. Health benefits would be provided to part-time employees who met specific service and hours-worked requirements. "Some of the recommendations were not considered high cost or high impact initiatives. However, the lack of medical coverage for part-time employees, referral bonuses, and recognition awards were cited as barriers to recruiting and recognizing employees. Once these programs were implemented, they were off the table as issues," said Jackie Barry.

Implementation Is the Key

An integrated implementation schedule was developed that positioned each recommendation for success. The communication theme for the implementation of the redesigned reward and recognition strategy was "Aligning for Excellence." All communications stressed managerial and employee ownership of:

- ▶ Their role to understand, use, and be accountable for these processes and the actions taken and decisions made within them
- ▶ A mutual accountability for meeting short-term and long-term performance expectations and for employee development
- ▶ Creating work schedules that meet the needs of the business and the needs of employees, and then complying with these work schedules
- ▶ The success of the organization and the appropriate sharing in that ownership

The implementation process began in early 1998 and is expected to be completed by July 1999.

One early success occurred as the new performance excellence process was being developed and implemented. The goal alignment process, called Fast Start, was designed to take business objectives and develop unit, department, team, and employee objectives. As managers were participating in this process, it became clear to them that this process wasn't just for performance management; it was the way they had to run their business. The leverage of aligning performance goals became apparent.

One recommendation of the design teams was to establish paid time-off banks rather than maintaining separate vacation, holiday, sick time, and STD programs. This approach was considered to be important to greater employee accountability. Those employees who were high users of paid time-off would have to manage their time better. However, when the recommendation was presented to senior management there was a concern that employees who hadn't been high users would use all of the additional time available. Further analysis was requested to ensure this program would be cost-effective.

CEO Dick Keyser believes the results of the reward and recognition redesign effort are in alignment with the strategic direction of the company. "If each one of us takes accountability, or ownership, for getting the job done, success will certainly follow."

MEETING THE COMPENSATION NEEDS OF A RAPIDLY EVOLVING
COMPANY
AT

Genzyme Corporation

Genzyme Corporation was founded in 1981 in Cambridge, Massachusetts. Over the last decade and a half it has evolved into a diversified healthcare products company with a worldwide employee base. With its roots in the biotechnology arena, Genzyme's compensation programs have been modeled after those traditionally found in start-up companies: lower cash with higher equity.

As the company has evolved and the diversification of products has become more pronounced, it has periodically paused to review the components of the total compensation program to ensure that it is still reflective of the business strategies and needs.

Company Background

Genzyme's recruiting brochure starts with the following:

> It began with a simple premise. Focus on developing products and services that address major unresolved health needs—not just in one country or continent—but around the world.

Genzyme has held true to that statement and now supports an employee population of more than 3,500 throughout the world. Its business units include Specialty Therapeutics, including Genzyme's premier products, Ceredase and its recombinant successor Cerezyme; Diagnostic Products, which develops and manufactures test kits for use by labs and hospitals; Genetics, a provider of prenatal and DNA testing services; and Pharmaceuticals, whose products include biomolecules and are increasingly involved in the research and development of alternate drug delivery systems.

Additional business units have been created when Genzyme products have been teamed with the existing product strength of its newest colleagues. Genzyme Tissue Repair represents the combining of the tissue research programs at Genzyme with former

Biosurface Technologies and its Carticel and Epicelsm products. Genzyme Surgical Products was formed when Genzyme acquired Deknatel Snowden Pencer, Inc., in 1995. This merger with a manufacturer of high-quality surgical products epitomizes the company's diverse growth strategy. "We are growing through a combination of internal development, strategic acquisitions, and collaborations with other companies that are leaders in their respective fields."

The newest business unit is Genzyme Molecular Oncology, a virtual business that has been charged with the development and commercialization of molecular approaches to cancer diagnosis and therapy by integrating four key technologies: genomics, gene therapy, genetic diagnostics, and small-molecule combinatorial chemistry drug discovery.

The Evolution of a Compensation Program

Genzyme has its roots in biotechnology, a world with many parallels to the more traditional pharmaceutical industry, except that research tends to emphasize biology instead of chemistry and many of its techniques, such as working with recombinant DNA, gene therapy, and transgenic animals, are considered cutting-edge.

Compensation in the biotechnology world tends to be modeled after other start-up industries using strategies that conserve cash in the short-term and provide for a large return on a longer-term basis—if the company is successful. The pharmaceutical compensation patterns mirror the more mature industry that it is. Cash is more available and equity compensation tends to be reserved for those who have a more pronounced impact on the long-term results of the company.

Genzyme is one of the leaders in the biotechnology industry in terms of age of products and revenue. It was one of the first biotechnology firms to bring a product to market and continue to have a pipeline of products in both basic research and clinical evaluation. To move the business forward, it needs to hire experienced talent. Sounds logical, but the experienced talent is in the pharmaceutical industry. When it loses talented employees, it is often to a smaller biotechnology firm. The compensation challenge has been to straddle the two compensation styles and create programs that allow Genzyme to hire from one world and keep it from losing to the other.

In 1994, it undertook a serious review of the base salary structures of the two industry groups. Through a thorough analysis of the available survey data, it made a key discovery. The midpoint line of the biotech companies did not contain the pronounced "J curve" of the pharmaceutical industry, an observation noted in Heinz Kohler's *Statistics for Business and Economics,* Second Edition (Glenview, Illinois: Scott, Foresman and Company, 1988, pp. 561, 564). Genzyme took a first step toward the pharmaceutical pattern and repositioned its midpoint line to more closely resemble the steeper curve shown in the surveys. This meant that midpoints for middle managers moved as much as 15%.

The second step was to determine how to adapt market pricing strategy to reinforce the company's look at both "worlds." Hiring managers were feeling pressured to match the pharmaceutical industry's cash compensation. The impact of wholesale adoption of that stance on the company's bottom line was too severe. Genzyme chose a philosophy that gave weight to market data from both the biotech and pharmaceutical industry groups. For positions where it could obtain data from both groups, it would calculate an artificial market rate weighted 60% to the pharmaceutical market rate and 40% to the biotechnology market. Psychologically, this acknowledged an evolution away from a purely biotech world.

The third aspect to be addressed was equity compensation. A comprehensive review and redesign of Genzyme's stock option program was completed in the fall of 1997. Within Genzyme's (and therefore compensation) culture, the annual, worldwide stock option grant is key. The senior management team is quite emphatic in its desire that all employees have stock in the company. A recent communication piece reflected this as follows: "Genzyme stock ownership by Genzyme employees is very important to the company. We are committed to promoting a culture of allowing employees to influence and participate in the success of the company."

The liability that a company faces in the extensive use of equity compensation is overhang, or a large number of outstanding stock options. There are a number of factors that can contribute to a company's having a large number of outstanding options besides high option usage—for example, low turnover or an unfavorable stock price (read that as options underwater).

It is common knowledge that shareholders do not appreciate large numbers of outstanding stock options because of their dilutive effect. In the popular press there have been articles suggesting those shareholders should accept outstanding options as high as 10% of shares outstanding. In the biotechnology world, 10% is fairly low. The "panic point" is closer to 20%, and Genzyme had been hovering near that dilution level for a number of years. Each time the company decided that it needed to overhaul the program, the stock price would swing and there would be significant numbers of exercises. It would reduce the number of options in the next year's annual distribution matrix, but keep the principles of the program intact. This was a Band-Aid; then in 1997 came the opportunity to perform the necessary drastic surgery.

Keeping the principle of the 60/40 split, Genzyme undertook an examination of the use of equity compensation in the pharmaceutical and biotechnology marketplaces. This included not only the value of options granted at various salary levels, but also the extent of eligibility within the organization and, beyond that, the actual extent of distribution to the eligible population.

Establishing the market-value line was a relatively straightforward task. Determining the actual distribution patterns within key competitors was a bit more daunting. The key discovery was that Genzyme was fairly unique in the generosity of its annual distribution, not just in the value of the options granted but in the extent of participation. Many of the larger biotechnology firms have extensive eligibility but few grant to over 90% of those eligible on an annual basis.

The company had extensive discussions with the senior management team and the board of directors on the cultural implication of changing its distribution pattern. It was obvious that the most expedient way to cut dilution was not to give out so many options. But how could the company hold true to the philosophy it had voiced and still give out about half the options on an annual basis, compared to what it was distributing previously?

Genzyme set about to model, as accurately as possible, the number of shares it would take to give each eligible employee a grant equal in value to the market line it had developed. This market line used values from the pharmaceutical and biotech industry competitors and the same 60/40 weighting used for the base salary program. Remarkably, the number of shares required was just about half of the average distribution over the last three years. The number presumed that everyone would receive the most popular performance rating and that all raises for the reminder of the year would be at the company average.

The models gave the company the confidence to report to the senior team and board of directors that it could achieve a significant reduction in usage and better control distribution by adopting the concept of an annual option pool funded as a set percentage of shares outstanding. This would allow the company to keep a competitive option grant value and, just as important, maintain the cultural statement that it is important for all Genzyme employees to participate in equity ownership of the company.

The 1997 annual option grant was made in October, which was a delay of six months as the company undertook this program redesign. Options were again to be distributed in conjunction with the annual meeting in May 1998, and thus are back on schedule.

The topic for 1998 is this: In an ever-diversifying business, can Genzyme maintain a single compensation program, or can it better support its businesses by further tailoring its programs to each area and their competitive practices (without creating an administrative or cost monster)?

Tune in again as Genzyme continues to evolve.

REDESIGNING THE SALES INCENTIVE PLAN AT

Key Private Bank

The banking industry began shifting from asset management to customer management strategies in the early 1990s to respond to increasing competition from other financial and nonfinancial competitors. Many banks began segmenting their customers according to their individual needs and providing tailored products and services via customer-focused delivery channels. Customer satisfaction, along with a full array of value-added products and services, became critical determinants of success in this new competitive environment.

Private bankers, who provide an integrated mix of products and services to affluent bank customers, evolved from order takers to relationship managers like their retail banking counterparts.

This new focus on relationship management required coordination across multiple functional areas and often led to the development of multiskilled teams to improve product and service delivery. Along with an emphasis on relationship management, retail and private banks began shifting the focus of their compensation programs from base pay to variable pay programs, driven by customer satisfaction, team productivity, and financial performance.

Background of Key Private Bank

In early 1995, KeyCorp was a super-regional bank with approximately $66 billion in assets, 25,000 employees, and banking operations in 18 states across the northern United States. Key Private Bank (KPB), KeyCorp's private banking arm, had reconfigured its delivery channels to focus on relationship management and customer segmentation. Multiple banking relationships had been consolidated into single points of contact for customers, and products and services had been realigned to focus on customer needs, as well as profitability.

KPB's compensation program had not kept pace with these strategic changes and was a growing impediment to the new customer-focused business strategy. Relationship managers were now expected to focus on customer needs, rather than product profitability, but were still rewarded on purely financial measures. Team members were expected to cooperate and partner with one another to better serve the customer's needs, but they received widely differing levels of compensation.

Design Guidelines for a New Incentive Plan

Based on this assessment of a growing disconnect between KPB's business strategy and its compensation program, the KPB management team decided in early 1995 to redesign its sales incentive plan. At the outset of this redesign project, the management team defined several success criteria for a new sales incentive plan. They were:

- ▶ The redesigned plan should build from and reinforce the private bank's business strategy. It must support the match-

ing of products and services to customer needs and reinforce seamless customer service from any team member.

▸ The redesigned plan should focus on building short- and
long-term customer value for the private bank. It must reinforce the notion that customers belong to KPB, rather than
the relationship manager initiating a sales contact or managing an ongoing customer relationship.

▸ The new plan should create a service quality focus for all
team members. Customer service must be a primary goal of
all team members in all transactions with new or existing
customers.

▸ The redesigned plan must take a total compensation perspective to accommodate widely varying compensation
packages for individual team members.

These success criteria for a new sales incentive plan were communicated to representatives from KPB sales management, human resources, and finance in a mid-1995 meeting on the current sales
incentive plan. As a result of this meeting, a steering committee
was formed to oversee the development of a new KPB sales incentive plan. This steering committee identified January 1996 as the
target implementation date for the new plan, engaged an external
consultant to lead the design effort, and defined a multifunction
project team to work with the external consultant. Project team
members were selected from KPB's sales management function, as
well as the human resources and finance functions.

The Conceptual Design

In a series of early meetings, the project team reviewed management's concerns and success criteria and interviewed a cross
section of current incentive plan participants. These success criteria and interviews led to the development of a conceptual design
for the new KPB sales incentive plan. This proposed design was
reviewed with the steering committee and private bank management in August 1995.

This conceptual plan design was based on the need for team
members with differing roles and technical skills to partner with
one another to complete the sales process. The private banking

relationship manager was primarily responsible for customer acquisition and management, whereas trust representatives and investment representatives were viewed as technical specialists with secondary sales responsibilities. These three jobs were supported by product specialists from trust, mortgage, insurance, and financial planning. Together, they formed a full-service team that provided one-stop shopping for customers

Base salaries for the three managers with direct selling responsibilities were targeted at market medians to avoid the need to "churn and burn" customer portfolios to earn reasonable levels of compensation. An umbrella incentive plan with team and individual components was designed to reinforce cooperation among the various team members. Each of the three managers with direct selling responsibilities had an individual sales incentive component, and all team members were eligible for the team component of this new incentive plan.

After reviewing the plan design proposed by the project team, the steering committee and KPB management team instructed the project team to complete the final KPB sales incentive plan from this conceptual framework. Based on management's endorsement, the project team conducted a total compensation analysis for all positions that would be eligible to participate in this new incentive plan, finalized measures for each plan component, and then modeled performance ranges for each plan measure.

Design Parameters

The sales incentive component of the new KPB plan was designed to focus on economic measures that were tied to broadening relationships with existing customers and acquiring new customers. The cost of replacing lost private banking customers was approximately five times higher than cross-selling to existing customers. Therefore, it was clear to the project team that maintaining and expanding relationships with existing customers was as important to revenue growth as acquiring new customers. Standard sales measures were adopted for this plan component, such as revenue generation, customer runoff, product mix, and assets under management.

The sales incentive plan component focused on the three core

jobs with direct selling responsibilities: the private banking relationship manager, the trust and the investment representatives.
After review and discussion, it was decided to maintain industry-
standard sales incentive payment cycles for this plan component.
As a result, the relationship manager received annual payments,
the trust representative received quarterly payments, and the investment representative received monthly incentive payments.

The team incentive component of the new incentive plan was
designed to reinforce the partnership aspect of the plan by focusing on group performance within geographic clusters that had
common markets and interdependencies. An important strategic
objective of the team component was rewarding team members
for effective customer handoffs and high-quality customer service.
Team incentive pools were funded by achieving a mix of customer
satisfaction and revenue goals.

Participants' share of the team incentive pool was based on
estimates of their job's relative contribution to overall team performance. The relative job value times the number of participants in
a particular job determined that job's share of the team incentive
pool. Team members in the same job category received the same
dollar award from their team pool. Team payouts occurred at year-
end for all team members.

The Results of the Plan

The new KPB sales incentive plan was implemented in January
1996, and by year-end it was evident that this plan was supporting
and reinforcing KPB's business strategies. Specifically:

▸ It helped shift the focus of KPB's sales process from a transaction orientation to a balanced focus on customer acquisition and
retention. This strategic shift was supported by weighting customer retention and acquisition goals equally for participants with
direct sales responsibilities.

▸ The new plan increased KPB's overall focus on customer satisfaction as a major driver of revenue growth. Revenue generation
was directly correlated with customer satisfaction and overall customer satisfaction began improving for relationship managers.

▸ The team component of the new incentive plan helped create a partnership or team mentality across the various functional areas that participate in the plan. Relationship managers willingly hand off customers to the technical specialists who can address specific customer needs.

▸ Revenue generation in 1996 exceeded KPB's business plan for the first time in three years, and senior management attributed a significant portion of this success to the organizational alignment and focus created by the new sales incentive plan.

One of the more significant achievements of KPB's new sales incentive plan is the interest it has generated in improving customer satisfaction. A new measurement system was developed by KPB, and an external vendor was selected to support the customer satisfaction aspects of the new sales incentive plan. This system is based on questionnaires that are sent to a statistically valid random sample of KPB customers following their transactions with any team member. These questionnaires tie the customer's response directly to the relationship manager and team members who supported that transaction. Returned questionnaires are scored and analyzed for statistical validity by the external vendor, and the results are provided to KPB in an online database.

Customer satisfaction is measured weekly on an individual and team basis, scored on a five-point rating scale, and the results are provided to individual and team participants monthly. KPB's goal is an average rating of four or better against this customer satisfaction rating scale. During 1997, KPB distributed approximately 60,000 surveys and averaged better than a 40% survey return rate. Approximately 30% of the returned surveys also had written comments, which were content-coded and analyzed by the vendor and KPB. By mid-1997, a growing correlation between customer satisfaction and revenue generation had been identified, as noted in Figure 9-1.

As the relationship between customer satisfaction and revenue generation became apparent, the focus on customer satisfaction continued to improve throughout KPB. This measurement-feedback loop created a "motivational effect" that helped to further improve KPB revenue generation. Figure 9-2 illustrates the customer satisfaction improvement trend in relationship managers' scores from March 1996 until July 1997.

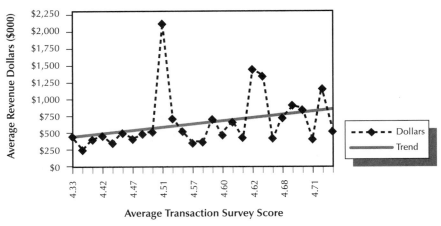

Figure 9-1. Revenue generation versus customer satisfaction at KPB.

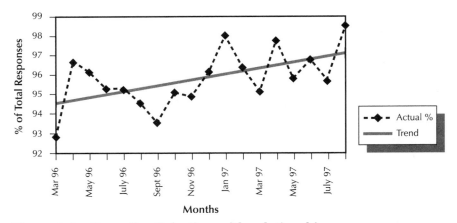

Figure 9-2. Overall satisfaction with relationship managers.

Lessons Learned

Several important lessons were learned by KPB and KeyCorp from this sales incentive design project. First, sales incentive plan design is often more than just changing financial formulas. Effective incentive plan designs that require a thorough diagnosis of the situation may require rewarding nonfinancial as well as financial results to achieve their strategic goals. By including a strong focus on customer satisfaction, a nonfinancial measure, in its new incentive plan, KPB was able to improve revenue generation.

A second learning from this incentive design project was that multiple roles can be accommodated within a single incentive plan to improve its overall impact. Team participation was crucial for the success of KPB's business strategy. By employing a mix of team and individual performance measures, the new sales incentive plan motivated product specialists and sales support staff to partner with revenue generators to provide effective customer service.

Finally, it may be necessary to create new measurement systems or modify existing measurement systems to focus on true measures of customer value. KPB's management information system needed to change in order to adequately measure and report customer satisfaction. Rather than accepting the limitations of their existing systems, KPB management bought customer satisfaction measurement services from an external vendor. This allowed KPB to implement the new incentive plan and realize the resulting revenue gains much more quickly than would have otherwise been possible.

INTEGRATING CORPORATE VALUES AND PERFORMANCE AT

Levi Strauss & Co.

Companies, both large and small, are often conflicted between the values they espoused and the performance they require. Values often define the character and working environment of an organization. Performance reflects its competitiveness and often determines the firm's worth in the marketplace. Levi Strauss & Co. (LS&CO) has found a way to optimize this balance, yet this requires continuing vigilance.

Over its 145-year history, LS&CO has struggled to retain the core values of a family-type business. This means caring deeply for employees' welfare, responding effectively to customers and changing markets, and generating strong profitability. This case study will explore how LS&CO has addressed challenges to these factors and used reward systems to reinforce the commitment to its formula for success.

Company Background

To truly understand a company's culture, one needs to examine
how it addressed several major crisis points in its history. Levi
Strauss & Co. began in response to a basic need. In California in
the 1850s, the gold rush prospectors complained that their pants
could not withstand the abuses associated with this work. Levi
Strauss, a Bavarian-born dry-goods merchant, believed that strong
cotton denim could solve this problem. Jacob Davis, a Nevada tailor who made pants with denim purchased from Levi, had discovered a novel method to reinforce the stress points on miners' pants
(or waist overalls, as they were then called). Davis put copper riv-
ets in his pants, but he needed $68 for a patent to use metal rivets
to reinforce pockets. Strauss provided the cash and material, Davis
provided the technology; their collaboration made the difference.
Their new product—Levi's waist overalls—was incredibly successful.

   During the depression of the 1930s, LS&CO faced the challenge of engaging in major layoffs at a time of historic unemployment. It felt a responsibility to its workforce to provide
employment. Consequently, the company retained most of its
workforce and engaged them in maintenance and development
projects. Throughout this period, LS&CO did not significantly reduce its philanthropic contributions.

   Buoyed by its products' becoming the preferred clothing for
the baby boom youth of the 1950s, 1960s, and 1970s, LS&CO saw
revenues and profits skyrocket. Yet it faced a dilemma in values.
The country was in the grip of pressures for social change, and
many of the executives wanted the corporation to live up to the
principles they were espousing. In the 1950s, LS&CO became one
of the first companies to racially integrate all manufacturing plants
in the South and other areas of the country, long before it became
fashionable. It established equitable wage rates for all employees
and invested in specialized training for its workforce. This enabled
LS&CO to live its values and build a highly productive workforce.

   In 1971, the descendants of Levi Strauss took the company
public. Then, responding to investor pressure, management diversified into related businesses, such as rainwear, men's suits, wom-
en's fashion, hats, and skiwear. They were driven by shareholder
pressures for financial gain. Most of these new ventures failed to

produce sustainable results. Furthermore, many believed the financial pressures were crushing the culture of the organization. By 1984, net income had plunged more than 80% from a four-year peak; the company sold or closed one-quarter of its factories and reduced the workforce by 15,000, one-third of total employment. The company was facing a crisis of its conscience; it had lost many of the family-based values it sought as an organization.

Strategies for Taking the Company Back to Its Foundations

Robert D. Haas, a fifth-generation nephew of the founder, assumed the position of chief executive officer in 1984. His challenge was to return LS&CO to many of the corporate values that had been the hallmark of the organization. As he told *Fortune* magazine, "Our focus became diffused. We became less attentive in our hiring, staff, and cost-control efforts. Management, including myself, all share responsibility." He began a strategy that reshaped the corporation.

The major commitment behind the change process was the importance of employee and customer satisfaction to achieving financial performance. Haas stated in many interviews and company meetings that employee morale, consumer satisfaction, on-time delivery, brand perceptions of quality, and meeting the needs of retailer customers were instrumental drivers of financial performance. Haas told *Fortune*, "I believe that if you create an environment that your people identify with, that is responsive to their sense of values, justice, fairness, ethics, compassion, and appreciation, they will help you be successful. There's no guarantee—but I will stake all my chips on this vision."

In the late 1980s, under the leadership of Bob Haas, LS&CO employees created the company's mission, business vision, and aspirations statements. The aspiration statement is a document that outlines the values that have become tenets by which the corporation operates. They include statements regarding teamwork, trust, diversity, recognition, ethics, openness, empowerment, promise keeping, compassion, integrity, and communication. These were communicated to all managers and employees worldwide and they set the stage for a variety of new changes.

The company was made private during a leveraged buyout in

1984. In April 1996, Levi Strauss & Co. completed a leveraged buy-out that was a recapitalization that further constricted stock ownership to family members only. This produced a debt of more than $3 billion in order to finance the privatization of the company. Most of the debt was acquired through standard financing. This debt load then placed substantial cost and cash flow pressures on the corporation. Yet the commitment to the aspiration statements has not faltered. In fact, it has become sharper and better defined as the standard by which decisions and actions are judged.

Reward Systems That Demonstrate Commitment

LS&CO has used a wide variety of reward systems to support the strategy and core values of the company. The philosophy and basic structure of these programs have enabled people to see the importance of the organization's operating principles. These programs have included salary, short- and long-term incentives, as well as special recognition.

Partners in Performance (PIP) is one of the programs that touches every employee. It is an annual performance review plan that includes an assessment of performance against corporate, divisional, and individual goals as well as the key components of the aspiration statement. There are a variety of feedback tools and links with incentive pay for eligible employees.

The annual performance assessment impacts salary adjustments and annual long-term incentives. The amount of money available is determined by the financial earnings of the corporation and divisions, as measured by operating earnings and return on investment. The results are compared to the corporation's business plan, and the payout opportunity is differentiated by level within the organization. By integrating salary adjustments with incentive payouts, managers are able to fully integrate the appropriate rewards with performance.

One of the optional features of the PIP process is to use 360-degree feedback tools as part of the performance assessment. If managers want their staff members to receive feedback from multiple sources, then a questionnaire is used to collect specific information about the individual's capabilities and impact. The connection between performance and the aspiration statement is measured with this tool. This process is not forced on business units but is offered as a highly attractive way to enhance the feedback one receives. As units find this process meaningful, the usage is increasing across the organization.

The number of people eligible for the long-term incentive plan was also expanded dramatically. When the program was originally established, it included 400 senior-level managers and professionals in the corporation. Through a series of training sessions, focus group reviews, and employee discussion groups, the message was sent that the exclusive nature of this program was inconsistent with the aspiration statement. Middle managers commented that senior managers were gaining more from the performance improvements, and they were not rewarded for their achievements in a similar manner. The program was consequently changed and the number of eligible participants increased to the 10,000 salaried employees worldwide.

The company has also integrated its piecework incentive systems in the manufacturing plants with team-based total performance incentive plans. There were several important objectives for this change. Traditionally, the key to successful performance with the piecework system was the worker's skills and stamina for the highly repetitive tasks of stitching fabric and assembling the apparel. This resulted in unacceptably high injury rates and problems with nonproductivity-based performance, such as on-time delivery, inventory control, and introduction of new systems and processes. The team's performance is now based on a combination of measures, involving productivity, safety, and on-time delivery.

In addition to these programs, the company has developed an innovative global long-term incentive program. When the company recapitalized, it assumed a $3 billion debt. The interest and principle payments on this debt need to be met each year from the operating earnings of the company. The sooner the debt can be paid down, the more resources it will have to reinvest in the business. To that end, a long-term incentive program was created. It is called the Global Success Sharing Program (GSSP).

The essential features of the GSSP is that if the company can meet the payback schedule for the debt and eliminate it within six years, every employee will receive approximately one times their annual salary in a special award. Regardless of where employees are based, they all share in proportion to their annual salary. This very large payout opportunity has encouraged people to examine costs carefully, seek ways to enhance revenues, and monitor the success of the corporation in personal terms. This incentive opportunity further represents the commitment of the executives to share the risks and rewards of building a strong organization with all employees.

Sustaining a Renewal Strategy

In order to remain competitive from a cost perspective, LS&CO needs a highly productive workforce. The reward systems have enhanced the commitment of the employees to the company and encouraged collaboration and process improvements at the most basic level of the organization. The company retains an aggressive approach to training and development, as well as providing opportunities for employees to make contributions beyond their standard job. This enhances its ability to compete.

LS&CO continues to reinvent itself as an organization. The Dockers and SLATES brands have become leading brands in their respective apparel categories. The corporation is also focusing its efforts on the population segment that provided the greatest growth—the youth market. The company is continually introducing new products and special promotions to connect with its new generations of consumers. This is an exciting and highly competitive time. Furthermore, Levi Strauss & Co. continues to prosper and develop markets throughout the world and sustain its commitment to high-quality products.

Levi Strauss & Co. has won numerous industry, national, and community awards. It continues to hold strong to the commitments that created a family-oriented business and reinforce these values as frequently as possible. The company shares its community recognition with employees and promotes their active involvement. The company promotes its efforts to develop and employ a highly diverse workforce in every dimension of race, nationality, religion, sexual orientation, age, and personal circumstances.

The 30,000 employees of LS&CO share a common bond to the success of the company, and each has a share in its achievements. In this way, the company has created a workplace in which performance and values strengthen the ability of the organization to serve the communities in which it operates and remain a global leader.

10

Not the Last Chapter

These case studies represent only a sample of what is occurring in organizations today and what is possible for organizations in the future. We are beginning to see a level of change and renewal that is unparalleled in human history.

These case studies also reflect a vast array of possibilities. They include retail workers and physicians, executives who would feel comfortable in the boardroom, and blue-collar workers who have seldom left the factory floor. Each organization approached rewards differently, reflecting its culture, management philosophy, and the degree of change needed. By moving through a deliberate process, guided by a simple mission, each of these organizations has created something special and unique. Each has found its own way to succeed, instead of adopting someone else's program.

Yet these organizations have one thing in common—they have reshaped the employer-employee relationship, creating an environment where people are valued for achieving desired results. And by creating this environment, in which rewards are aligned with the corporate strategy, they have managed to improve their overall performance and gain a competitive advantage. This was done by people taking desired actions.

Similar to politics, behavioral change is a local issue. These organizations and the units within these firms have developed their own plans. Their situations are unique and their response has been tailored to local circumstances. There is no universal "right" reward system, but every reward system will not be equally effective. Therefore, there must be core principles that determine how to make them work.

Lessons From the Leaders

The case studies presented in this book have much to teach us. Like stories from ancient civilizations, they provide a sense of how these organizations operate and what they value. They show what can be done, as well as how these organizations will continue the process of improvement. There are important lessons from these leading organizations in how they were able to make their unique reward systems work. However, it is more important to understand why they were successful than to adopt one of these programs and expect similar results.

To aid you in developing your own approach to change, I have summarized the 10 key factors that seem to most accurately determine what makes reward systems successful. While this list summarizes common characteristics, the true significance is in applying these principles to your own situation and to learn from the direct application of experience. Then, the value of these pages will be multiplied.

1. Reward Systems Play a Crucial Role in Performance

Every organization has some type of reward system. Whether it is formal or informal, principally driven by cash, stock options, or special recognition, it shapes the culture of the organization. The reward system sends messages to managers and employees about what is important and valued by the organization. It defines what the organization wants to pay for and what behaviors it wants to reinforce. The extent to which the reward system is aligned with the strategy and key success factors of the organization often determines whether the strategy is implemented effectively.

Leadership and effective management practices can inspire people to achieve great results, but people will ultimately ask, "What's in it for me?" Rewards, likewise, do not create performance; they only encourage and reinforce actions. Exercising their discretion, employees may barely achieve what is expected of them, or they may excel well beyond what is expected.

Rewards increase the probability that any given employee will perform at a higher level, but to make a long-term difference in performance, effective reward systems must be coupled with effective leadership. In short, they contribute directly to building commitment to the organization's goals—a prerequisite for success.

2. Measures Give Rewards Relevance; Rewards Give Measures Meaning

Reward systems work in the operating context of an organization. To be effective, they need to be linked to what is important to the organization. Performance measures create this linkage. When performance is measured but there are no consequences to the results, the data quickly loses its credibility and has no lasting impact on behavior.

Initially, employees who never received meaningful feedback will find feedback data to be of great value. They may exercise significant additional effort and produce short-term improvements. However, unless the feedback data is paired with some form of recognition or reward, the impact will not endure.

Data is objective and does not carry a message. Data takes on meaning when people expect something to happen to them because of the messages the data brings. If the consequence of the feedback is usually negative, people will likely resist, fear, or refute the data. When the response to the feedback is usually positive, such as providing some meaningful encouragement, people often make great efforts to understand, learn, and apply additional efforts. Measures, and the data they bring, can create opportunities for reinforcing performance. Look beyond the financial transactions and into the hearts and minds of the participants and you will recognize what people expect from the data they receive. The role of rewards, therefore, is to create a system of positive consequences for achieving desired performance.

3. Alignment and Consistency Are Essential

Every profiled company spent considerable time making certain the measures of performance were aligned with the organization's strategy and key success factors, and ensuring that the structure of its reward systems was consistent with its management philosophy and values.

People can often see through the rhetoric of organizational communication. When the words announcing a new compensation program do not match the actions that follow, employees stop listening to the words. They believe only what they experience. This will hurt leadership credibility, which can take years to rebuild.

In an environment where commitment to an organization is key to its responsiveness to a changing marketplace, credibility is essential and precious. Some compensation programs, by their nature, structure, and communication, are not intended to make payouts. They fail because employees do not believe the organization is sincere about sharing the gains. It is better to place people on straight salary than to set expectations that are never intended to be met.

When meaningful rewards are directly linked to the success factors of the organization, the power of this alignment cannot be replicated by a competitor. The agility of the organization is enhanced because people feel a common stake in its success. Combined with a strong strategy, adequate resources, and other key factors, aligned rewards create an enduring competitive advantage. This has been a major learning for many of these leading companies.

4. How People Are Paid Is Often More Important Than How Much They Are Paid

Many organizations see compensation merely as a fixed cost that is necessary to attract and retain a workforce. They view the competitiveness of compensation as the central issue. This is reflected in compensation strategy statements that spend considerable time defining a marketplace and a desired level of competitiveness. Some organizations spend thousands of dollars on compensation surveys and thousands of staff hours analyzing data to justify their compensation arrangements.

While rewards cannot make up for a poor market position for salaries, the way people are rewarded often has a greater impact on their performance and commitment than the amount they are paid. Some organizations have found that if they do a poor job of creating valuable rewards, they need to increase the amount of the rewards. Others have found that as long as pay is generally competitive, other rewards can make the difference in their ability to attract and retain talent.

When it comes to the design of a sales incentive program, a retention bonus program, or a performance recognition process, some organizations invest limited time in design, implementation, or communication. Why? Where is the greatest value to be gained—determining how much people should be paid or how they should be paid? The lesson is to understand what is important to people and how to use reward systems to give them what they are looking for in return for the level of performance the organization strives to achieve. Then, a true win-win condition is realized.

5. Build Programs With a Vision, and Then Improve Them Over Time

Teams that design new pay or recognition programs are often excited by the tasks and want to create breakthrough programs. But they often find that the most they can accomplish is to upgrade the existing programs. As they conduct reviews and seek approvals, they may face many criticisms. Their program is seldom perfect, and inherent weaknesses of the plan are accentuated during the review process. Even when the program is being introduced into the organization, criticisms of its design or sincerity emerge with the participants.

Challenges and criticism of the recommended program often reflect resistance to change and a fear of repeating past mistakes. The value of the new program may not be appreciated, even though it may be better than the current program. The program's design may not live up to the original expectations because of the lack of effective measurement systems, managerial skills, or resistance to change.

To overcome these issues, a strong belief in and commitment to the new program are necessary. Remember why the design effort started and the importance of what can be achieved. Clearly state the concerns with the current process and the reasons why the change is important. Then review the objectives and philosophy of the new program—the vision for what it can accomplish. The benefits need to be stated in terms of the needs of the recipient. What is important to executives is different from what is important to operational employees, sales staff, or managers. Complete the design even though it may not be perfect. As you implement the new program, continue the process of upgrading it as the measurement systems and work procedures improve. This will get you started on the desired path, build confidence in the program, and keep it refreshed and focused.

6. The Value of the Reward Should Exceed the Cost

In addition to the financial impact, rewards have a psyche value to each employee; for some it is found with financial pay-outs, for others it comes from recognition. The organizations profiled realized this and made an effort to provide employees with multidimensional rewards for their performance.

The value of the program is determined by how it is designed, how features are communicated, how feedback is provided to participants, and the level of effort managers put into supporting the program. The companies profiled rarely missed an opportunity to provide participants with celebrations or special events that recognized their achievements. They created value greater than the financial or tangible awards, enhancing the positive impact of the culture. Organizations that direct-deposit bonuses with little or no recognition will likely need a substantially higher amount of money to gain the same impact.

7. The Program Begins After the First Payouts

Typically, a small group of employees and managers (and sometimes consultants) spend a great deal of time and effort designing the company's new reward system. They prepare analysis, presentations, publications, and promotions to announce the program. And then they become surprised—and disappointed—when the program participants fail to share their enthusiasm.

It is important for the design team to recognize that the program is not real for most participants until the first payouts are made or a special award is presented. Until then, the program is theoretical. Employees may even be skeptical of its authenticity. After the first payout, though, they will begin to take notice. They may be pleasantly surprised by their awards, or they may realize that they could have earned more if they had tried a little harder. Even if they react with jealousy or anger toward those who receive larger rewards, they will recognize that management is serious about the program. They will pay more attention next performance period, and even more in the next period. They are likely to start asking questions about how the program works and what is needed to succeed. They will be more active participants in the future. Managers and employees need to support this new level of interest and provide the answers people seek about what they need to do to win.

8. Translate Measures Into Action

Many organizations spend a great deal of time developing an elaborate business plan, but the plan fails to be executed effectively because employees never knew what they had to do differently. Strategies are not translated into meaningful measures, and measures are not supported by articulating the actions needed for success. A major series of disconnects occur between the strategy of an organization and the actions its people take.

Improvements are achieved when employees start doing things that align with the desired plans, and not until then. But before employees significantly alter their performance, they need to know what needs to be done. If management is serious about using the reward program to improve performance, people need to know what to do differently, have the skills to do it, and receive frequent feedback, coaching, and encouragement. Managers should then take the following actions:

- ▸ Translate performance measures into descriptions of activities.
- ▸ Measure progress and results in meaningful ways.
- ▸ Provide the participants with frequent feedback.
- ▸ Train employees to improve their skills in highly focused areas.
- ▸ Make needed resources available that will enhance the participants' opportunity to succeed.
- ▸ Recognize achievements during the performance period and when the period has ended.

Taking these steps can engage employees in the process of achievement, and this will help ensure that the reward program generates a high return on investment for everyone.

9. Make Rewards Meaningful

Some believe that money is the only meaningful reward. Others believe noncash rewards are the key to motivation and condemn cash awards as being destructive. Both points of view have merit and need to be carefully understood, but neither is completely accurate.

If the reward is nonfinancial, how can employees benefit beyond personal satisfaction from what they've accomplished? If their achievements create greater profitability, higher revenues, stronger competitive advantage, and improved shareholder value, shouldn't they share in the financial gain? However, many compensation-based reward programs are inherently unable to influence specific behaviors. With a financial incentive plan, what do you do for an individual or team making a major contribution *during* the performance period? Must they wait till the end of the year to be recognized?

Several of the case studies demonstrate how nonfinancial recognition and rewards reinforce the behaviors that lead to improved results. Others show how financial incentives or stock options have become the real "stake" in the success of the company.

The truth lies in using financial and nonfinancial rewards in combination. Together they create a multiplier effect, making rewards more meaningful to employees than when either type of reward is given alone.

10. Take a Strategic, Systematic, and Holistic Approach

It is intriguing how companies spend considerable effort in justifying large capital expenditures and use sophisticated analytical tools that determine the return on investment. Yet compensation represents the largest expense for many organizations, and few organizations seek to use these dollars as an investment. Instead, they seek ways to reduce costs or build in automatic escalations in annual budgets.

The problem is that organizations do not see performance improvements as a return on the investments related to compensation. For example, the cost of variable compensation plans is usually considered without the context of the performance improvements they are expected to encourage. The organizations profiled here have achieved remarkable results because they understand how to utilize rewards as strategic management systems within the organization. They gain powerful business results because they effectively design, implement, and manage the systems as important priorities of the business.

Reward systems are only a part of the process of management. They are not the only determinant of human behavior. Their role is to encourage and reinforce desired actions. A well-thought-out strategy, strong leadership, effective organizational structures and systems, and advanced facilities and equipment are all essential elements of the high-performance organization.

However, when employees are not committed to achieving desired performance goals, the organization cannot transform into a high-performance enterprise. Commitment cannot be dictated; it can only be developed and earned. Rewards can aid in building a spirit and culture that cannot be replicated by any competitor. If all these parts are working in concert, the organization will achieve and sustain a competitive advantage.

To develop a reward strategy, build the link between performance requirements and needs of employees. Understand what each element of a total rewards system needs to do to support the strategy and values of the organization. Then design and use each program as part of a total system, not as independent, discrete programs. The power of each program is in how it works in combination with the other programs. They multiply their impact on people and performance.

The People Dimension

The people who are employed by the organizations profiled in this book view their organizations very positively and often take great pride in the work they do. Many other stories could be told that would demonstrate the human dimension of these programs. They may not be measurable, but they exist. They may not immediately affect the bottom line, but they are primary determinants of success. They create those conditions in which employees feel they can overcome challenges and have confidence in themselves and commitment to their organization.

As stated in the first chapter of this book, these organizations represent only a handful of companies that are changing the way they relate to their people. These stories are a partial view into these organizations. Their workplaces are not perfect and without issues. But somehow their people are able to overcome the challenges and take part in creating solutions, because they want to.

It is my hope that those who read, learn, and apply the principles that have been demonstrated in these pages will become agents of change. Regardless of how large the platform on which one operates or the role one performs, we can each make an important difference. Many of the programs and systems developed in these companies started with a single individual who had an idea, cared enough to take action, and remained committed to the possibilities. They knew what could be accomplished and knew what needed to be done. They have, in ways large and small, changed a piece of the world.

Your challenge is to do the same. In an organization where winning is recognized often, winning becomes a habit. As such, this is not the last chapter. It is only the beginning. Accept and enjoy the challenge.

Bibliography

Bardwick, J. M. *Danger in the Comfort Zone.* New York: AMACOM, 1991.

Belcher, J. G., Jr. *Results-Oriented Variable Pay System.* New York: AMACOM, 1996.

Caldwell, W., ed. *Compensation Guide.* Boston: Warren, Gorham & Lamont, 1994.

Cohen, A., and D. Bradford. *Influence Without Authority.* New York: John Wiley & Sons, 1990.

Collins, J., and J. Porras. *Built to Last.* New York: HarperBusiness Publishers, 1997.

Deming, W. E. *Out of the Crisis.* Cambridge, Mass.: MIT Press, 1986.

Freiberg, K., and J. Freiberg. *Nuts! Southwest Airlines' Crazy Recipe for Business and Personal Success.* Austin, Tex.: Bard Press, 1996.

Gupta, N., and J. Shaw. "Let the Evidence Speak: Financial Incentives Are Effective." *Compensation and Benefits Review,* March/April 1998, p. 26.

Heskett, J., W. E. Sasser, and L. Schlesinger. *The Service Profit Chain: How Leading Companies Link Profit and Growth to Loyalty, Satisfaction and Value.* New York: Free Press, 1997.

Kanter, R. M., B. Stein, and T. Jick. *The Challenge of Organizational Change.* New York: Free Press, 1992.

Kaplan, R., and R. Nolan. *The Balance Scorecard.* Boston: Harvard Business School Press, 1996.

Lawler, E. *Strategic Pay.* San Francisco: Jossey-Bass, 1990.

Nelson, R. *1001 Ways to Reward Employees.* New York: Workman Publishing, 1994.

Schultz, H. *Pour Your Heart Into It: How Starbucks Built a Company One Cup at a Time.* New York: Hyperion Publishing, 1997.

Schuster, J. R., and P. K. Zingheim. *The New Pay.* New York: Lexington Books, 1992.

Wilson, T. "Establishing Reward Systems That Support Change." In J. Lowery, ed., *Culture Shift: A Leader's Guide to Managing Change in Health Care.* Chicago: American Hospital Association, 1997.

————. "Group Incentives: Are You Ready?" *Journal of Compensation and Benefits,* November-December 1990, pp. 25–29.

————. *Innovative Reward Systems for the Changing Workplace.* New York: McGraw-Hill Publishing Company, 1995.

————. "Is It Time to Eliminate Piece Rate Incentive System?" *Compensation and Benefits Review,* March/April 1992, pp. 43–49.

————. "Key Issues in Designing Group Incentive." In H. Risner, ed., *Pay and Performance: From the Board Room to the Shop Floor.* New York: AMACOM, 1999.

————. "Re-Energizing the Performance Management Process." In W. Caldwell, ed., *The Compensation Guide.* Boston: Warren, Gorham & Lamont, 1997.

————, and C. Phalen. *Rewarding Group Performance: An Approach to Designing and Implementing Incentive Pay Program.* Scottsdale, Ariz.: The American Compensation Association, 1996.

Index